The Changing Outer Hebrides

Galson and the meaning of Place

The Changing Outer Hebrides

Galson and the meaning of Place

FRANK RENNIE

First published in 2020 by Acair.

First reprint in 2021 by Acair,
An Tosgan, Seaforth Road, Stornoway, Isle of Lewis, HS1 2SD

www.acairbooks.com
info@acairbooks.com

Text © Prof. Frank Rennie, 2020
Photography © Prof. Frank Rennie, Fiona Rennie (Sradag Creative), Malcolm Macleod
Photos from Urras Oighreachd Ghabhsainn
Photos from Museum & Tasglann nan Eilean Collections.
Illustrations © Fiona Rennie (Sradag Creative)

Text and cover design by Fiona Rennie (Sradag Creative) for Acair

A CIP catalogue record for this title is available from the British Library.

Printed by Hussar Books, Poland
ISBN: 978-1-78907-083-5

Scottish Charity Regulator
Registered Charity SC047866

For Agnes, Fiona, and Catriona

Contents

Acknowledgements

Piecing together a book of this sort involves many conversations, false trails, and serendipitous comments that lead to wonderful discoveries. There are almost as many stories and anecdotes that remain to be retold as there are the stories that have been included here. Frequently, the nuggets of information shared or the encouragement that is given, is barely noticed by the individual informant, but to the author following a theme they are invaluable. My very special thanks go to my good friends Dr. Finlay Macleod and David Green for reading and commenting on various chapters, and thereby improving the final manuscript. Also to Sandra Corbett, my niece and proofreader extraordinaire, who read every chapter and mercilessly corrected my inconsistencies.

Numerous of my colleagues at the University of the Highlands and Islands, have been invaluable, offering information, recommendations, and chance remarks, including Prof. Hugh Cheape (material culture), Dr. Arne Vogler (marine science), Catriona Murray (Gaelic folklore), John Alexander Smith (Technical), Dr. Martin Carruthers (Iron Age archaeology), Dr. Melanie Smith (ecology), Dr. Iain MacInnes (Scottish history), Dr. Rebecca Rennell (archaeology), Iain Angus MacAulay (nautical studies), and Dr. Edward Graham (meteorology). Also a bevy of UHI librarians, Ruth Priest, Morag Llewellyn, Elizabeth McHugh, and Laura Jeffries for their untiring support in seeking out my obscure archival request, as well as the numerous unnamed staff at the National Library of Scotland for their consummate professionalism.

In the wider academic environment, I have to thank Christopher Fleet (Scottish National Map Library), my long-standing colleague and friend Prof James Hunter (history), Dr. Rachel Barrowman and Dr. Chris Barrowman (archaeology), Dr. Cathlin MacAulay (School of Scottish Studies), and for geological input Dr. Graham Leslie and Dr. Maarten Krabbendam, (British Geological Survey, Edinburgh), Dr. Adrian Hall (Swedish Geological Survey) and Museum & Tasglann nan Eilean Collections.

More locally, Margaret Martin and Mary Margaret Morrison at the Stornoway Public Library are always willingly helpful, and conversations with Janet Marshall (whales), Roderick (Rodaigan) Martin (local history), Mary Ann (Thoudy) Matheson (wells) and Dolina MacLeod and Annie MacSween (Gaelic) have always been fruitful.

Many others have helped along the way, both by encouraging me and by not discouraging me, and I thank you all. I hope that you all enjoy the final result.

Foreword

Despite the repetition of a melodramatic cliché such as "... time stood still..." time does not stand still. Since whenever time began, it has progressed, and a self-evident conclusion from this is that whatever we now see, whatever now exists, in fact whatever we are, is simply a natural continuation of something that has already gone before. Change is as inevitable as time itself. Change is not necessarily good nor bad, it simply happens, but perhaps understanding the reasons for that change, and the subsequent consequences, can enable humans to minimise the production of unwanted futures, and also to come to some acceptance of the things which we absolutely cannot change.

This book took just over a year-and-a-half to research and write, but in actual fact it seems that I have been building towards this for my whole life. The topic of this book brings together many of my formative experiences and interests. The geology, the natural environment, the social history of the communities in this book, are not isolated topics in my own head; they are seamlessly integrated and inter-related. I have listed the references for many of the facts mentioned in these pages, but I have avoided, in general, giving precise page numbers for quotations, for these sources should be enjoyed by reading them in full, not dipped into to collect random, disjointed facts like some historical smorgasbord.

Many of us have a place, or places, that we especially treasure. For some it is in the mountains, or a particular stretch of coastline. For me, it is the area where I have been based for most of my adult life, the village of Gabhsann and its surrounding countryside on the northwest tip of Scotland's Outer Hebridean islands. In choosing to explore the story of this place in detail, I am not necessarily saying that it is better than your favourite place, but it is certainly distinctly different.

To a very large extent, a location is simply space until we engage with it and give it some social context. That context can be in relation to another known place, a certain distance and direction from it, or it can be as a result of some intrinsic property of that place. It might be characterised by a particular configuration of the landscape, or the abundance of a recognisable species of plant or animal, or perhaps the site of a historical event, such as a battle or an incident that happened to a predecessor. It might, in fact, be all of the above. In these spaces which we now recognise as named places, we construct layers and layers of different sorts of meanings. Those meanings change and interweave over time, and are perpetuated - or not - by our subsequent interactions with that place. This in turn culminates in the development of a sense of place. What this sense of place is, may be different for every one of us, though collective experiences and community memory can evoke every form of human emotion from dread, through nostalgia, to sheer exuberant delight. For some people, the sense of a place is learned, for others it is as instinctive as breathing. Whether or not we, as individuals or as a community, place any value or merit on the sense of place that we possess, is another matter, and that too will change with time.

I have swum in the Dead Sea and snorkeled on the Great Barrier Reef; I have climbed Mount Kilimanjaro, trekked in the Bhutan Himalaya, and sailed down the Amazon River. One year I was in Svalbard, barely 1,050 km (650 miles) from the North Pole, and soon after that in Stewart Island in the far south of New Zealand, the last inhabited landfall before the Southern Ocean and the continent of Antarctica. I am not telling you this to boast of my travels, merely to put into context that I have visited scores of countries and hundreds of wonderful geographical localities, but I have never found a place that I like better than the few hectares on the north-western edge of the Outer Hebrides that I call home.

If reading this book encourages you to rediscover your sense of place with your own favourite locality, then it will have served my purpose.

More images are at   https://bit.ly/2XbJYYv

CHAPTER 1

The first 3 billion years

On the rocks

When is "here" not actually here?

This is not such a Zen conundrum as it might first appear.

The centre of my world is at 58° 26' 34" N and 06° 23' 37" W but this spot has not always been at this precise location on the surface of our tiny planet. For the geographically challenged, this location currently corresponds to the middle of the village of South Galson, (Gabhsann bho Dheas, in the Gaelic language indigenous to this place) in the north-western edge of the Isle of Lewis, on the north-western edge of the Outer Hebrides, on the north-western margin of the continent of Europe. The township now comprises the small villages of Gabhsann bho Thuath (North Galson) Gabhsann bho Dheas (South Galson), and Mealabost (Melbost) but these precise places have changed names and locations over the centuries, and for simplicity I will simply refer to the whole area as Gabhsann (pronounced like "gow [as in the English 'how'] - sun").

Over many millions of years, the crustal land masses have been shunted back and forth on the surface layers of Earth, driven by slow but inexorable convection currents of partially-molten rock, deep within the mantle of the planet. The familiar shapes of countries and continents that we recognise today are just a relatively modern and very transitory phase of geological artwork. Continents and supercontinents whose shape we would not recognise, whose boundaries we only tentatively appreciate today, with fantastical names that would not be out of place in *The Lord of the Rings* or *The Hobbit*, were the only solid land for 99% of Earth history. Vaalbara, Ur, Nuna, Rodinia (the first confirmed supercontinent), Avalonia, Gondwana, and latterly Pangea and Laurasia, are only a scattering of the names given to enormous lumps of continents that formed, broke up, and reformed without our assistance, without our knowledge, and without even a recognisable life form to observe their creation and disappearance.[1] The forces required for these global reorganisations, and the time-span needed to accomplish these changes, are staggering in their immensity, but are well-documented by radiometric age-dating and palaeomagnetic evidence. That is the first significant change in the story of "the changing Outer Hebrides"; they were not always where they are now. In fact, the current location of these islands is a relatively modern resting place, but we will come back to that palaeomagnetic data in a little while.

Some people may find starting with the geology of an area to be a daunting task, but the complexities and intricacies of reading about the formation of the ground that we now stand upon is as integral to a place as the climate of that place, the local ecosystem, or the social history of the communities that have lived there. In Gabhsann, like most of the rest of the northern part of the Isle of Lewis, the solid bedrock is exposed at the surface mostly around the edges of the island only, along the considerable length of the shoreline and occasional cuttings along a riverside or a road-verge. I walk along this shore at some point during most weeks, and it is difficult to appreciate that we are actually walking along the remnants of the root zone of an ancient mountain chain – the deep interior of a range every bit as high as the current Himalaya. What is now exposed at the surface, twisted and contorted rock, challenging the pounding of the Atlantic Ocean and the ravages of the elements, was once 35-40 km underground, formed at temperatures of around 900° C and pressures in excess of 10 kbar (that is, roughly 10,000 times the normal atmospheric pressure at sea level).[2]

The current landscape is low and gently rolling. In the distance there is a horizon of small rounded hills in soft focus, the remnant stumps of a once-great range of mountains. In some places, the bare rock protrudes as dark coloured slabs, or small broken crags, indicating how shallow is the thin covering of infertile soil, but mostly the landscape is draped in a sinuous covering of deep peat. The colours of the country seem to be an infinite dappled variety of greens, browns, and washed-out yellows, with areas of contrasting splashes of exposed black peat and the fluffy white tufts of Bog Cotton. In Autumn, the palette is transformed as the purples and blues of heather blooms stretch trembling to the near horizon, like a gently sloping sea.

Lewisian Gneiss is the type locality to define the nomenclature of a rock assemblage of minerals and tectonic structures found in the UK only on the north-western fringes of the northern Highlands and Islands.[3] To the south and east of a sharp dividing line from near Durness, on the north coast of the Scottish mainland, running roughly south-southwest to the Isle of Iona, there is no Lewisian Gneiss. North and west of this dividing line is the ancient, stable, basement of a long-disappeared continent, or in fact, several continents. The Scottish rocks are just a tiny remnant of that ancient basement (or shield, as geologists call it) for there are similar rocks in north-eastern Canada, East Greenland, and Scandinavia, and even a non-geologist could correctly speculate that these scattered areas were near neighbours before the opening-up of the Atlantic.[4]

To really understand the intricate nature of the overlapping, intersecting, and tightly convoluted relationships of regional geology over long spans of time, we need to envisage the land as a three-dimensional jigsaw. Geographers refer to the expansive view of the surface topography of a landscape as the terrain, but to geologists, the *terrane* of this area of surface topography extends downwards to include a chunky block of crust several kilometres deep. The terrane of the Gabhsann area includes the folded and faulted rock features that we now observe on Earth's surface, but also extending to include the deep and complex subterranean structures which we can only begin to illustrate through the interpretation of the bewildering arrays of subterranean reflections produced by the mathematical calculations of seismic exploration.[5]

The Lewisian Gneiss is a metamorphic rock, meaning a classification of rock which has been transformed from its original rock-type, usually igneous rocks such as granite, or sedimentary rocks such as sandstones and shales, to create different constituent minerals and distinctively changed tectonic structures. Usually this transformation is as a result of heat and/or pressure applied to the rock, and in the case of the Lewisian Gneiss, both heat and pressure were extreme. Stop at any outcrop and look at a freshly-broken piece of rock (weathering tends to alter and obscure the details of surfaces exposed to the atmosphere). This gneiss is coarse-grained, with a distinctly striped appearance. The piece of gneiss from Gabhsann that I hold in my hand just now is a striking combination of largely black and white crystals - in various shades of black and various hues of white - with thousands of small crystal faces shimmering in the sunlight. As I rotate the rock at different angles, different crystal faces sparkle, while others lose their glint. There are frequent flashes of beautiful deep green minerals - epidote, pyroxene, amphibole - and occasional studs of pinkish-red garnet. Many of the darker crystals are roughly rectangular and crudely orientated parallel to each other to form alternating bands of light and dark stripes.

A few metres away from where I am standing the rock-type is an eye-catching, metre-wide slash of massive pink-and-white crystals of a pegmatite, formed by the extremely slow cooling of hot, granitic fluids which were once injected into the solid rock of the grey gneisses. These mineral stripes may vary from a few millimetres to a metre or so in thickness, depending upon the effect that heat, pressure, and water content had upon the original rock type. There are three broad types of gneiss that have been formed by these intense Earth movements. Rocks which were once sediments – sands, muds, limestones, clays – have been transformed into 'metasediments'. Then there are 'granitic' gneisses, which are rocks originally formed by igneous processes – such as granites, gabbros, basalt lavas, and so on, before they too were altered by metamorphic activities. Thirdly, there is what the British Geological Survey term "undifferentiated gneiss" - or 'grey gneiss' - meaning simply that the resultant rock is too complex, too mixed, and too variable to be certain beyond doubt what the original parent material was. Tantalisingly, Gabhsann has all three varieties within the relatively small land area of the village.

Here is revealed a second major change in the Outer Hebrides, for nothing of this solid rock structure – the ground that we walk across and can observe from every angle – remains in its original form. When trying to infer past changes, a frustrating aspect of the rocks affected by metamorphism is that each metamorphic episode, each mountain-building clash of drifting continents, each injection of molten rock rising from the depths of the mantle, will alter and distort what was there before. Each metamorphic event partially or totally obscures any previous event, and we are left with only the evidence of the most recent event overprinted on the pre-existing structures. This can make the geology of the Lewisian Gneiss very complicated very quickly, and the further back in time we go, the more complicated and obscure the details can become.

Comprehending the relationships of time is a key factor in understanding the geological history of any part of our planet. In some regions of the world, the interrelationships of sedimentary rocks, frequently with characteristic 'marker horizons' of strata containing particular fossils which are known to indicate a specific age, can be used to date the relationships of different rock types with each other. In the case of the rocks of Gabhsann, however, and indeed throughout the Outer Hebrides, the ultra-high temperatures, pressures, and physical distortions to which the rocks have been subjected, mean that no fossils have been preserved to enable identification. Fortunately, within this convoluted terrane there are occasional slices of the original, unmetamorphosed rocks - called protoliths - which have been enveloped, and to some extent protected from subsequent extensive alteration, by the surrounding grey gneiss. Some small samples of the ancient protolithic granites can be found in sections of the foreshore of Gabhsann bho Dheas, and have been used for dating purposes.

Instead of relying on fossil creatures, we can utilise an ingenious system of the physical properties of our solar system, and this is another measure of the changing fabric of the Outer Hebrides. The same physical understanding of radioactivity which enables us to generate energy in nuclear power stations, and to build nuclear weapons of destruction, can be used to calculate the age of formation of a wide variety of rocks. Many radioactive elements are included in the mineralogical 'recipes' to create new rocks, both the molten igneous rocks of volcanic regions, and the re-heated, highly-pressurised metamorphic rocks resulting from colossal collisions and folding deep within the Earth.

The nuclear clock

Radiometric dating is a simple concept which is difficult in practice, because it requires the precise measurement of very, very small quantities of chemical elements. We cannot simply stand on the shore of the beach in Gabhsann and calculate the chemical proportions of the various elements making up the rocks, we need to take some of those rock samples to a laboratory. In that laboratory we can rely upon the fact that we can accurately measure the abundance of different isotopes in a rock sample. Isotopes are different forms of a single chemical element that can have the same number of protons, but different numbers of neutrons in their nuclei. Some of these isotopes are unstable, and as they shed their nuclear particles over time (radiation), they slowly change towards a final, stable, isotopic composition.

The key factor in this process of isotopic decay is the fact that this decay occurs at a known rate. The half-life of any radioactive element is the constant amount of time that it takes for the parent isotope to decay to half its initial value. By measuring the exact quantities of the parent and the daughter isotopes it is possible to calculate how long it has been since that rock sample cooled from an active, molten state, and crystallised into a solid rock. Several radioactive isotopes are particularly useful for geological dating: for instance Uranium^{238}, which decays to Lead^{206} (U-Pb) at a half-life of 4.47 billion years (b.y.). (That is, every four thousand, four hundred and seventy million years, there will be half as much U^{238} than you started with). Other useful isotopes, such as Rubidium to Strontium, and Potassium to Argon, with half-lives of 48.8 b.y. and 1.25 b.y. respectively, or even Samerium^{147} decaying to Neodymium^{143} with a half-life of 106 b.y., have been used to date the ancient gneisses which underlie the whole of the area of Gabhsann. Measurements of each pair of isotopes give different opportunities to calculate the age of geological activity long, long ago, and to cross-check the dating processes with greater and greater accuracy.

In the area of Gabhsann, most of the exposed rock available for our scrutiny consists of the undifferentiated 'grey gneiss' category, which spreads below most of the northern part of Lewis, and is currently buried below many metres of peat. A sliver of Precambrian metasediments, recognisable by their mineral chemistry and their fractured, slabby appearance, lies just north of the point where Abhainn Gabhsann bho Thuath (the North Galson River) enters the sea. This is no surprise, really, as the Ness Assemblage, just a few miles further north, consists of a vast crustal slab of metasedimentary material which was itself mashed onto an already ancient pre-existing continental crust around 2000 million years ago.[6] Think of a large sedimentary basin, such as the North Sea, in which layer upon layer of sands and muds slowly accumulate on an ancient rock basement, then become buried, dragged down to the zone of intense compression and re-heating by the radioactive elements of the Upper Mantle, and then become 'cooked' into a new combination of the original chemistry. With modern geophysics, we can use seismic imaging and sophisticated dating techniques, to visualise this process happening today, for as the 'father of modern geology', the early Scottish geologist, James Hutton, proposed in his doctrine of uniformitarianism, "the present is the key to the past".

A little bit more surprising is the slice of Archaean granitic gneiss which stretches along the foreshore from the mouth of Abhainn Gabhsann bho Dheas (the South Galson River) south-westward for about a kilometre-and-a-half. Surprising, because this metamorphosed remnant of an ancient granite appears not to be an offshoot of the much later Lewisian granitic complex in Uig, to the far west of the island, and is at least 1000 million years older than the already ancient grey gneisses which surround and encompass it. Walking a transect section along the present-day foreshore, there is nothing obvious to indicate that there is any real distinction between the rocks, but the chemistry observed in the laboratory tells a different story. Recent evidence provided by the isotopic dating of key minerals, such as Zircon, which is highly resistant to change, indicates that the Lewisian Complex is not just one crustal plate, but rather a complicated amalgam of several different ages of crustal slabs, squeezed and sliced into their present position to form one continuous Precambrian terrane.[7]

Minerals in remnant patches of protoliths - those fossil-like fragments of the original rock-types - now enveloped by the grey gneiss which predominantly forms the shoreline of Gabhsann, have been dated as being formed between 3,120 and 2,800 million years ago (mya), while the re-worked metasediments which are now found in Gabhsann bho Thuath, and more extensively a few kilometres further north in the Ness Assemblage, date from a comparatively young 1,860 mya. A deep and fundamental earth fault along the eastern margin of the Outer Hebrides separates the Lewisian Gneiss of the outer isles from apparently similar rocks of the north-west mainland of Scotland. In contrast, the earth-building events and the specific rock types of the Outer Hebrides appear to have more in common with their (now geographically distant) neighbours in East Greenland.

Let's try to imagine this time-scale in a more contemporary context, although even this comparison might stretch the imagination of most people. Supposing we were to make a year-long documentary film chronicling the formation, growth and development of planet Earth: each day would cover just slightly less than thirteen million years of real time. When we are watching this documentary film, the grey gneisses of Gabhsann and most of northern Lewis would not be formed until the viewing period between 3rd and 26th May. We are already more than one-third of the way through the passage of Earth history since the formation of our planet, yet for all the information we have amassed about the chemistry, the palaeogeography and the interrelationships of the solid landforms over this period, we are merely trying to piece together fragments of knowledge. It is akin to picking up a "whodunit?" novel with twelve chapters and trying to follow the plot of the story despite the fact that the first few chapters just contain sketchy unfinished sentences on every page.

Around 9th July in our film, we see the appearance of the metasediments that now form the northern tip of Lewis, in the area of Nis, squashed up against the already ancient grey gneisses and other pre-existing crustal fragments. These rocks have been pushed together, in the same sort of massive tectonic movements which we are currently witnessing as the subcontinent of India drifts inexorably northwards and crashes into the Asian crustal plate. In both situations, the tectonic collisions cause the two plates to fold, buckle, and become raised up to form mountain ranges along their junction, such as the resulting chain of the Himalaya. In this cinematic time-scale we do not see the end of the global Precambrian metamorphic complexes until the start of the Cambrian era about 540 million years ago – corresponding to around 20 November in our film. As it is today, the surface of the planet at that time was probably covered more by oceans than by solid land, but the first fish do not make a starring appearance in our film until sometime around 22 November.

All of which takes us back to the initial question, when was 'here' not here? To be more exact, where exactly was the spot where we are standing right now before it came to be here, at the present location on the surface of our globe? Conventionally we measure the position of a location on the planet by plotting the latitude, the degrees, minutes, and seconds north or south of the equator, and similarly the longitude, which is the angular difference from London. But longitude is a relatively modern invention. In 1851 Sir George Biddell Airy, the U.K. Astronomer Royal, snatched one of the most significant prizes of cultural hegemony in human history when he established the meridian of zero degrees to pass from Pole to Pole through the Royal Observatory at Greenwich in London. From this date onwards Greenwich is conceded as the central point for any journey around the Earth, both 'East' and 'West' now being given a cultural as well as a geographical context.[8]

Not so with latitude, because latitudinal distance is measured both north and south from the equator, that imaginary yet very real line around the broadest part of Earth which is exactly midway between the North Pole and the South Pole. Throughout the history of the planet, as continents formed, merged, and broke up, these huge slabs of continental crust were shunted, folded and pushed across the surface of the globe. We cannot measure their longitude, but by clever and precise measurements we can determine their location north or south of the equator.[9] The deeply driven movements within the mantle and the outer core of the planet, which are caused by differences in temperature, pressure, and chemical composition, produce convection currents as cool, dense matter sinks and warmer, less dense matter rises. These convection currents of iron-rich minerals, whipped into whirlpools due to the influence of Earth spinning on its own axis, produce a flow of charged particles, resulting in a continuous current of electricity, which in turn produces a magnetic field which engulfs the entire planet. Imagine a giant bar-magnet with the north and south poles at each end.

As minerals crystallise from molten lava or metamorphic re-mixes form new rocks, the charged particles in the crystals adopt the magnetic field of the location on the Earth where they are being formed. If you think about the bar-magnet again, and the orientation of the magnetic field, the inclination of the field varies, from being parallel to the Earth's surface at the equator, to steeply dipping at the poles. By measuring this orientation, which is fixed as the rock cools, geologists can back-calculate the latitudinal position of that rock at the time of its formation, and by this process we can recreate the shifting palaeography of the surface of Earth. We can literally follow the path of various rock types as they drift and are pushed across the surface of the globe.[10]

By the start of the Cambrian, (mid-November in the film) around 540 million years ago, and for the next 150 million years or so, the site that would eventually become the location of Gabhsann was around 25° south of the equator, about the latitude of Rio de Janeiro or Pretoria according to our present-day configuration of geography. Previously, around 2,500 million years ago when the Lewisian Gneiss was starting to form, Gabhsann was down near the South Pole, with the landmass drifting very, very slowly northwards.[11]

By the Early Ordovician (485 mya - around 23rd November in our epic earth-science movie) what is now southern Britain was located off the west African margin of Gondwana at around 60°S, although it had moved to a latitude of around 20°S by about 400 million years ago.[12] The south of 'England' was still separated from what would become northern Scotland by a wide stretch of the Iapetus Ocean; they were as far apart as Lisbon and New York are today.[13]

Wearing down and raising up

From the end of the period of the formation of the Lewisian Gneiss until the next big geological event that has left its mark on Gabhsann is a huge stretch of time, during which we would be watching nothing but a continually blank screen in our Earth-movie). In other parts of the world, of course, rocks were being created and destroyed, animals and plants were emerging, evolving, or disappearing into extinction, but in Gabhsann, none of this record remains. We know that lots of tumultuous geological events occurred during this time, for the evidence of these events is documented close by in the Highlands and Islands, but around Gabhsann itself, the inexorable forces of erosion have stripped away all traces of this part of Earth history.

A few kilometres southeast of Gabhsann, in the vicinity of Steòrnabhagh, a thick, thick sequence of coarse sandstones have been preserved for our observation by a quirk of geological disruption.[14] During the geological periods known as the Permian and the Triassic, the area we now know as Gabhsann was still deeply buried below the surface of Earth. To the north-westward of what is now Gabhsann, there was at this time a range of high mountains, probably as large as the present day Himalaya. Like all upland areas, almost as soon as the tectonics have buckled them and forced them skyward, the water, ice, wind, and sand-blasting begin to break the rock down and transport the fragments downwards and seawards. The evidence from the sandstones of the Stornoway Beds indicates that those Permo-Triassic mountains were rapidly worn down, transported southeastward towards lower-lying valleys, and dumped as huge alluvial fans in hot, desert conditions.[15] These conditions undoubtedly extended over the whole of the northwest Highlands and Islands, but subsequent erosion has removed most of these sediments and relocated them elsewhere on the planet. In our cinematic time-frame, the Permo-Triassic sandstones of the Stornoway Beds were laid down over an extended period of ninety-eight million years, somewhere between 9th and 17th December. These are very coarse sediments, from muds and rough sands to rounded pebbles and small boulders, characteristic of a high-energy fluvial environment, such as powerful mountain streams gushing off the highlands and dumping their load of river-sands and stones where the force of the river was checked by meeting the flatlands of the valley floor. In the vicinity of Steòrnabhagh, from the banks of the Inner Harbour eastwards to a line between Garrabost and Suardail, an angular block of these coarse sediments has sunk down in the floor of a localised rift valley, probably connected to the tectonic readjustments of the mountain building, and these sediments gained protection during the following millennia from the erosion that has deleted this period from the history of Gabhsann. Over the subsequent millennia, the terrane of the village has progressed from mountain topography to arid desert, and then evolving to temperate coastal uplands without leaving any indication of the many other landscapes and climates which must have prevailed at this spot, sometimes lasting for many millions of years.

A further piece of ancillary evidence is literally earth-shattering. Comparatively recently (around midday on 19th December in the Earth-documentary) the convection currents churning in the interior of the Earth began to tear apart the region now occupied by the Atlantic Ocean. Opposing convection currents began powering the solid crust of the North American continent away from the European plate, forcing them apart with the injection of new volcanic magma along a mid-Atlantic crack which has its surface expression in the expanding landscape of Iceland. That process continues to this day. By now, Gabhsann has almost arrived at its present-day latitude and longitude, although the constant speed of ocean-floor spreading (about 2 cm per year) means that Canada and the USA are about 1.2 metres further over the Atlantic from Gabhsann than where they were when I was born. Curiously, the current site of Gabhsann occupies an ocean-edge, continental-margin location, much the same as it did those millions of years ago when it sat on the rim of Pangea, and like that time the ocean pounding continues to change, reshape, and readjust that coastal edge. The coastline of this island is a constant negotiation between the land and the ocean.

So, that was the next major Hebridean change – the surface of the land that we can see now –   the rolling landscape and every visible hollow and hillock, was once deep, deep underground, or under the floor of marine sea, and has been sculpted, worn-down, and eventually revealed in its present form.

There now comes another long, long gap in the geological record around the Gabhsann area. The excitable volcanic eruptions and injections of molten rock which accompanied the opening of the Atlantic and affected surrounding areas such as the islands of St Kilda, the Shiant Isles, and Skye, did not penetrate the ancient, stable basement that now hosts the site of the Gabhsann township. Instead, the surface of the land continued to be ground down and reshaped by the forces of nature. The present-day look of the land, in every direction, bears the imprint of the last major ice age. There have been many separate ice ages which have carved and reshaped this landscape, and technically we are currently merely in an interglacial period (waiting for another ice age to begin) but, similar to subsequent metamorphic episodes, each period of engulfment by the ice reworks and at least partially masks the effects of the previous glacial action. Depending on the severity, duration, and extent of the ice coverage, landscape features are cut out, built up, or simply remodelled. Needless to say, this can make it difficult now to interpret the sequence of events that have produced the current geomorphology, so it was good to be able to spend several days in the field with Dr. Jost von Weymarn, whose research has specialised in the glaciation of this island.[16]

Under Jost's expert analysis I began to appreciate how the climate had produced a local ice cap over the uplands of south Lewis and north Harris, and how that active ice accumulation spilled outwards radially in slow-moving rivers of ice to spread across the Outer Hebrides.[17] As is common with extensive ice ages, the colossal weight of the ice cap pushed down on the land and depressed it, so that when the ice eventually melted, the land, relieved of its encumbering load, bounced upwards slightly. This effect is called 'isostatic rebound' and the evidence for it is clear, even to non-scientists, by the way that previous shorelines have been lifted high above the contemporary shoreline. Around much of the coastline of the Highlands and Islands there are examples of these raised beaches which have popped upwards as the ice retreated. Seven-and-a-half metre lifts are a common feature, but nearer the core of the enveloping ice blanket, where the ice was thickest, the rebound has been greatest, and sometimes it appears that several coastal terraces of sand and gravel have been formed, one above the other, as the landscape jumped upwards in fits and starts with the disappearance of the ice covering.

Visiting a number of key locations in company with Jost, he showed me that much of the raised beach material in the southern half of Lewis and Harris has been scraped away by subsequent streams of moving ice. In the northern part, however, the area now covered by the north Lewis moor, the ice appears to have been relatively static for a period - a large flat icefield rather than a constantly moving glacier - which has left the unconsolidated gravels of the northern raised beaches relatively intact. This is of major significance for our understanding of the geomorphology of Gabhsann, for as we walk today from the dog-leg corner of the road in Gabhsann bho Dheas, down towards the shore, we walk over the old seabed of a raised beach. As the ground drops away smoothly below the line of the village houses, a straggling scatter of small broken cliffs mark the boundary of the pre-ice age coastal edge. The gently shelving crofts dip down to the present-day shoreline, and along their seaward margin, the top of the stony beach, the old sands and gravels of the former seabed are now compacted to resemble a barrier similar to naturally occurring concrete. (Geologists call this loose accumulation of compacted sand, gravel, and water-rounded pebbles, 'beach rock'). Even this, though, is no match for the Atlantic, and steadily this coastal margin is still changing. To stand with your back to the ocean and look inland over the emerging landscape of Gabhsann is to include over 3,500 million years of Earth history in your gaze, yet that is only the end of the beginning of a complex inter-relationship with this place.

To conclude our epic year-long documentary movie of Earth-history, a mention of the earliest known hominids would appear in our film about one o'clock in the afternoon of the last day of the year, with our first recogniseable Homo sapien ancestors putting in a tentative appearance on the planet shortly before 25 minutes to midnight. It will take many more thousands of years before humans will arrive in Gabhsann.

The last ice age to cover this north-western tip of Europe only receded from the Outer Hebrides about 1 minute before the end of our film. The stage is now set for the arrival of life in Gabhsann.

CHAPTER 2

The living blanket of the land

The dirt beneath my nails

On top of this rock and gravel, the rest of our world was assembled. Not all at once, but slowly and steadily, with many false starts and reversals. All rock, once it is exposed to the atmosphere of Earth, is at once subjected to the forces of erosion. Rain, perhaps slightly acidic with its load of atmospheric carbon, begins to react chemically with the surface rocks, weathering them into slightly more decayed versions of themselves. In cracks and small fissures, the water freezes, and the expanding ice prises apart the surrounding rock. Earthquakes tear and shatter the landscapes dramatically, rivers and glaciers pick up broken rock and gravel to grind their winding channels while wind-blown sand scours and shapes exposed rock slowly but inexorably, as efficiently as a stone-mason or a woodcarver. Above the land area we now know as Gabhsann, the surface of Earth was progressively worn down over a period of 3000 million years, from a surface topography which would have been similar to the present-day Himalaya, to a topography resembling the present-day Alps, and finally to the familiar reduced altitudes and rounded contours of the Scottish Highlands and Islands as we view them today. Except of course it is not the final stage, for this wearing-away of the rock surface, its reshaping and redeposition as sands and gravels, is still taking place today.

At the area called Breibhig, on the southern coastal margin of Gabhsann, the beach is overlain by till, and on the exposed rock platform of gneiss, glacial striations can be discovered which indicate that the ice was moving north-northwestwards. Along the coastline further to the south, the raised beaches have been entirely removed, so Gabhsann is pivotal to our understanding of the late glacial period in Lewis and Harris, with Breibhig perhaps marking a localised northern boundary of the moving ice. There has been some scientific debate about whether or not the coastal area from Breibhig to north of Gabhsann bho Thuath was an ice-free area during the last ice age, and while the evidence is patchy, it would seem that, at the very most, any ice-free area was small and localised, and that the landforms suggest that the whole of north-west Lewis was glaciated during this period. The fact that remnants of the raised beach in Gabhsann have not been worn away, unlike similar deposits further south, is probably a fortunate result of them being to some degree protected by the backing cliff-line and the localised direction of the moving ice.[18]

In these cold, northern climates, the soil which covered Gabhsann is slow to form, and has been wiped away by surface processes many times. Under these circumstances, it is surprising to discover a small patch of deeply weathered rock, visible where I am standing just now beside a small roadside cutting a couple of hundred metres south of the Lodge (Loidse Ghabhsainn).[19] By a quirk of geological fate, this small pocket of weathered material was not entirely scraped away by the dominating mainland ice as it advanced across northern Lewis at the height of the last major Ice Age.

All around this sheltered spot of old soil, which was itself a relatively recent addition to the local landscape, the retreating glaciers dumped millions of tons of till, a sticky, unsorted mixture of mineral materials that the moving ice had picked up, ranging from fine-grained clay to large angular boulders. This 'boulder-clay' was spread like a thin layer over most of northern Lewis, and so an unpromising start was made on developing the subsequent soils from this slow-draining, nutrient-poor glacial remnant. There are half-a-dozen factors which affect soil formation. Apart from the length of *time* in the development process, the underlying *geology* and the *climate* play an important role. The ancient gneisses on which Gabhsann is located are highly resistant to chemical erosion, and so the resultant soil and gravel is silica rich and nutrient poor. The cool, damp oceanic climate does nothing to hurry the process of chemical decay. A fourth factor is the *site* of soil formation itself, is the soil developing in a poorly-drained hollow of the landscape, or on the crest of a protruding knoll of bedrock? And lastly, leaving aside the modifying *work of humans*, for the moment, the ground *vegetation* and its associated micro-organisms have a profound effect on the type of soil that is created. For such a small land area, Gabhsann has a diversity of soil types, from sandy grassland, to bare rock, but it is fair to say that the deep accumulation of blanket-bog peat is the feature which usually dominates most first impressions.[20]

Towards the northern coastal edge of Gabhsann, at Tobha Ghabhsainn, a thin organic deposit which is interbedded with sand is sandwiched between the rock platform of the gneiss below it, and overlain by broken material from the glacial edge and by the raised beach gravels. This assemblage can give us some evidence of the sequence of soil formation, and the relative dates of when things happened in this landscape. Radiocarbon dating of the organic material gives an age of between 39,000 and 47,200 years ago[18] and an analysis of the pollen contained in this deposit indicates the development of vegetation consistent with grassland and heath, with an absence of trees. This organic deposit was the start of a soil beginning to form in the time-space between periods of glaciation, and it was subsequently covered by till from the retreating ice and by the raised beach gravels.

Standing on the main road, with my back to the sea, looking inland towards the area north of Tom na Bà, it is obvious that Gabhsann, and indeed the island as a whole, has not always been treeless. It is here that our family peat-banks are, which have been cut for our fuel by at least four generations of islanders. The flat face of each peat bank is about a metre-and-a-half deep, and over the years two layers of banks have been cut, forming a flattish, step-like, double-terrace of Heather-topped peat exposures. The top peats are light and fibrous, but at the bottom of the lowest bank, the intense black of the caorann (the lowest peat) with its almost plastic texture is sharply contrasted against a mass of tangled branches with identifiably silver bark which lie buried within it. The branches range from twiglets a couple of millimetres in diameter, to branches as thick as the thigh of a big man. Not only is it astonishing that this layer of tree relics is so extensive, but the contrast between this and the surrounding moorland, which does not display a single tree from horizon to wide horizon, is itself thought provoking. Tree remains like these are not uncommon at other locations in the Hebrides, but despite the ample evidence, it is only quite recently that scientists have pieced together the evidence from a variety of sources to describe the evolution of woodlands in the island, which show that in the past, the islands were neither treeless nor uniformly covered.[21]

With the departure of the ice, the first plant colonists were bryophytes – mosses and liverworts – and contemporary comparisons with the colonisation of new land in Iceland demonstrates that this process can be quite rapid, creating a vegetative landscape not dissimilar to the Gabhsann moor at present. In common with most of the rest of Scotland, the end of the last Ice Age left a landscape almost entirely devoid of trees, but over the following centuries, there was a fairly swift colonisation from mainland Europe, firstly of Birch around 8,000-7,600 BC, then by Hazel (7,500-7,000 BC) and various species of Willow - Grey Willow, Goat Willow, Eared Willow, and perhaps Tea-leaved Willow. Pine expanded through the Highlands after 5,500-5,000 BC, but it appears that although it reached the Hebrides, Pine never really became established in Gabhsann, with this northwest coast retaining a slightly different plant assemblage due to the wind exposure and the moist oceanic-edge climate. Pollen evidence, along with radiocarbon dating at numerous sites [22] suggests that in western Lewis, the Gabhsann landscape consisted of sedge-rich grassland and heathland communities and that by 9,300 years ago, the area was dominated by open, extensive, but not continuous woodlands of Birch scrub, with a mixture of Rowan, Aspen, Willow, Juniper, Hazel, and some Alder. It was possibly a similar habitat to areas of southwest Greenland today. Closed canopy forest probably did not exist at all in this region. There were cyclic phases of woodland decline and regeneration, broadly equivalent to changing ocean climatic patterns, and at this north-western edge of tree growth, it would not take much to initiate soil waterlogging, which would inhibit woodland growth and encourage the mosses and grasses to grow.

There has been contradictory speculation about the level of involvement of early human settlers in the clearance of tree cover in the islands,[24] with Viking raiders and early farmers getting anecdotal blame for burning the landscape. More recent ecological evidence, however, shows a more complex ecological pattern, which began thousands of years before the Vikings made any appearance.[24] About 11,600 years ago the vegetative cover started to increase, with Willows, Docks, ferns and grasses amongst the earliest colonisers. There was a major woodland decline around 7,900 years ago, and within 100 years, pollen analysis indicates that there was a covering of blanket peat communities similar to those which dominate today. This sudden demise of these western woodlands is more likely to have been from natural climatic fluctuations rather than human clearance, but the changing conditions, and the rapid growth of peatland vegetation progressively inhibited tree regeneration. There was a further and more extensive woodland decline around 5,200-4,000 years ago, possibly assisted by humans creating clearings for livestock grazing early agriculture, which resulted in the slow spread of blanket bog throughout the islands, to dominate a predominantly treeless landscape by around 2,500 years ago. Through a long series of continually changing environmental situations, the formation of blanket peat vegetation began in the Gabhsann landscape around 9,000-

8,000 years ago, and with the occasional presence of small woodland communities, has continued for thousands of years to the present day.

Perceptions of place

People see the landscape that they want to see.

There is a stereotypical perception which is typified in the romanticised writing of William Black, who in his setting for the Lewis-based 1874 novel *A Princess of Thule*,[25] begins his book;

> *"On a small headland of the distant island of Lewis, an old man stood looking out on a desolate waste of rain-beaten sea....";*

and later

> *"... what a wild and dismal country was this which lay before and all around me ..."*

Over the course of the book, the quaintness of the people is continually counterpoised with the bleakness of the landscape, and this is a formula lazily repeated by a number of other writers. For several generations around the turn of the nineteenth century, the Hebrides were depicted as a fantastic, magical land, full of supernatural drama which was reflected in the monstrous landscape and the strange people. To some extent this was understandable, if inaccurate, because the visitors who had left their comfortable urban homes in London and Edinburgh to travel north-west with some effort and discomfort, wanted to impress on their readers how *different* it all was in the islands, how heroic they had been to venture there, and how *wild* everything had been. Perhaps they lacked the knowledge or the subtlety to understand the complexities of the landscape and culture that they found, and covered their amazement the only way that they knew how, by embroidering their ignorance as mystical and the landscape as monotonous and fearsome.

The language that we use to describe the landscape is not value-neutral, however, and it has suited a certain metropolitan mind-set in various historical settings, right up until the present, to refer to rural areas, the Highlands and Islands in particular, and to Gaelic as the language of that landscape, in derisory and pejorative language. My friend, Professor James Hunter, in his writing on the linkages between the history of the Highlands and Islands and the different attitudes towards its natural environment, has commented frequently on the links between the Gaelic language and the land from which it developed, and highlights the *"... intimate relationship with community and place, land and language..."* [26]

Even those who should know better, occasionally lapse into the easy pretensions on the importance of (*their own*) place. In the regional *Flora of the Outer Hebrides* [27] one of the last regional guides of the flora of the UK to be published (in 1991) it was noted[28] that "*Lewis is a wilderness of bog and loch, Harris abounds in bog interspaced by bare rock…*". The editors noted that large areas of the mainland of Lewis have not been thoroughly explored, and that "*…This remains substantially true even now. The centre and east coast of North Lewis is still mainly unknown.…*". What they mean, of course, is unknown to *them*, and they betray their own perspective in the preface when they described the islands as "*some of the more distant and less accessible parts of the British Isles.*" From the perspective of my family, it is not distant or inaccessible. It is right outside our door, and I am continually entranced to discover that previous generations of residents, some long forgotten, have named and described this land in intimate detail, although they normally did not commit this knowledge to paper in order to be shared with the world community. There are sweet-water wells and other landforms which are specifically named after the ancestors of people who are still living in this area, and other locations of particular significance to former inhabitants of the village. This is not an unknown landscape - to those who have the empathy to enquire.

In a dissection of the importance of local knowledge and the impact of urban biases, Robert Chambers analyses the predicament precisely.[29] Although primarily referring to issues of development in Least Developed Countries, his observations are equally apt for most of the Highlands and Islands throughout history, and even today. He noted that when the urban visitors arrive from afar, they predominantly come in the summer, and so only have the vaguest notions about conditions at other times of the year. They rarely leave the tarmac, and so only have roadside experiences of places to which they can drive. Most frequently they will visit 'projects' where they have heard that 'something is being done'. Even before they arrive at these destinations, they will have a bias towards people who speak the same language as them, and frequently only the most articulate members of that community who are conversant with the professional language of their business, often only the males and only those of a certain age-group. These recurrent biases, even when unintentional, severely limit the exposure to the realities and complexities of the landscape, and of the social fabric of the communities (human and non-human) residing on that land.

My former colleague Andrew Currie described the history of botanical exploration as having taken place in four phases.[30] Not until 1964 was the classic work published that brought the natural history of the Highlands and Islands together as an ecological system.[31] In the period until 1830, the descriptions of the flowering plants and the general vegetation of the Outer Hebrides were restricted to the casual notes taken by the early visitors, such as Skye-man Martin Martin (who had travelled widely and studied at the University of Leiden); but botany was a very superficial interest, and many of the early 'explorers' focussed more on the oddities rather than on general descriptions. Next, in the period 1830-1930, came those travellers with a specific interest in natural history and plant-hunting, who made detailed lists and descriptions of what they found. Notable among them were the meticulous observations of William MacGillivray, who was of Harris descent, and lived for a time with his family in An Taobh Thuath (Northton). Later the Professor of Natural History at the University of Aberdeen, he wrote sensitively and carefully detailed accounts of his travels and produced beautiful, stunningly detailed, bird paintings, all of which is still valued today, but of course he was still a child of his time, with many of his descriptions described from birds that he had shot and plants that he had plucked in order to study them. Despite his obvious love of this land, he too once described it as *"the desolate isles of the west"*.[32] Significant too is that Arthur Bennett, a tradesman who lived in Croydon and for over a quarter of a century devoted himself to the study and publication of records of the Scottish flora, did not once visit Scotland during this time, relying instead on specimens which were sent to him. From 1930 until around 1980, the newer breed of botanical visitor did not simply compile lists of plants, but attempted to relate the plants to their habitats and the detailed ecology of the landscape, often returning year after year to produce valued methodical studies. Unfortunately an element of 'exploring the remote wild' still frequently persisted, and the perceived glory of being the 'first' to record the presence of some new, exotic plant, or to 'confirm' some personal biological theory sometimes led to controversial claims which proved difficult or impossible to confirm, and sowed a doubt of scandal among the more rigorous scientists.[33]

The final phase of botanical study began in the 1980s and was stimulated by - ultimately exaggerated and misinformed - claims by some conservationist organisations about what they perceived as threats to the natural environment of the islands from the State investment in an Integrated Development Programme for the Outer Hebrides. The fear was that crofting villages like Gabhsann would intensify agricultural production, and in so doing would damage the complex ecology of the machair and the moorland which make these wonderful habitats unique. The good outcome is that a considerable amount of detailed ecological study was conducted to document habitats, explore ecological relationships, and to establish baselines for future comparison, but though the forecasted damage never really resulted, the public outcry against 'external' specialists whose interests in the islands was only prompted by a concern for the wildlife rather than the people, left a bitter aftertaste which has taken years to redress. Most crofters and many other locals felt that the rich biodiversity of the crofting landscape had been created and nurtured by their land-use activities at a time when the 'conservationists' had regarded this region as not much more than a remote wilderness.

The moor

Over this topography, since the departure of the ice, two main soil types have developed to swathe the Gabhsann landscape with their constituent components. In a line roughly following the main road heading north-northwest up the coast, the landscape is bisected; to the east of the road the view is dominated by tens-of-thousands of hectares of peat, whereas to the west of the road, there are smaller patches of moorland, but these are interspersed with crofting villages and their long, linear fields of agriculturally re-worked land. This land, to be sure, is poor-grade agricultural land, mostly rough grazing, mostly shallow soils overlying the till, and frequently wet, but the green and yellow of the grasses between the lines of fences which demarcate the individual crofts, immediately distinguish it from the vegetation of the rolling moorland towards the centre of island. A common Gaelic epithet for the Isle of Lewis is *Eilean fraoich* – the island of Heather – and standing at the end of the village road looking to the horizon north, south, and east, this folk-name can be appreciated. It is a wonderful landscape, with waves of Heather on every rise and stumpy varieties of moor-grass in the hollows between, giving a dappled pattern to the land surface, like the sea changing its appearance every day, but with a more sensitive colour palette than the ocean. There are sensitive distinctions of brown and yellow, and washed-out green in the winter, flushes of bright greenery and vivid yellows, with the occasional dark sigmoidal traces of open peat-banks in the summer, changing to breath-taking ridges of shimmering purple as the Heather blooms in the autumn and re-starts the colour-cycle of the changing year. At times, stretches of white of fluffy Bog Cotton delineate the damper hollows and produce a cloud-like haze just above ground level. And in between the Heather and the Deer-grass lie the exotic gems that can be seen only by those who have eyes to notice and perception enough to recognise the importance of those treasures.

It is easy to look at the vast moor as a hostile, unchanging and monotonous landscape, but that is to look with eyes which are themselves hostile, unobservant, and which over-value novelty. Many of the early visitors to the islands combined plant-hunting as a respectable activity for a gentleman traveller. As they did throughout the British Empire, the Victorian 'adventurers' (and earlier) used the pseudo-scientific pursuit of botanical collecting as a means of attaching meaning and understanding to the landscape that they traversed. Initially, 'collecting' was a euphemism for shooting birds from the sky and digging up plants from the soil in order to convey them back to a comfortable study for identification. It is only relatively recently that peat-bogs and moorland have become valued in their own right as complex adaptive systems in which each component part is critically linked to another, and each species is uniquely adapted to survive and multiply in microhabitats where other species might flounder and die.

The geographical location of Gabhsann, at the junction between the landmass of Western Europe and the great stretch of the Atlantic Ocean, has a profound effect on the formation of the soil, and to a more noticeable extent, on the growth and survival of the plant-life covering the landscape. At a similar latitude to Juneau in Alaska, Perm in the Ural Mountains of Russia, and the settlement of Churchill on the Hudson Bay coast of Manitoba in Canada, the contrast in climate between those locations and Gabhsann is startling. While those other areas experience severe winters and deep snow, the area of Gabhsann normally experiences mild winters and summers which are warm, but not hot. If snow falls in Gabhsann, it frequently melts before it has time to accumulate on the ground. Snow or hard frost rarely lasts more than a day or two and it is not unusual to sit snow-free and watch the rest of the country grapple with blocked roads and cancelled services. Severe frosts are rare. Rainfall is not heavy, but a little bit is spread throughout the year and the oceanic influence contributes to a high humidity, averaging 85%.[34] Although the moderate temperatures mean that evaporation is generally low, the constant wind can be a challenge to both plants and animals (including people!) The lighthouse at Rubha Robhanais (the Butt of Lewis), about 14 Km to the north, regularly registers around 30% of the year winds of 'strong-to-gale-force' (in excess of 24 mph /36 k.p.h.). Winter storms are frequent, and the massive 29.41 metre (96.5 feet) wave which was measured trough to crest about 15 km off the coast of Gabhsann on 4 February 2013 shows no indication that waves of this magnitude are in any way unique to the area, simply that on this occasion, the appropriate technology was in the correct area to measure it.[35] Even with the milder temperatures, the desiccating effect of wind-chill can have negative effects on both humans and the vegetation.

Conventionally, the Gulf Stream and its North Atlantic Drift, an ocean current commencing in the Caribbean and bringing warming water to the west coasts of Scotland and Norway, is credited with producing the difference between the warmer Hebridean winters and the frigid temperatures at this latitude in North American and central Europe, but recent evidence suggests that this is only part of the story. There are transitions across isanthers as we move north and west, and even the flowering plants of Steòrnabhagh bloom two-to-three weeks earlier than they do in Gabhsann. While it is true that some subtropical plants grow here (I have several Cabbage-palm trees in my own garden) this is mainly a result of warmer winters caused by the seasonal storage and release of heat by the ocean and its interaction with atmospheric circulation producing warm maritime southwesterly winds.[36] Only along the northern areas of the Norwegian coast does the warming effect of the ocean by itself have any marked climatic warming effect, and this contributes to the melting of sea-ice as a knock-on impact.

Regardless of the specific mechanism, this combination of climatic factors produces a rich combination of environmental and biological effects. The changing of the seasons can be subtle gradations, with warm, frost-free temperatures in winter and rainy days in summer, but the contrasts can also be stark and magnificent. On a calm summer's evening it is often possible to hear a normal conversation between two people a kilometre or so distant, and the stillness and clarity of the air has the effect of shortening distance to bring far-away features of the land into sharp focus so that they appear to be much closer than they actually are. In contrast, the noise and physical fury of a winter's gale, or the intermittent tail of a hurricane, can be terrifying in its intensity, even for the most experienced of local residents. Both extremes have a way of making a lasting impression on a lover of the natural environment, and memories of specific evenings at both extremes can remain fresh for a lifetime.

The roadside ditches can be a linear riot of brilliant yellow, large-headed, Marsh Marigolds, with their vibrant green leaves, and the delicate but resilient blue flowers of Water Forget-me-not seeking out the damp hollows. They form living necklaces of colour across the field of view. The line of the main road also marks the transitional area of an ecotone between the sandier lime-rich soils of the coast with the acidic peatland vegetation - the so-called 'blackland' - which is fertile and so encouraged the establishment of villages along its route.

Ultimately, for most visitors to Gabhsann and the west coast of Lewis, it is the huge extent of moorland that dominates their first impressions, but most of this impression is gained from a car, or the solid safety of the tarmac road. True, walking across this vast moorland, one of the largest unbroken extents of blanket bog habitat in the world, can be very challenging and exhausting. Innumerable peat lochans and patches of broken ground mean that you can hardly ever walk in a straight line, and the tussocky vegetation necessitates constant detours and backtracking. In some areas, the narrow peatland drainage channels might be only 20cm wide, but camouflaged by vegetation and perhaps a metre or more deep. They are suddenly encountered fissures deep enough to twist an ankle or break the hip of an unwary walker. Walking straight out eastwards towards Loch Rumsagro, on the southeastern margin of the Common Grazing land of Gabhsann township, is a journey through time, with the skinned land and oldest exposed peat-cuttings in Gabhsann adjacent to the main road, and a steady accumulation of peat until it thins as the land begins to rise on the conical slopes of Sgritheabhal in the central moorland. Peat forms because the damp, humid, oceanic climate brings more precipitation than evaporation, so the shallow soils become waterlogged and the Sphagnum mosses become like a huge, saturated sponge draping over the land. In these waterlogged, oxygen-poor conditions, the micro-organisms which break down dead vegetation are inhibited, so the plant remains do not decompose and can accumulate to several metres depth. Peat forms at different rates, accumulating up to 5m deep in the damp rock basins or just a thin covering on the more exposed ridges, but a blanket-bog such as the Gabhsann moor will normally grow deeper at the rate of about 1 mm per year.

There has been a lot written about peatlands generally [23] and about blanket bogs, but one of the few detailed ecological studies of the peatlands of Gabhsann, one of the few which got well away from the road into the centre of the moor at Blàr nam Faoileag,[38] gave a rich analysis of the small intricacies and complexities of this habitat. In this vast peatland, covering about 430 km², or 79% of the island north of the main road from Steòrnabhagh to Calanais, it is possible to walk for days without seeing a single human, but the discerning eye will notice subtle but distinct gradations in the vegetation. There are zonations from the damp hollows to the drier edges of slightly higher land. There are innumerable pools of water, from the size of a large puddle to a small loch, on which there is abundant pink-and-white Bogbean sticking above the surface, or perhaps the large white-and-yellow flowers of White Water Lily, with their flat, almost circular leaves, floating on the waters. Sporadically, there are peat mounds, strange structures of obscure origins of formation, protruding up to a couple of metres in height above the surrounding land, and covered with Heather, Crowberry, and Hare's-tail Cottongrass. More commonly than not, ecologists describe their discoveries in the arcane descriptors of a dead language, but while Latin specific names can be highly descriptive of the morphology or colour of a species, and might even include a reminder of the name of the original discovering botanist, they are not syllables which spring lightly into common conversation. But surprisingly, these names too are part of this place too - hidden from many people due to the precision of the science, but nonetheless, native to this place. (See appendix 3)

Within this bogland there are many surprises, from the colourful micro-habitats of different mosses, each with their own invertebrate communities, to the delight of finding a gnarled Dwarf Juniper, hugging the ground to avoid the wind - how old it is, it is impossible to judge just by eye. There are small green patches on the moor, like islands of lushness among the browns of the heathland vegetation, such as at the land south of Tom a' Mhile, where the guano and seeds carried by the Lesser Black-backed Gulls fertilise the tough sward, or like at Àsmaigearraidh, where the attempts at agriculture and disturbed drainage remain as evidence of abandoned human activities. Heather is classified as a sub-climax vegetation in this part of the world, meaning that the natural ecological succession has not yet proceeded to a condition of final climax, which in the case of Gabhsann might revert to a low, open scrub covering the ground. In many areas of the moor nowadays, the Heather is tall and difficult to walk over, because few of the crofters are grazing their livestock on the Common Grazing - it is easier to manage a small sheep flock or a few cows on the fenced-in croftland. Much of the vegetation is a combination of variations upon a common range of species, but there are moorland delights like the multiple flower-spikes of Bog Asphodel - a small pyramid of yellow petals with orange tips - which is not really an asphodel at all, but loves the acidic, low-calcium soils. Or the startling discovery that there are many varieties of Orchids scattered throughout this one village, some like the Heath Spotted-Orchid on the moor, or the Hebridean Spotted Orchid on the croftland outside my window. Others such as the Early Marsh-Orchid or the Frog Orchid, or the Northern Marsh Orchid prefer the sandier grasslands of the coastal fringe. There are several other species of orchids and many hybrid varieties, incredibly difficult even for many experienced botanists to differentiate, which are unique not just to different islands, but to different microhabitats within the same landscape. There are exotic delights lying hidden in this landscape, but they do not disclose their treasures easily to those who do not put in the effort to discover them.

A square metre of discovery

It often intrigues me that professional botanists can spend several hours on their knees in a bog, minutely examining and recording a single square metre of random vegetation. I do mean random, because a key factor in the scientific recording of plant communities is to avoid, accidentally or on purpose, selecting sites which look 'typical' or 'interesting'. To be accurately representative of a plant community, the precision of the biological recording has to be matched by the randomness of the selection of the sample site. Despite our best intentions, we frequently get tempted to be drawn to the exceptional rather than the recurrence of the dominant species. The botanical recorder carries a very light wooden frame exactly one metre square, cross-hatched by thin wires of gut dividing the internal dimensions of the frame equally into nine smaller squares. This wooden frame then gets tossed over the shoulder, or with eyes closed, sent whizzing like an awkward giant frisbee, to land at random on the habitat to be explored. If this is a long-term study – for habitat management, for example – a corner is then marked with a wooden peg (so that the location can be found months or years later) and the square is aligned to the cardinal points of the compass. Only then can the slow, delicate, and meticulous process of documentation begin, as the botanist seeks to note the identity and approximate abundance of each species within each of the nine small squares within the delineated square metre.

I have been out on the moor of Gabhsann on many days, having a nose-to-ground inspection of the vegetation, sometimes as part of a study to estimate the grazing impact of the roaming herds of Red Deer, and sometimes just to explore what is out on that moor. In an area of deep blanket bog, such as at Blàr nan Stearnag, or perhaps far out at Blàr nam Faoileag,[38] I have squatted down on damp knees to see what I can find. In the midst of the dominant covering of Heather, Deergrass, and Cross-leaved Heath, the diversity of plant species in those randomly-chosen square-metres can be truly astonishing. Common among the plants are Bog-sedge and Common Cottongrass, often with some small patches of White Beak-sedge, or perhaps straggling trails of Bog Pondweed or Bogbean among the wetter areas. In summer, when it is easier to locate and identify plants that have been sheltering for the winter months, there will usually be several Great Sundew or maybe its relative, the Round-leaved Sundew, studding the ground beneath the quadrants of the wooden frame. Tough, gnarled Tormentil, with its delightfully small yellow flowers, is never far away, and if we are lucky, a splash of colour is added to our species list with spiky yellow heads of Bog Asphodel, and the gentle flowers of a Common Butterwort with its violet petals fading to a white 'throat' lightly suspended high on a slender stem above its star-shaped, insect-loving leaves. There will be Purple Moor-grass within many of these recording frames, and Many-stalked Spike-rush. There will be several species of sedge, but here things begin to get complicated, for it takes training, patience, and lots of experience to differentiate between the fibrous tufted stems of Carnation Sedge, or Slender Sedge, or Dioecious Sedge, or Few-flowered Sedge – plants that most non-botanists do not know even exist.

Then there are the ubiquitous Sphagnum mosses which might form most of the ground-cover of our square-metre frame, and here our problems of identification really step up a notch or two. There may be six or seven separate species of Sphagnum within a very small area, and it often may require an experienced field botanist to retreat to the security of a microscope in the laboratory to ensure accurate identification – even a photograph may not provide certainty. There will commonly be the dainty Slender Cow-horn Bog-moss forming loose mats of golden-orange ground-cover, and frequently Lustrous Bog-moss in dense cushions and small hummocks of green-and-salmon-pink branches which look top-heavy when they absorb water. There will be large shoots of Feathery Bog-moss, which can range from green to almost washed-out white, or perhaps the distinctive Red Bog-moss, with its flat-topped shoots which can form extensive carpets of spongy moss and from which it is easy to extract a single shoot without pulling apart the whole clump. If we are lucky, there will be Soft Bog-moss, the smallest of the British Sphagnum species, which falls apart when handled, but is unlikely to be confused with any other species because it is a rich yellow-orange colour and is often found in low, flat patches about the size of a dinner plate. Similarly, Magellanic Bog-moss occurs in low cushions intermediate between the tops of hummocks and the rolling hollows and is a deep wine-red or perhaps a mixture of red-and-green, whereas the Papillose Bog-moss seems very similar, but is a pale ochre-brown or yellowish-green, but is never red. Seen at close quarters this simple, random square metre of ground can be a kaleidoscope of colours and textures which can baffle all but the most experienced and the most dedicated observers. Did someone say that this landscape is monotonous? I have yet to get a definitive answer from any botanist who can tell me exactly how many diverse species of plants survive in the security of the Gabhsann moor.

Carnivorous plants, and other delights

As we were walking on the moor one early-Spring morning, following a narrow stream-side sheep-path, winding beside the Allt Grunndal, my eye was captured by a small splash of vivid green among the uniform grey-brown clumps of Heather. The Heather had not yet begun to develop its new-season growth, so the contrast with the lime-green moss was quite startling, and when we drew closer, the reason for its presence became obvious. Wedged among the Heather tussocks was the dried and decomposing remains of a gull which had perished over the winter, probably snuggling inside the maze of tussocks for a last, fruitless attempt to gain shelter and warmth. The green moss was growing on the white carcass. In this nutrient-poor soil, the carcass of the gull would have been a bonanza for the moss, adapted to take advantage of any passing opportunity to suck up sustenance whenever a chance presents. Nor is this uncommon, for several species of plants on the moor of Gabhsann are wonderfully suited to this challenging environment. Among my favourite plants, although they are fairly common here with their red-and-green starburst outlines, are those that are exotically, and intriguingly, carnivorous.

When we hear mention of 'carnivorous plants' most people probably imagine strange Amazonian man-eaters, or perhaps something in a dreadful B-list movie Hollywood horror film, but there are half-a-dozen delightful species dotted across this northern landscape. Delightful, that is, unless you happen to be a Midge, or a small fly, because a couple of species of Butterwort, and three or four species of Sunflower specialise in trapping and digesting small insects to secure their scarce supply of nutrients. It was Charles Darwin who first demonstrated that some carnivorous plants capture insects as a source of nitrogen and phosphorous, but if you get your nose right down near ground-level and search among the moss, it is easy to observe the process for yourself. Over the short northern summer, the little green buds of the Sundew burst into a new phase of life and develop a rosette of sticky green leaves covered with tiny hair-like, red fibres. Apart from the clue in their English names, the Round-leaved Sundew and the Oblong-leaved Sundew are perhaps difficult for the botanically inexperienced observer to differentiate, but the leaves of the former are roundish and lie mostly flat on the peat and grow on the higher, drier parts of the bog surface, while the latter have leaves which are gently inclined or even erect, and prefer the lower and damper parts, even on open and water-covered areas of mud.[39] Small insects are attracted to the colourful leaves, but get covered in their sticky coating, and are eventually dissolved by the enzymes which are released by the plant to secure its nitrogen intake. Once trapped on the sticky leaf, the struggles of the insect only serve to encourage the production of more digestive enzymes, and hasten the consumption of the insect.

There is also another species locally, the Great Sundew, but while the three species share the same geographical coverage across the Gabhsann landscape, they each prey on a slightly different range of insects and prefer to occupy subtly different microhabitats on the moor. Botanists have shown that the rate of insect capture increases with the area of the leaves, and that the growth of new leaves is directly related to insect capture.[40]

Surprisingly, the Sundews are not the only carnivorous plants on the Gabhsann moor.[41] Despite being regarded as botanical oddities, it has been discovered that several plant species have adapted to survive in sunny but wet and nutrient-poor habitats such as peat-bogs, where the nutritional benefit gained from capturing insects can give them an edge on survival.[42] Although unrelated, two species of Butterwort are also found on the moor of Gabhsann and they too obtain their nutrient intake by capturing and digesting insect prey. The Common Butterwort and the Pale Butterwort can be harder to find among the ground vegetation, because they do not have the self-advertising red rosette of the Sundew, and they can be difficult to find among the Sphagnum mosses until the flowers bloom. Called 'pinguicula' after their fat, glistening leaves, and 'butterwort' because of their application by early peoples to curdle milk and produce a yoghurt-like fermentation, the Butterworts have a distinctive delicately blue flower, held on a long stem just high enough above the sticky leaves to ensure against trapping potential pollinators instead of a potential meal.

The Gaels, who have inhabited this landscape longer than anyone can remember, have named every part of it that was familiar to them (which is in fact everything) as did the Norse settlers, who came, stayed a while, then left or intermarried. Some people say that, as a general rule, the names of places which can be seen as landmarks from the sea, have names derived from the Norse, while the inland names were given by the Gaels. Superficially this has some truth, but as always there are many exceptions and oddities. There are names of places which betray a Norse derivation, but which are rendered now in the Gaelic mode of spelling. There are place-names whose meaning and origin are now lost beyond time. What is clear from the topographical nomenclature is that the Gaelic-speaking inhabitants were intimately familiar with every part of their landscape. The naming of the configurations of the land is intimately connected with the Gaelic language, and the Gaelic language is intimately reflected in the nature of that indigenous landscape. Land which might be simply called 'moor' in English has a wide diversity of descriptive names, based perhaps on the geomorphology, the colours, the predominant covering of vegetation, and/or the perceived usefulness of that land. This land is not the deep, fertile farmland common further south, but it is neither a wilderness, nor is it bleak. Neil Gunn, in one of his Highland novels *The Other Landscape*,[43] explores the concept of a hidden landscape beyond the visible one. He describes it to be like having two similar conversations with different men and liking the first man but distrusting the second because some 'other conversation' in the subconscious background led him to detect features and characteristics which gave different interpretations of what he could actually see. Some people read landscapes like this, and these are the impressions that I have as I walk, and work, and live in Gabhsann.

There are subtle distinctions between a knoll (*bacan*), a little hillock (*cnoc*), a hill (*beinn*) a rounded hill standing apart (*cruach*) and the ridge of a hill which is the edge of a precipice (*faobhar*). A Gaelic-speaking traveller would welcome the descriptive terminology of the land, in much the same manner as Aboriginal songlines, which give details of the landscape that travellers expected to encounter. Navigational points such as an *abair* (the confluence of two streams) a *blianag* (a green, level spot of land) or a *bugha* (a green spot by the windings of a stream) and a *dronnag* (the highest point of a ridge) are as distinctive as they are self-descriptive. Enthusing over a map today, I am left in my imagination, wondering who in the past made use of a *cro-sheilg* (a hiding place for hunters), or a *dìon-aite* (a place of refuge or sanctuary) or who practiced *falach-fuinn* (land-hiding: taking advantage of every natural feature on the landscape to hide themselves). (See appendices 1 and 2.)

It was necessary for those who worked the land for their survival to know the difference between *artach* (stony ground) and *banbh* (land unploughed for a year), between *claigionn* (the best field of arable land on a farm) and *daibhir* (the worst pasture of a farm). Wildlife was an intimate facet of life to those early residents of Gabhsann; the coastline to the north of the village is guarded by Sgarbh Sgeir (the reef of the Shag) and to the south by Stac an Dobhrain (the sea-cliff of the Otter), while in the interior moorland, Blàr nam Faoileag (the level, flat spot of the gull) and Blàr nan Stearnag (the level, flat spot of the Tern) advertise their faunal residents. (I once had a friend visiting, who enthusiastically announced that he had found a 'new colony' for the survey of terns that I was doing at that time, and when I produced an Ordnance Survey map in anticipation, he plunked his forefinger down on Blàr nan Stearnag, which has been known by that name probably for several hundred years: it helps to understand the language of the land that you are passing through.) The description of the land is also recorded in fine gradations of detail according to the most distinctive flora, so an area is *fineagach* when it is full of Crowberries, or *eachrann* (a place where Brambles grow) *dearcach* (abounding in berries) or named according to the very many trees and bushes that provide ground-cover, such as *coille-challtuin* (Hazel wood) or *conasgach* (abounding in Gorse) or *bùnnsach* (a spot where Willows grow). This landscape was neither 'bleak' nor 'monotonous' to those who named it; each slope and turn of the topography was significant and full of detail.

At the eastern edge of Gabhsann, lots of small *feithean* (very small channels in the bog that have been opened by seeping water) feed into a slightly larger conduit, such as Feadan Hiadagro (the small watercourse of Hiadagro) which in turn flows into a marginally larger stream (*allt*) such as Allt Stiuacleit, or the burn in Gleann na Siga, which empties itself into the even larger Abhainn Gabhsann bho Thuath (North Galson River) and then to the ocean. Such is the capacity of the moor to absorb and retain precipitation that these waters run all year long, although in the drier summer months the smaller rivulets may flow quietly underground (a *còs-shruth*) through the peat, unregarded and unnoticed by human visitors. The Gaelic names for wet places seem almost innumerable. The common term 'bog' that has descended into English use is a poor, shorthand version for a myriad of different hydrographic and vegetational situations ranging from the welcome *fìor-thobrach* (a place abounding in perennial springs or wells) (there are at least five wells in the village of Mealabost, five in Gabhsann bho Dheas, and another four in Gabhsann bho Thuath) through the *càthar* (mossy, soft ground, in the dry part of a peat bog) or a *currach* (a bog where shrubs grow) to the place which is *boglach* (quagmire) and could spell the end for careless livestock, or the crofter who goes to look for them.

For the Gaelic-speaking travellers across this landscape, their route is well marked-out - even if they have never travelled there before - because the nomenclature of the land *describes* this land in detail. Neither so fluid nor so formalised in tradition as the Aboriginal Songlines of Australia,[44] nevertheless, the Gael would know the specific shapes of the landforms to be encountered on the journey, the colours of the land, perhaps the dominant vegetation to be travelled across. This is not a landscape which has been deprived of people. This is not a landscape which is unknown, even if fewer people now traverse its mosses. This landscape is neither barren nor bleak. This is not a wilderness.

Let's face reality, among the many definitions and the many arguments for and against 'wilderness' (if by the term 'wilderness' we are referring to a landscape untouched by humans)[45] then there is no wilderness left in the UK. In fact, even 'wild land' is often a somewhat pejorative term, mainly used by urbanites on their recreational excursions to the countryside. The contemporary concept of 'rewilding the countryside' is a rather misguided and somewhat delusional understanding of ecology. Much of this 'wild land' in the Highlands and Islands is only empty of people at the present time because the people who once lived on this land were ruthlessly cleared by a previous generation of economic missionaries who were allowed to put their personal gain ahead of the public good. The great natural scientist and writer Frank Fraser Darling perceptively chronicled much of this interconnection between humans and the natural environment in his monumental work *"West Highland Survey"* (subtitled, incidentally, *"An essay in Human Ecology"*).[46] Although he famously called the landscape of the Highlands and Islands a *"wet desert"* because of the generations of ecological damage done by overgrazing by sheep, moor-burning, and human-impact, elsewhere in his writing he emphasised the benefits of multi-purpose land management and noted:

> *"This has resulted in a considerable increase in the beauty of our countryside because, let me emphasize, much of what we call beauty in the countryside stems from conditions of ecological repose. We sense the beauty even if we have not a clue about the ecology."*[47]

From the main road, looking southeast across the great expanse of heathland vegetation, the Gabhsann moor may appear to be monotonous and unchanging, but venturing out into this landscape with an open mind and an alert vision reveals an enormity of great and complex beauty. Standing on the slopes of Beinn Dail, having made the strenuous effort to reach this landmark, and looking back towards the three villages of Gabhsann, is to sense a deep and overwhelming absorption into this landscape. If you think the Gabhsann moor looks endless when regarding it from the comfort of your car, it seems positively immense when you stand at the centre and look towards the sea horizon. Only from your experience gained by walking those many kilometres over difficult bog, by retracing your route around the intricate network of lochans and marsh, stopping to examine those abandoned sheilings and to admire those rare and beautiful flowers, do you become aware that this land is not 'empty'; it is simply invisible to those who cannot see.

In a philosophical frame of mind, Barry Lopez has said, *"it is precisely what is invisible in the land… that makes empty space… into a place."*[48]

CHAPTER 3

A metropolis of birds

The first residents

Occasionally I speculate on the possible first residents of Gabhsann. At this distance in time it is impossible to say with any certainty, but if I were a betting man (which I'm not) I would say that the Shag might have a pretty good claim to being the first living vertebrate to move into the area.

Despite being seabirds that spend their lives in and around water, the plumage of Shags is not waterproof, which accounts for the images of them commonly sitting with their wings outstretched on the broken reef-rocks just off the Gabhsann coast. They are drying their feathers. Their glossy black silhouettes against the white background of the surf, with their wings partially extended, and that long beak, slightly hooked at the tip, suggests a hangover from many millennia of geological time, and that would be correct. There are fossils of the ancestral cormorants dating from 60-65 million years ago. Think about it, this is a bird species whose ancestors were around when dinosaurs walked the earth, and then when the rapid climate change swiftly drove the dinosaurs into extinction, the Shags adapted so perfectly to take advantage of their changed environment, that their descendants have survived in an easily recognisable form to the present day. The earliest fossils of a distinctively European Cormorant appear in the

Late Oligocene, perhaps 25 million years ago, and while Cormorants and Shags may appear to us to look so very similar today, their morphology is the result of convergent evolution in a similar habitat,[49] for although they are related deep in the geological record, their relationship is so distant that in human terms, it would not crop up in a casual family conversation about the relatives. Those features shared by the Shag and the Cormorant are common characteristics which have enabled them to thrive in a hostile environment, and to survive to pass those survivalist advantages to a subsequent generation.[50]

The Shag is a bird of the north and west, favouring the islands and living off a variety of small fish, for the species is an opportunistic predator, diving on average thirteen metres below the sea surface (although a dive of 38 m was recorded) to hunt for middle-zone and bottom-living fish species.[51] They are birds of both land and water, and can remain submerged for up to 3-4 minutes at a time. There are not very many days that I walk the shore at Gabhsann and do not see a Shag, fishing, or drying its wings, or a lone bird flying purposefully over the sea, or simply sitting motionless, waiting to identify the next meal. Their cocky crested head feathers at breeding time and their intense, steadfast eye give them a primitive, predatory look, but that's what they are. (Ironically, their Latin Family name, *Phalacrocoracidae*, means 'bald crow'). Their nests are seldom seen in the village area, because Shags prefer low cliff edges and offshore skerries to construct – build is too grand a word – their shambolic nests of gathered seaweed, looking like a rope-basket made by a very young child. The Shag is ideally suited to the environment of this rocky coastline, and as their breeding success is thought to be closely related to the sea temperature and the abundance of food, they make excellent ecological indicators of the state of the marine environment. Although an individual Shag in its first winter may wander a considerable distance, the majority of them return to their birth areas and remain close to their nest-sites, usually foraging within 5 km of this base. They are tenacious survivors, and they reside here all year long. They are residents, and they are here to stay, and that's something that I like about them.

But I will come back to the resident birds in due course, because if you think that the local bird population is sedentary and unchanging, you would be very far from the truth. Perhaps even more so than the human population over the centuries, the birds that can be found in this small area of the island are regular global travellers, to an extraordinary degree.[52] Reading through the bird-ringing records of the Outer Hebrides compiled by the British Trust for Ornithology is an exotic experience of travel-by-proxy. Poised at the edge of the European landmass to the east, and the swirling waters of the Atlantic Ocean to the west, the Isle of Lewis is the last stop (or first stop) of the wandering birds that are blown off-course, or simply using the island as a staging post in their annual migrations. Looked at in this light, Gabhsann has the appearance of a big, green, side-room in the International Departures lounge of a huge modern airport. Year by year, and month by month, the local bird population steadily changes. Some birds simply pass through Gabhsann regularly but don't stay, like the sleek white lines of darts of Gannets heading north and south, flying low over the sea and pausing to plummet vertically in pursuit of fish. Or the White-tailed Sea Eagle spreading its huge wings to cruise over the area with its sharp-eyed reconnaissance. Standing on the raised beach watching long lines of hundreds of black-and-white Guillemot, out of the hundreds-of-thousands that breed in the region, urgently flapping their way past the village, heading north-east or south-west, is an exhilarating prospect. These visitors may not breed here, and they are certainly are not seen in their thousands, like the Gannets nesting on the island of Sula Sgeir just 90 km to the north, nor the awesome sight of eight Sea Eagles soaring together in the sky above the local wildlife reserve at Loch Stiapabhat in Nis, but their passage through Gabhsann is a regular occurrence and an important landmark in the pattern of their lives.

There are winter visitors to Gabhsann and summer visitors, although even to categorise birds as 'wintering away' is to imply a false and human-centred perspective on their behaviour. Breeding species such as the Arctic Tern (more common here than the "Common Tern") defend their short-grass, cliff-top nesting sites with relentless ferocity against intruders, but once the frenetic burst of egg-laying and fledging is over, like many other bird species, they head south. The Arctic Tern, however, does not just make a short hop to the warmer countryside of the Mediterranean. Every year of their lives, perhaps for 30+ years, these individual Arctic Terns quit the breeding grounds of their Hebridean summer, and towards the end of August they begin their incredible, meandering migration to the southern ocean of Antarctica. Following two broad flight-paths along the African or the South American coast, they stopover in a few regular areas of high marine productivity, spend a few months in the Antarctic summer, then begin their return to the Hebrides, taking perhaps only 40 days in each direction to make the trips. It is nonsense to think of those Arctic Terns that are swooping at our heads on the cliff-tops of Gabhsann as 'wintering' in the south, for it is only we humans who are wintering. It is staggering to realise that this small, frisky creature can annually travel a round trip of around 70,900 km (44,000 miles), perhaps the longest individual migration of any species on this planet, from almost-Pole to almost-Pole, living in continual summer, and seeing more daylight and less darkness than any other species.[53] They 'return' to Gabhsann to breed, but like any truly dedicated traveller, is anywhere truly their home?

Nor are such long-distance flights unusual. A sporadic but intriguing visitor, the Red-necked Phalarope, appears here at the southern extremity of its breeding range, and its short visits - arriving mid-May and leaving by the end of August - simply add to the novelty of its appearance. Its habit of spinning rapidly in an aqueous ballet on the loch surface as it feeds on insects, together with the fact that it is the male who takes the responsibility for incubating the eggs and raising the young, are well-known. But its nest-sites are not, and it is going to stay that way. Nor has it been clear where the Scottish birds go when they leave the nest, although recent tagging with geolocator devices has shown that most birds cross the Atlantic towards Labrador, travel down the eastern seaboard of North America, and winter between the Galapagos and the north-west coast of South America, a total migration of 22,000 km.[54] Even the tiny, white-rumped Wheatears that seem to flit along the fence-lines of every single croft in the village, depart to equatorial Africa each Autumn and return to Gabhsann in mid-March to herald the arrival of our Spring with their nest-building activities.

There are four basic habitats in the area known as Gabhsann, several smaller micro-habitats, and one ecotone (where different communities of plants and animals meet and integrate) which bisects the village boundaries. There is the shore and the coastal zone, then perpendicular to the coast runs the shallow valley of the Abhainn Gabhsann bho Dheas. The river cuts through the agricultural areas of the crofts (known collectively as the "inbye") and has its main catchment in the extensive area of blanket-bog moorland lying to the south and east of the main road. Of course, many of the animal inhabitants, especially the birds, move comfortably between these four main habitats to conduct the different purposes of their behavioural activities. Some species, such as the gulls, appear to be happy in every habitat, sullen optimists watching their chances on the shore, or the fields of the crofts, or at their nesting sites on the moor. Other species show a definite preference; the Greylag Geese, previously only visitors but now year-round residents, prefer the grassy fields of the crofts, and leave their fecal remains widely scattered as proof of their occupancy. They are often joined by their distant relatives the Barnacle Geese, who strut their black-and-white dress-sense between late September and late April as they pass through to or from their nesting sites in Svalbard or East Greenland.

The ubiquitous gulls

Out on the reef at Reidheadal, just beyond where the road from the former farmhouse goes down to the shore and meets the beach, crowds of gulls frequently gather on the rocks. There is a 'club' area where unpaired and immature birds gather during the day, although they glide back to their moorland nesting areas to roost at night. Some of these gulls, such as the formidable Great Black-backed Gull, and the smaller but no less numerous Herring Gull, are residents in the village, dispersing around the islands of the Hebrides and the west coast mainland during the winter, but returning to Gabhsann to nest with the arrival of each spring. Mixed among these, the plentiful Lesser Black-backed gulls can easily be distinguished from their larger black-backed relations by their smaller size, and yellow legs, and from the Herring Gulls which have a light-grey back and pinkish legs (like the Great Black-backed).

These Lesser Black-backed Gulls have an interesting story to tell, for although they return in the spring of each year to a flat, grassy area of moorland just beyond the horizon of the village, they leave at the end of summer, to wander down in stages to the south of Spain, Portugal, and to North Africa. To understand why birds migrate, it is important to realise that migration is a response of the species to the need for survival, it's not just random movement. This realisation helps to explain why the Lesser Black-backed Gull does not migrate south by the shortest possible route, but instead makes substantial detours and largely follows the coast in short stages, stopping frequently to forage.[55] Like many gulls, this species is an opportunistic feeder and also utilises a variety of different flight techniques at different stages, from flapping to soaring or gliding, depending on the thermal conditions. It combines these traits to minimise the biological cost of migration. This fly-and-forage technique is useful, as it saves the energy needed to expend on flight, together with allowing stoppages at plentiful feeding localities to sustain them as they travel.

The return journey each spring follows a similar behaviour, although in both directions individual Lesser Black-backed Gulls, unlike many other migrating species, tend to follow a diversity of routes and stop over at different locations to congregate. Just how they navigate back to Gabhsann, is still a mystery, although recent studies seem to indicate that many seabirds somehow maintain 'mental maps' of huge swathes of geography enabling them to have a spatial awareness of both seasonal feeding locations and their "home" nesting sites.[56] For the Lesser Black-backed Gulls of Gabhsann, the visual cue of the colourful bright green, guano-enriched splash of moor amid the tussocks of fibrous Deer Grass, the dark clumps of woody Heather and straggly lochans, must be a powerful stimulus to land. Once they have met their mates and started to nest, they make this small corner of Gabhsann their own, and it is a brave walker who will risk the wrath of their aerial bombardment in its defence. The Black-backs are mixed with Herring Gulls, lying on an eroded blanket-bog, with the nests perched on tussocks of Soft Rush, Hare's-tail Cottongrass, and Woolly Fringe-moss.[57] (Do they prefer the slight ridges because they are drier, or because they give better observation from the nest?). We used to go out to this green sward every year to gather sheep from the moor for shearing. The sheep liked to nibble the fresh green grass, and passed slowly among the nesting gulls, largely unmolested, but any human approach always produced a whirling, screaming, wing-flapping cacophony of aerial gymnastics. The gulls would not usually actually strike intruding humans, but the frenzy of their contorted flights was fast, multi-directional, and enough to intimidate all but the most stoic shepherd. These days, the village sheep are not normally put to the moor, and the gulls are left largely undisturbed.

On the edge of the gull colony there reside a growing number of Bonxies - the Great Skua - (and the intermittent explorations of its relative, the Arctic Skua) - whose UK breeding grounds were once only in Shetland. I can remember exactly when the first Bonxies came to nest in Gabhsann. One early-April day in 1981 they were suddenly there, solid, brown, and humourless, keeping watch on a small hillock overlooking the Lesser Black-backs.[58] I was already familiar with their behaviour from close encounters on Hiort, the largest of the St Kildan islands, so as I walked nearer the hillock I was prepared for the pair to rise effortlessly into the air and commence their broad, circling flight-path. Nothing, however, equips you for what comes next, not even when you have prior experience of the bird's behaviour. After a couple of low fly-passes as you get nearer the nest-site, a swoop perhaps a mere two metres above you, which feels close for a bird with the bulk of a Bonxie travelling at speed, the intimidation becomes serious. The next aerial interception comes swooping in quickly about waist height, and even the most familiar Bonxie-watcher feels compelled to flinch ever-so-slightly, and perhaps to duck their head. This is an elemental mistake, for the next swooping attack comes careering in at knee-height, and with this impetus, the human instinctively bends almost doubled-over to avoid being hit (and they *will* thud the head and draw blood). The contest is normally over, and all but the most ardent birder will retreat quickly, pursued by a close fly-past from the victorious Bonxie. For this reason, most people will remember their first encounter with a Bonxie, and this makes it easier to recognise them, count them, and indirectly to test a theory of mine. Bonxies have probably been nesting in the Outer Hebrides since the early 1950's - an overspill from their core breeding areas in Shetland - but their appearance was limited to the Druim Mòr area near Griais, on the east coast of Lewis.

Their arrival in Gabhsann, on the opposite, western, edge of the great moor of northern Lewis was at first surprising, but then later understandable.

After a lot of long-distance moor walking, and Bonxie-watching, it became clear that the expansion of the Bonxies beyond the Druim Mòr followed a clear pattern of association with established gull colonies, dotted like a living necklace across the wide expanse of moorland between the Druim Mòr and Gabhsann. There is a well-documented kleptoparasitic relationship between the Bonxies and the gulls, with the Bonxies simply following their food supply of the eggs and young chicks which are supplied by the gull colonies.[59] The gulls and their young are numerous, and no match for the strongarm tactics of the bumptious Bonxies. Their defensive response is so finely-attuned that it is easy to delimit the breeding territory of each individual Bonxie pair simply by walking towards the nest-mound and noting the point where the birds rise into the air - then step a few paces back and they will land again. Do this by approaching from different directions and the borders of the Bonxie territory will become clear. All intruders are left in no doubt about who 'owns' this piece of Gabhsann.

Not long after the departure of the Lesser Black-backed Gulls, other gulls frequently choose to visit. When we have been in the right spot, at the right time, and been sufficiently alert, these winter visitors have been recognised as an Iceland Gull, or a Glaucous Gull, both arriving from the Arctic north, from East Greenland, or even further west from Baffin Island, or perhaps north-east from the Barents Sea.[60] On one memorable occasion on Hiort we spotted a Laughing Gull as a rare summer visitor, but recording rarities and isolated birds like these is so heavily dependent on chance – that a bird should land within sight of a human who is interested enough to recognise something different, and knowledgeable enough to positively identify an uncommon species - that many, many stray visitors to the island must pass through unrecorded. A stray wind from the Arctic north has occasionally brought a Snow Bunting, (normally at the southern limit of its breeding range) an Arctic Redpoll, or a Lapland Bunting with its distinctive triangle of chestnut-brown at the back of the neck (both from Greenland north of the Arctic Circle). They land in Gabhsann, rest awhile, then move on as their strength recovers. In a delightful explosion of flitting and fluttering, the Redwings arrive from Iceland, the Faroe Islands and from Scandinavia in late September, living at the westermost limit of their breeding range. These beautiful thrushes have a pale stripe above the eye and elegant flashes of red on their flanks, and they fill the bushes along the village road. They scatter over the croftland and whirl around cars and houses as they make their way to the south of Europe and the western Mediterranean.[61] The duration of their stay in Gabhsann is short, but memorable.

The visitors

One year a Snowy Owl appeared in the village, perhaps a victim of the periodic collapse of the Lemming population in north-west Russia, or from beyond the Urals (it is instructive to note the interconnectedness of our global ecosystem where a disruption in one country has an effect in another, perhaps 4000 km away). The Snowy Owl was obviously lost, and stood waiting for a mate for several weeks, clearly visible from the main road, like a large white fertiliser bag among the peats, until it eventually gave up and moved on. Before it left, hundreds of twitchers – those extreme birders who obsessively tick off the species that they have seen – arrived in Gabhsann from all over the UK. They came by bus, by chartered plane and by hired car to stand in groups at the edge of the village to observe the bird, perhaps to snatch a blurry photograph, and to tick *Nyctea scandiaca* off their 'must-see' list, before heading for the ferry or the airport and making their own journeys back home.

Another year, a Glossy Ibis appeared in Gabhsann, blown off-course from somewhere in the Balkans, and looking distinctly out of place as it strutted stiffly around the crofts, pecking the ground energetically and searching for food. Within hours the news spread mysteriously on the social network grapevine: some local twitchers appeared, but with less ostentation than the Snowy Owl followers, and the bird quietly left before the twitchers outnumbered the locals.

From the window of my study I can see the patch of Yellow Iris down by the river, at the edge of the croft grassland, where there is occasionally an enigmatic visitor to Gabhsann. The Corncrake has its core UK population in the Hebrides and the northern isles, with over 90% of the 1300+ UK breeding birds concentrated here. These birds are at the extreme western edge of their species range, which extends across Europe (where numbers have generally declined) to its main breeding stronghold in Russia and eastern Siberia, where agricultural management is less intense. The Corncrake has become iconic for the modern conservation movement because its continued decline across western Europe since the end of the Second World War has been strongly correlated with the introduction of intensive agriculture and mechanised mowing techniques.[62] Despite a global population of between 5.5 and 9.7 million individual birds, early grass-mowing and lack of alternative cover have reduced Western European numbers so severely that the crofting islands of the Hebrides and Orkney remain their only significant UK breeding localities.

I say that the bird is enigmatic for many reasons, but mainly because it is very rarely seen, yet most of the locals know of its presence. This small,

Coot-like bird hides all day in marshy field margins and the tall grasses of hay or silage meadows, and the males make their mating availability known during the long, bright nights of northern summers, usually between 23.00 and 04.00, by their monotonous, repetitive and quite distinctive call. The usual Gaelic name for the Corncrake is the *Traon,* but some older alternative names *Corra-ghoirtean* (the long-legged bird of the little cornfield) and *Rac an fheòir* (croaker of the grass) are typically descriptive. Its Latin specific name is *Crex crex*, which neatly articulates its rasping call. This throaty call-sign can be accurately imitated by dragging a stiff plastic comb against the edge of a credit card in two short swipes per second. With my study window open I can hear the male call even at this distance of 250 metres, (only the males call) and there can be few local residents unaware of when the bird is in the area. Although it will drive sleep to distraction when a bird is near your house, a great many locals will fondly mention in conversation their first hearing of the Corncrake song each year, in much the same way as people further south record the arrival of the Cuckoo. When it is considered that individual male birds will sing almost continually for at least four hours every night, and that over a summer each bird will repeat the call between half-a-million and one million times, it is hardly surprising that the call drums itself into your subconscious.[63]

The Corncrakes arrive with us in April or May, navigating their way from their wintering grounds in south-eastern Africa, and departing again in September, although their precise migration route south is a bit of a mystery. The Eastern European birds appear to prefer a direct route over Egypt and down the eastern countries of Africa, to winter in the savannah grasslands from southern Tanzania to northern South Africa. The Scottish birds have a migration route which is less clear, but may be over Spain and North Africa, then south-east across the Sahara to join their Russian relatives on the savannah.[64] Ringed Corncrakes have been recovered from thirty-five African countries and in such disparate destinations as North America and New Zealand, so although they may not have the agile flight skills of the gulls, or the navigational acumen of the Arctic Tern, they are clearly competent fliers. Whatever their flight-path, the migratory journey, for such a small animal, is prodigious and full of danger, both from hunters and from the environmental conditions of drought or predators encountered en route.

Against these survival odds, the Corncrake is enigmatic for another reason. The bird that I hear calling in Gabhsann is unlikely to be the same bird that I heard last year, for although both genders are reasonably faithful to their breeding areas, there is a very high level of mortality. Only about 20% of adult Corncrakes present in one spring will survive to the next. The endless nocturnal calling of the male birds will lessen when they mate successfully, and a little while after the female has laid a clutch of about ten small eggs, the males will drift off a few hundred metres and begin to call again, in the hope of attracting another mate. To be fair, once the female has fledged her clutch, she too will try to breed again with any calling male and raise another large clutch, for it is only by producing a large number of young that the species can overcome its environmental stress and enable continuing generations to breed.

Through targeted species conservation measures, the population in the core areas has increased significantly in recent years, but breeding success is always fragile. A combination of increasing suitable breeding habitat, delaying the mowing of hay and silage, and introducing new mowing techniques which begin cutting in the centre of the field, driving chicks to the edges rather than trapping them in the centre, has, at least for now, reversed the Corncrake decline of the past seven decades. The 'familiar' Corncrake that I can hear on a calm summer evening might even be the son of the bird that was calling last year, but at least there is a nostalgic satisfaction that the bird heard calling down on the banks of Abhainn Gabhsann bho Dheas is probably a descendant of the birds that have been heard here for as long as Gabhsann has been a place settled by humans.

Along this shore, Oystercatchers are present in summer and in winter, with their black-and-white markings and coral-red bills. Every hundred metres or so, a bird stands conspicuously alert on sentry, and it is almost impossible to walk any distance at all without one bird or another setting up its piping cry of alarm, warning every other animal within a kilometre radius that an intruder is approaching. They like the shingle beaches for their nest-scrapes, and although they are often observed breeding inland in other areas, they are seldom seen lingering on the sandy machair or the crofts of Gabhsann. An intriguing feature of this species is that, although they may look so similar from a distance, the bills of Oystercatchers show striking variations in shape.[65] Prolonged study has shown that there are three main forms, pointed, chisel-shaped, and blunt, and that these shapes arise through different types of feeding specializations. The bill shapes of individual birds may change over time, but broadly speaking the pointed bills are used for foraging for buried prey such as invertebrates, the chisel-shape is used to lever open shellfish,[66] while the blunt bill is used for hammering the shells of molluscs. Biologists call this type of intra-species variation 'resource polymorphism' and in the case of the Oystercatcher it used to be thought that these subtle differences in feeding ecology and behaviour which result in the wide variations of bill shape might be an indication of different subspecies of Oystercatcher, but we now know that is not the case. Nevertheless, it is still uncertain whether young birds learn their predominant feeding techniques from their parents, or by trial-and-error, or a combination of both.[67] Feeding on a particular prey results in changes to trophic structures (in this case, the bills) and repeating this generation after generation may lead to greater specialization, so it is interesting to speculate that we might be witnessing the slow evolution over a large geographical area of differing regional subspecies.

Belonging to a place

Nor is this species variation a unique feature in this part of the world, for the Hooded Crow predominates in the Hebrides and the west coast of Scotland, while the Carrion Crow predominates in the east, with an overlapping form of hybridisation running down the middle of the country in a continuous band from John O' Groats to Galloway.[68] The Hooded Crow, like its relatives, is a clever and opportunistic feeder, and while young birds may travel considerable distances throughout the region, the adult birds can normally be seen in Gabhsann throughout the year in almost any of the main habitat types. They perch quietly on the landscape, on walls and buildings, with their slightly-shabby, almost-elegant, dinner-party dress of black head and wings set against a grey back and breast, watching for the next meal.

There is a noted difference too in the other members of the crow family, with normally the total absence of Magpies, Rooks, and Jackdaws, and the striking abundance of the much larger Raven, (the largest of the European crows) normally avoiding the proximity of humans, with their distinctive croaking cry as they leisurely soar over the village and fly down the glen. They are as large as the Buzzard, which also has its breeding site on the moor, but can be seen almost every day over the village, and it's impossible not to be impressed watching Buzzards quartering the landscape and gliding effortlessly above the open ground, their extended wings curling up confidently at the tips. Buzzards are a good illustrative example of the constantly changing avian population of Gabhsann, being rare-to-absent during the 19th Century, their numbers falling and rising with intermittent but continued persecution, then making a steady recovery since the middle of the 20th Century, at least partly as a result of the Second World War, to now being the most abundant raptor in the Outer Hebrides.[69] The fortunes of raptors have lurched back and forth with the dominating ethos of persecution or conservation, and the Gabhsann Buzzards may occasionally share their hunting areas with stray Merlin, a passing Peregrine, and the twin delights of wandering Golden Eagles and Sea Eagles, but the Buzzard is the resident attraction. The sight of a Buzzard, dark-silhouetted against a clear, pale-blue Hebridean sky, dwarfed by the massive profile of a majestic Sea Eagle in the background airspace, is a breathtaking experience never to be forgotten.

Moving from the largest avian (a female Sea Eagle can weigh 5-6kg, with a wingspan of 2370mm) [70] to perhaps the smallest resident bird in Gabhsann (a Hebridean Wren weighs around 12-13g, with a wingspan of only 170mm) is by no means to disparage the smaller resident. Of course, in fact, these are serial residents, because the lifespan of a Wren is barely two years, and the bird that I see each year is probably a different bird every time. Still, I always look forward to spotting that flitting ball of brown-speckled feathers, bobbing up-and-down, and darting between the boulders of the dry-stane wall down by the Abhainn Gabhsann bho Dheas. On another occasion, far out on the moor in a crook of the same river, where the ruined shielings are slowly being reclaimed into the landscape, I met another noisy Wren. Again, it was peeping here and there between the gaps in the boulders, perfectly suiting its scientific specific name of *Troglodytes troglodytes*, the cave-dweller, or hermit. This one was not in the slightest frightened or intimidated by a human, and told me loudly and persistently that I was the one who did not belong there. There is undoubtedly some justification in this, because the insular breeding of the species has produced six distinctive sub-species breeding in the oceanic islands of the north-west Atlantic, with one, the Hebridean Wren, *Troglodytes troglodytes hebridensis*, restricted to the Outer Hebrides (although there is another sub-species *Troglodytes troglodytes hirtensis* in St Kilda). [71] All of these island races have colonised the islands from mainland Europe during the last 12,000 - 22,000 years as the last remnants of the ice-age retreated. Like island species in many other parts of the world, these island Wrens are slightly darker and slightly larger than their mainland relatives, and incredibly, they also have slight differences in song structure and length. [72] Unlike Wrens further south, these island Wrens are largely sedentary, and so breeding and natural selection among the relatively isolated populations produces their distinctive characteristics. The Hebridean Wren has lived so long in these different islands, breeding within relatively local populations and producing successive generations so rapidly, that they truly belong very particularly to this landscape, even to the extent of adapting their appearance and behaviour to vary between the island groups.

We all tend to see the world from our own perspective, naturally, so we can only ever be voyeurs on the natural world. Some of us may be more intimately connected, or watch wildlife more closely, while others remain detached in their suburbs and city commutes, but really all of us are merely observers of wild animals. What do we really know about their motivations and inter-relationships, or where they go when they leave the stage of our world? Is that opportunistic Grey Heron that I can see from my study window, standing motionless by the village river, the same one that I saw yesterday down on the shore by the rock-pools?[73] Or is it his mate, or his son, they are so alike, even under close examination, that normally it is impossible to distinguish. Is it the same one that I saw in the same place last year (more than 70% of Grey Herons move less than 100 km from the place where they were born) or a different bird?[74] How long has that family of birds been coming here to breed, to hunt, and to live? We continually refer to them in the terms of our own world, using anthropomorphic descriptions and comments such as "wintering away" when it is only us who have the winter, while they follow the sun to warmer habitats.

Nature can be confusing too, like the exquisitely coloured Golden Plover who nest around the edges of the village with their plaintive single-note piping, but migrate south for our winter, only to be replaced here by Golden Plover from Scandinavia who pass through or perhaps stay with us a short while before returning north in the spring to breed.[75] (Their name in Gaelic is *Feadag* - The Whistle - and how very appropriate this is). There are slight gradations in the plumage marks, but who among us can get close enough for long enough to become acquainted with each individual bird?[76] Who would have thought, before the days of satellite tracking, or even bird-ringing, that these birds that are so familiar in our village are such global travellers? From the Arctic to the Antarctic, all across Africa and Europe, to the oceanic edges of the Americas and to the vastnesses of Asia, or simply ocean wandering, the birds of Gabhsann travel far, and return here to make their nests and raise their young. Even the ubiquitous local Wheatear is an intercontinental voyager.[77] This place is not 'on the edge' to them, it is the centre of their life, from where they travel to do other things as the need arises. They are not 'getting away from it all' when they come to Gabhsann each year, they are returning to regenerate life and introduce their next generation to the habitat where they belong.

This element of continuity is important, but nature is constantly changing too, and the Outer Hebrides reflect this. Even within my own life-time the bird populations have changed. As elsewhere, the stocky Fulmar has reduced its breeding range and is now seldom seen in the village, whereas the Skuas have made an appearance, thrived, and consolidated their expansion. For the Skuas, and for every other animal, including humans, the world is full of opportunities, and also full of danger. Small islands offer unique environmental conditions to study ecology, being both connected yet isolated, with clearly defined boundaries of ocean, but caressed by global winds and currents.[78] There are indigenous residents and fascinating sub species, and there are regular visitors with a pedigree of family visitation that stretches back into deep time. Humans are the 'johnny-come-lately' species. Each of these inhabitants of Gabhsann brings an intimate local knowledge which is embedded in a world-view that is difficult for another species to recognise, let alone to comprehend.

Is it not ironic that so many scientific ornithologists spend their working lives in urban offices, making summer field trips to 'the periphery' to observe their chosen species. In the 21st Century, with online libraries, digital data, and professional networks at the touch of our keyboards, how much more appropriate (and exciting) it would be to establish an ornithological research base in these islands, focus our study attentions at the centre of our natural world (as the birds do) and make the occasional visit to a city if it became relevant.

CHAPTER 4

Animals come (and go)

The Ark in the Archive

It seems oddly appropriate to be reading about these long-departed animals in this particular setting - the Readers' Room of the National Library of Scotland. The book-lined walls reaching in stages to the high ceiling, and the exaggeratedly hushed tones of the patrons, almost reverential with their respect, are about as far from the uninhibited world of nature as could be imagined, but the animals that I am reading about belong in the archive of history. I had already read the book at my convenience as an ebook on my iPad, courtesy of the University of Michigan and their digitisation scheme, but this scholarly book is itself a part of the iconography of the natural history of the Outer Hebrides and deserves to be consulted, at least once, in its original, with its thick-paper pages and well-handled hard-backed binding. The book is A *vertebrate fauna of the Outer Hebrides* compiled by John Harvie-Brown and Thomas Buckley.[79] Harvie-Brown was a very distinguished amateur naturalist who, being of independent income (he was a Laird at Dunipace, near Stirling), devoted much of his considerable energy and intellect during the late 19th Century to documenting the vertebrate fauna of the Highlands and Islands. He visited the Outer Hebrides several times, pioneering an early scheme to monitor bird migration based on the records of lighthouse-keepers. During his visits he certainly became familiar with the island coastline and although there is no direct evidence of it, I like to think that his considerable travels took him through Gabhsann, either by land to the lighthouse at Rubha Robhanais, or passing offshore on his private yacht, the *Shiantelle*.

John Alexander Harvie-Brown was an enthusiastic amateur naturalist, and he was amused when a lighthouse-keeper interpreted his initials as John Always Hunting Birds. He did much more than hunt birds, however, although he followed the practice of his time by collecting eggs and shooting birds in order to identify and describe them. Over a period of many years, Harvie-Brown and a small circle of like-minded friends amassed a store of records and anecdotes which resulted in several volumes of remarkably detailed publications recording the vertebrate fauna of most of the north and west of Scotland. Unusually for his time and his class, he also took note of the Gaelic names of the species he recorded, and there are several unexpected records which might surprise his readers today.

Some people tend to think only of the iconic large vertebrates when considering the indigenous animals of islands, and I will come to them below, but the records of Harvie-Brown show that environmental change is continual, and on the short time-scale of human collective memory, it can be misleading. A good example of this is the fact he records that,

> "*about the year 1860, [Pine] Martens were still abundant. In 1879 they were reported as being present in Harris, but not abundant. There being few trees in Harris, any Martens which are procured are usually found in cairns of stones amongst long heather on the hill-sides...*"

He also notes that early accounts of Polecats are probably Pine Martens, and this is surprising in our modern context, because Pine Martens are now exclusively found (and comparatively rarely) in forested areas, and only on the Scottish mainland.[80] He chronicles several other introductions and extinctions, such as the introduction of the Mountain Hare to Rodel in 1859, and comments, somewhat naively, on the introductions of Rabbits, both of which have since spread throughout the island and are now found in Gabhsann (the latter in great numbers!) Despite the valuable work that Harvie-Brown has left us, recording the presence of species and logging unusual sightings, his terminology jars with us today because we find his enthusiasm for wildlife to be an inherent contradiction with his acceptance of the collecting methods of the time. We note, for example a rare Snowy Owl "*shot at the Butt*" in 1855 and another shot in Uig in 1859, and the Surf Scoter, "*The only specimen up to date of 1871, known to have occured on the west coast of Scotland, is recorded by Gray as 'shot in the winter of 1865 at Holm, near Stornoway'...*" In several other paragraphs he complains about the "*difficulty of obtaining eggs...*" or rejoicing when he has been successful.

Extinctions and introductions of species should not surprise us, but frequently they do. There are some general 'rules' in the science of ecology that islands tend to have fewer large animals than the adjacent mainland - fewer species in general - and that large-bodied species tend to become smaller on islands, while small-bodied species tend to become larger.[81] The effects of this are variable, depending on the size of the island and the distance or degree of isolation from a larger landmass. Varied too are the diverse theories that attempt to account for these observations. In general, it seems that the limitations of island resources (together with high population densities and habitat competition) preferentially select smaller individuals among the larger vertebrates because they require less energy to survive. In contrast, small-bodied species acquire fewer advantages by continuing to remain small and gain a selective advantage over others of the same species by a slight increase in size.[82] These interrelated biological circumstances have a profound impact on the animal species found in Gabhsann. Throughout the Outer Hebrides, there are only three large vertebrates found regularly, the aristocratic triumvirate of island mammals - the Red Deer (a long-term resident, though not indigenous) the Otter, and the Grey Seal (although not breeding in Gabhsann). There are no Squirrels, Foxes, Badgers, or deer apart from Red Deer. There are no Badgers or Wild Boars, although their bones were found by archaeologists in An Taobh Thuath in Harris (which might have been an early attempt at species introduction) [83] and there are no Wildcat despite remains that were found in an Iron Age midden in Gabhsann (although how to distinguish between a 2000-year old Wildcat bone and that of a feral domestic cat seems problematic). Island biodiversity is strongly influenced by four factors of population dynamics - introductions, extinctions, the survival of relict populations, and the evolution of distinctive species or subspecies due to long-term adaptation which is influenced by the relative isolation and/or the particular environmental factors of the island habitat. Fascinatingly for such a small land area, Gabhsann has examples of all these four factors.

Of the several deliberately introduced species - Rabbit, Mink, Polecat, and Hedgehog, more could be said, but for the moment it is simply worth noting that all have made an appearance in Gabhsann as they have spread throughout Lewis and Harris, resulting from the stupidity of the humans who have brought them onto the island. Stupidity might seem a strong accusation, but it is worth noting that, as with many introduced species which have been encouraged artificially to spread beyond their natural habitats, all of these introduced species have had a destructive impact upon the natural environment of the island. Mink and Hedgehog, both voracious carnivores with no natural island predators other than humans, have locally decimated the indigenous populations of ground-nesting birds. While there have been concerted attempts to control the populations of all these species, at present only the campaign against the Mink appears to have been successful, but perhaps it is unwise to speak too soon.

The extinctions recorded offer a tantalizing glimpse of past environmental conditions. Although there is the general reference to the Pine Marten in Harvie-Brown's book, there is no direct evidence of their presence in Gabhsann. Archaeological remains excavated in Gabhsann on a number of occasions have shown evidence of Wildcat, Wild Boar, and deer. In the mainland district of Assynt, within sight of Lewis on a clear day, are the Bone Caves of Inchnadamh, where the remains of Lynx, Reindeer, Brown Bear, Arctic Fox, and Arctic Lemming bones have been found.[84] However, while deer antlers are common recoveries from Iron Age sites, and even the occasional boar tusk, these discoveries do not prove that the animals were living locally, as antlers and tusks were valuable commodities for tool manufacture and decoration - antler picks and weaving combs have been recovered in Gabhsann - but it does indicate that early humans were acquainted with these species.

There have of course been other extinctions and introductions; one year a large, fat frog appeared on our croft - undoubtedly an introduction from mainland Scotland - and its absence in subsequent years may either be because it has moved on, or, more likely, it has succumbed to a member of the ever-watchful gull population, of which we have many. Introductions and extinctions happen in our own lifetime - regrettably, there are no longer any Fulmar nesting in Gabhsann - but on the human time-scale, slowly-changing features are often hard to detect, only a dramatic change is (barely) noticeable. Over time, the natural isolation of an island encourages selective breeding specific to the dominating environmental conditions, so varieties of some species develop and change - not necessarily into distinctive species or even subspecies (although this too might eventually occur) but simply a local variation evolves which is selectively retained in the local gene-pool. Many Hebridean bird species tend to be darker than their mainland relatives. In these islands, there is a local race of Starling, intermediate in size between the nominate - (common) - and the two subspecies found in the Faroe and Shetland Islands. (Incidentally, Starlings have been present in large numbers in the Atlantic islands for much longer than in the central mainland of Scotland).[85] Five Hebridean subspecies of birds are recognised (Wren, Twite, Hedge-sparrow, Stonechat, and Song-thrush). There are also Hebridean subspecies of the Long-tailed Field Mouse, and Field Voles, but now genetics becomes even more difficult due to scientific deliberations on the original source of the variations. In this debate between taxonomic 'splitters' and 'lumpers' it is important whether the genetic variation is a response to the island ecology, or as a result of a distant historical introduction. For example, it is believed that 'stowaway' voles were introduced to Orkney from the area of Belgium in imported grass for livestock. Another consideration is whether the organism is an example of a relict species (i.e. a population of a species which is now only found in a particular area, but whose original range was far wider during a previous geological period). For most amateur naturalists passing through Gabhsann, it is probably enough to learn that nothing is quite like it might appear at first, and that even common garden birds such as that Starling or Hedge-sparrow bobbing along the village walls, have an exotic genetic history embedded in this place.

Harvie-Brown focused only on the vertebrate fauna, but these islands have other ecological distinctions. The unique combinations of the mild oceanic climate, the relatively frost-free winters, and the certain degree of physical isolation that islands enjoy mean that there are Hebridean varieties of many species of butterflies, moths and bees. The Lepidoptera (butterflies and moths) of the Hebrides are melanistic (darker) varieties than the rest of the UK, so the Meadow Brown, and the Large Heath that flutter through my garden in Gabhsann are just slightly distinct from their mainland relatives. There are others, however, the Pearl-bordered Fritillary, the Common Blue, and the Grey Mountain Carpet, which have forms that occur only in the Hebrides, so that almost every fluttering creature that I come across I need to look at very, very carefully in order not simply to identify, but to ascertain if it is something idiosyncratic and wonderful which originates in this place. The various anecdotal theories of their biological origins have a long history among species enthusiasts. Almost none of these species have been recorded on the UK habitat distribution maps for this place, but they are here (although the biological recorders seem to be thin on the ground).

If you had been thinking that the comings and goings of the birds are complicated, then the ecology of the Bumblebees in Gabhsann introduces a whole new level of complexity. Throughout the Hebrides as a whole, there are local strongholds of certain bee species which are now nationally rare, but their origin, distribution, ecology, and even their existence can often be both problematic and mysterious. Of the 25 species of UK Bumblebee, there are about half-a-dozen different species in Gabhsann, but this fact can also be contested; even many experts often find it impossible to distinguish some species in the field, and require to resort to the laboratory microscope and dedicated computer software to confirm identification. The Heath Bumblebee, as its name suggests, prefers the habitats of acidic moorland as does the White-tailed Bumblebee and the Northern White-tailed Bumblebee, although the former seems to prefer to forage on Bell Heather, while the latter zig-zags among Heather and the flower-rich meadows of the adjacent croftland. The Cryptic Bumblebee also prefers the moorland habitat, and seems to be by far the most abundant species locally, although it is so closely related to the two white-tailed species that to most people they are indistinguishable, and there is still debate whether they are three related subspecies or three distinct species.[86] Until very recently, the Cryptic Bumblebee was not even considered to be present in the UK, but a survey in 2010 found that 84% of the bees caught in the Outer Hebrides were of this species.

Two of the rarest Bumblebees in the UK are the Great Yellow Bumblebee and the Moss Carder Bumblebee, both of which prefer to forage among the flower-rich coastal grasslands, as does the solitary bee called the Northern Colletes.[87] The loss of meadow grasslands throughout the UK has resulted in a dramatic decline in bee numbers, and while the Outer Hebrides might be a key location in the diminishing refuge for these bee species that are retreating before the spread of intensive agriculture, there remain lots of unknown factors about bee ecology.[88] Their preferred habitats and food (which varies with the seasons and the vegetational cover) their population numbers, and their geographical distribution, are all just sketchily known, especially in locations such as the Outer Hebrides where there very few recording experts on the ground, and a lot of ground to cover. We don't know how many bees there are of each species, or what their nesting and feeding choices are, far less their complex inter-specific relationships and ecological preferences. It would appear that several species have overlapping ranges, but differ in their choices of habitat and forage. As I walk around Gabhsann, with my eyes intent on the flying visitors to the flower-heads, different species of Bumblebees appear in different areas, but I have no way of knowing if that is their most common habitat, or if they have strayed from a neighbouring area of this place. The small-scale, non-intensive land-use of crofting produces an intricate patchwork of microhabitats – a mosaic of moorland, grassland, arable, silage, grazing, and fallow – which encourages a high biodiversity. Crofts are managed this way through a combination of historical legacy and personal lifestyle choice – not simply for economic gain – and if the the birds and the bees benefit from this style of land management, it is a happy outcome which benefits both humans and wildlife.[89] If we are to avoid several species of Bumblebees joining the Ark of the Extinct, however, perhaps our society needs to consider other ways of rewarding the labours of this style of land management so that these benefits are intentionally encouraged, rather than accidental results of a system which is subject to the fickle changes of political whim.[90]

Last but by no means extinct, despite its diminutive body-size, is the island Midge. Actually, the term 'midges' is just a common name for a very wide group of small flies that are found across all of Europe, North Africa, and Asia north of the Himalaya. They are not unique to Gabhsann, in fact there is not even a unique Scottish sub species, despite their notoriety among tourists for their summertime habit of collecting in clouds and biting any exposed flesh. (I have a theory that midges annoy tourists more because they are out-and-about all the time, whereas, on calm, dry days, apart from peat-cutting and hay-making, locals will retire indoors or to another midge-free environment!) Only the females bite, (to obtain oxygenated blood to nurture their eggs) and though they may leave an irritated spot for a few hours, for most people the irritation soon vanishes, as do the midges with the slightest breeze (which is usually omnipresent in Gabhsann except on occasional extremely calm days). Anyway, for most of the time I am prepared to tolerate midges, because without them in the food web there would be fewer small birds, and even fewer raptors. Individually they are tiny creatures, but the many millions that take to the air in late spring and summer form a collective biomass of such colossal proportions that it is impossible to calculate. Every time that I see the Swallows that nest in our stable feeding on the wing in their aerial gymnastics over our croft, I am thankful for the plentiful supply of midges and flies to sustain the insect-loving Sundews and the diet of these beautiful birds, (in Gaelic, Swallows are *Gobhlan-gaoithe* - literally, "the forked bird of the wind").

On land - Red Deer

Even in the span of a human lifetime, animal populations expand, contract, and change territories. In recent years, Red Deer have increasingly moved into Gabhsann from the inner reaches of the north Lewis moor. Seldom a week goes by without seeing them prancing across the main road, or even scuttling intently into the trees along the Allt Meagro, or to the greener, sheltered hollows of the village croft land. It is mostly not that the herd numbers have increased, but rather that crofting practices have changed; like other island townships, most Gabhsann crofters no longer put sheep out to the moor to graze all summer, so as nobody needs to go far out on the moor to gather them. The deer are largely undisturbed and therefore are emboldened to encoach further into the domain of humans in order to snatch a tastier bite. Occasionally in winter they are to be found licking the salt off the main road. At all times of the year, especially in the twilight in the shoulder months of summer, they can appear suddenly on the roadside verges and drivers have no way of knowing if they will remain where they are, or suddenly become spooked and dash across the road towards some unspecified destination. More than one car has been written off by a collision with 110kg of muscled deer.

I often go out to this moor by myself (locals say, in both Gaelic and English 'out' to the moor and 'in' to the shore - it is a linguistic relict of a dependency on the ocean. By the same token, we refer to going 'down north' using the same colloquial speech as our exiled relations in Cape Breton.) In walking the length and breadth of the moor of Gabhsann, all 2,200 hectares, although there is no physical boundary between this place and the rest of the vast moor from the tip of Nis to the hills of Harris, the presence of the Red Deer is never far away. Mostly they are detected by their delicate hoofprints in soft peat. They have a knack of finding the easiest ways to cross this landscape, either winding their way through the dried-up peat pools, or along thin dark paths that meander around and between the raised obstacles of drier heather-topped peat hags. This is a difficult country to walk over, for it is usually impossible to follow a straight line and the Heather is frequently waist-height and tough from lack of grazing control. Damp areas of soft moss or irregular shallow pools appear without much notice, forcing the walker to detour, double-back, and scramble down-and-up slippery black gullies - the feithean - of eroded peat. Inevitably, when you discover a good place to cross a burn, or leap over a narrow boggy area, there will be small cloven indentations in the soft ground to indicate that the Red Deer have found this crossing before you. As that early pioneer of meticulous field observation of natural history, Frank Fraser Darling, observed, the deer know their own ground intimately, and have an intuitive understanding of the best ways to cross rough ground.[91] For all their apparent pattern of homogeneity, each tussock is unique, with a slightly varied structure and vegetational composition, an asymmetric profile, a slightly different angle to the sun, a derangement of drainage, a contrast in height.

Far out on the Common Grazing of Gabhsann, near Malagro, a flattish area running along the outer border-country where the village marches with the more extensive moor-grazings of Nis, there can faintly be detected the remains of the Gàradh Dubh - the black dyke - which was a long, low wall constructed of turf to mark the boundary of the township. The Gàradh Dubh is slowly crumbling back into the surrounding ground, but to gaze along even this short portion of it provokes incredulity at the labour that must have been involved in its construction, even for a period when labour was cheap and hard, physical work was the norm. The dyke is barely half a metre high and runs for at least 10km in a wide polygon from the main road in Mealabost, out to Loch Striamabhat, curving round towards the northwest, passing south of Loch Shiabhat and just north of Loch Bharabhat, to reach the shore between Gabhsann and Dail bho Dheas at Geodh a' Phìobaire (the sea-gully of the piper, although who the piper was is lost in time - or does it refer to a bird call?) Far out on the moor, this part of Gabhsann can be confusing, for a slight dip in the landscape means that all signs of human habitation vanish, and the horizon is without navigational orientation in all directions, even in broad daylight. In darkness or the mist of a summer haar, an unwary person could walk all day and all night without knowing exactly where they were going.

Following the lie of the land down north into the shallow valley of Gleann na Siga, ('the glen where calves are suckled') I come upon a small family group of three hinds and their two calves. They are standing close together on a slight hillock because it is a warm, calm day, and in this formation they can disrupt the flow of air and help to gain some respite from the flies and the midges that plague them when they stand still. At first they seem astonished to see me, for I am approaching from an unexpected direction - humans are supposed to be in towards the township, not on the slopes behind the herd. Then the lead hind gives two soft, throaty barks, and they are off without hesitation, only stopping for a brief backward glance when they are a safe two hundred metres away, before slipping out of sight over the near horizon. Darling has written that, "*the most important part in their life history is that Red Deer are social animals: their herds are more than mere aggregations.*" [92] For more than ten months of each year, the genders live apart, the stags ranging widely in their all-male group, and the hinds much more localised within their territories, for this is without doubt a matriarchal society.

The lead hind is the one to look out for, usually easily identified by the calf following her closely. There is normally a high mortality with calves, about 50% will probably die in the first winter, so the mothers are highly protective of them. The lead hind is almost always the first one to spot an intruder and the first to bark the alarm. During the mating time of October, even the dominant stags will follow the lead of the wary hinds and trot off in an instant once a warning has been given. It is at this time of the year too when the deer retreat into the farthest and highest parts of Gabhsann moor to engage in the social stimulation which accompanies their breeding cycle.

Travelling carefully across the landscape, making use of the scant cover available, I have suddenly come across two young stags challenging each other. They were not actually clashing their formidable antlers together, that would be a high risk strategy through which any injury could finish their hopes of attracting any mating partners, but they were pacing back-and-forth, making small thrusts and feints, and much too preoccupied with the threat from each other to even notice me sheltering in the hollows. On another occasion I spotted a large stag through my field-glasses, a fearsome creature which had been wallowing in the damp peat-flats and was coated with dripping, black peat. He did not bother to hide his presence, for he was too absorbed in displaying to any other deer in the landscape. You have to hear the primitive roaring of a rutting stag in display before you can appreciate the awesome power of its effect. One time, in another location, a rutting stag saw its own reflection in the window of the bothy where I was living, and roared at himself with such force and volume that the window glass began to hum with the vibrations.

As a result of the way that the deer blend in with the landscape, the way that they survive, even thrive, on so very little, it would be normal to expect they have been here forever, an indigenous element of the land itself, but that would be incorrect. The presence of Red Deer in the Outer Hebrides in the Neolithic (5,500-4,500 years ago) has been recorded, (there were deer remains in the Iron Age midden in Gabhsann) although there is little evidence of how they arrived here. Earlier thinking speculated that a pre-Ice Age land-bridge with the mainland may have allowed animals to cross to the outer islands and that a small population survived in a few ice-free zones, but this is highly unlikely. Arguments for a post-Ice Age land-bridge have been systematically disproven[93] but it is known that there have been several introductions of new breeding stock by nineteenth century sporting estates in Harris and Lewis. Speculation that large mammals could have crossed on the ice during the glacial period has also been dismissed as unlikely, due partly to the ecological requirements of suitable habitat and sources of food, and it is considered most likely that Neolithic humans introduced most, if not all, species of mammals to the offshore islands.[94] As the outer isles are too far offshore for deer to swim from the Isle of Skye or the mainland, human intervention in their distribution is a certainty.

Stunning new genetic evidence in 2016, however, revealed that the Red Deer of the Outer Hebrides and Orkney are unlikely to have originated from mainland Scotland or the Inner Hebrides.[95] Norse sea-travellers were known to drop off numbers of their indigenous breed of sheep on islands along their sailing-routes, as a 'living larder' for their anticipated return to that location. (They are small, brown or black fleeced, with two, three, or even four horns, and some of these Hebridean Sheep have recently been reintroduced into Gabhsann). It is possible that deer might also have been translocated by the Norse, but again there is no genetic match between the Red Deer of the Outer Hebrides and Scandinavia, so current thinking is that the appearance of Red Deer in the Outer Hebrides in the Neolithic is as a result of the deliberate redistribution by humans from an unknown but distant source. It used to be said that "*only two species (the Pygmy Shrew, and the Red Deer) can be fairly definitely asserted to have arrived without the intervention of man*" [85] but the recent evidence on the deer leaves only the shrew as indigenous, and even this is in serious doubt.[83] As is frequently said in academic circles, 'further research is required.'

Like the blue remnants of partially-digested Blaeberries on a rock, which is often the only obvious sign that a feeding species has been present in the locality, often the only tell-tale sign of Red Deer in Gabhsann are their footprints left in the damp peat. These deer are always on the move. Unlike the higher land of the west-coast mainland, there is little differentiation between the 'high ground' and the 'low ground' and Red Deer have strong diurnal movements, so these deer are constantly back and forth. They do not belong to Gabhsann, rather Gabhsann belongs to them, and they choose which part to inhabit as their inclinations take them in search of food, or shelter, or simply in response to their age, breeding condition or season. Walking across this moor you can occasionally see where they have nibbled the tops of a tussock of Heather, for though they graze both Heather and grass, they browse on Heather more than sheep do, and their lower stocking densities on the land result in them grazing lightly but widely.[96] Red Deer populations have been around in the Gabhsann area for thousands of years, and in that time they have had a close association with humans, as food, as a source of tools from their antlers and bones, and as a fellow-traveller on the land that needs to be discouraged from raiding agricultural holdings.[97] Prehistoric Red Deer were substantially larger than present-day animals, and there is no doubt that there have been several introductions of new stock into the gene pool, largely through relocation by humans, but they are survivors well-bred for this natural environment.[98] They are our largest land animals. Nobody who has walked laboriously over the Gabhsann moor to the land beyond Loch Striamabhat and lain low among the hollows to watch a stag scraping furiously at the ground, or flailing the Heather with its new antlers in agitation to remove the velvet at the start of a new breeding season, would doubt that this animal is exotic and deserves its place in this ecosystem.

At sea - An Ròn Mòr

The Atlantic Grey Seal is a beast of legend, quite literally. They are not mythical, they are quite real, and they are far too private in their personal behaviour to actually live in Gabhsann permanently, but their presence is felt in every breaking wave of surf on this rocky coast. Nationally and globally, the Grey Seals are much less abundant than the Common Seals, but as is frequently the case along this northwestern edge of oceanic Europe, the 'common' is less common here. Numbers vary as populations oscillate, but more than 50% of the UK breeding stock of Grey Seals are born in the Hebrides. That is about one-third of the total world population. Mostly they reserve their presence on land to a dozen or so small, rocky, uninhabited islands off the west coast of the Outer Hebrides, islands with entrancing names such as Ronaidh, Shillaidh, Pabbaidh, and Hesgeir.[99] Although the indications are that they are approaching carrying capacity over much of their range (the maximum population number of a species that an ecosystem can support on a long-term basis), fish-farmers may complain that the seal population is increasing,[100] and on the geological scale, that is certainly true, though hardly noticeable within a human lifetime. Grey Seals appear to prefer the shallow offshore ocean shelf - less than 200 metres - and a narrow range of temperate water, so the habitat that was available to them during the last period of maximum glacial activity was probably only about 3% of what is available now.[101] Over the past 12,000 years since the end of the last Ice Age, seals have been expanding their range, and as global warning creates an increasingly ice-free Arctic, they will probably expand there too.

They love the wild surf and seem perfectly comfortable there, much more so than the Common Seal, which is often called the Harbour Seal for that reason. When you see the dark dome of a seal head, floating almost stationary among the breakers, silently observing its human neighbours, it is almost certainly a Grey Seal. *Ròn Mòr*, it is called in Gaelic, the big seal, for it is much larger than its common cousin. The textbooks will tell you that the two species can be distinguished by the different angles of the nostrils on the snouts - the Common Seal having a V shaped configuration and the Grey Seal being almost parallel - but unless you are very lucky it is virtually impossible to differentiate between them when all that can be seen is the tip of a snout poking out of the surf at a distance of a hundred metres or so.

Very little was known about the complexities of their breeding behaviour until Frank Fraser Darling went to live near the seals in order to study them.[102] Now, with tags that can be tracked by satellite transmission, even the movements of individual Grey Seals in the summer months when they take to wandering the broad ocean, are becoming better known.[103] Like the tussocks of Sphagnum mosses on the moor, the colours of the Grey Seal are highly individual. No two animals are identical, with a grey or brown fur and splashes of white and black, the variety is infinite, which allows the careful observer to identify individual beasts. In the changing Hebrides, Grey Seals appear to feed opportunistically by area and by season on the riches of the North Atlantic, with Herring, Mackerel, Horse Mackerel, Megrim, Witch and Sandeels appearing in their diet,[104] but with an apparent preference for Cod, Ling, and Whiting. Living among such a smorgasbord of seafood, it is little wonder that Grey Seals are so seldom seen on land or on the surface of the ocean. They commonly dive over 100 metres deep and a dive of 477 metres has been recorded.[101]

Although I have seen them occasionally hauled out on the skerries offshore, I have only once come upon a Grey Seal on land in Gabhsann, a young pup, still with patches of its natal white fur, and obviously lost. It is easy to see why traditionally there has been a strong human fascination for the Grey Seal, the almost-human gestures as they scratch themselves, or the cry made by the young, which sounds from the middle-distance like the cry of a human baby. The hooting noises which several cows make together in the breeding colonies have often been described as 'singing'[105] and they have a curiosity which attracts them to watch humans - from a safe distance - and even to respond to music and human singing.[106] Three hundred years ago, in some parts of the Outer Hebrides, Grey Seals were hunted for food, but, probably because of their reluctance to come ashore here, and also because of the lack of a safe harbour to sail and hunt from, I am glad to say that I have never heard of the slightest suggestion of seal-hunting by any former inhabitants of Gabhsann.

In the Celtic and Norse folklore of the northwestern edge of Europe, there are many tales of seals who become human, or vice versa. The family of MacCodrum in North Uist, who were hereditary bards to the chiefs of Clan Ranald, claimed their descent from 'the seal folk', although how this was substantiated remains unclear. There are local variations on similar themes; a hunter stabs a seal which escapes, and only later the hunter meets a stranger who bears a stab-wound in the same part of the body. Or stories of a seal (male or female) who sheds their skin and becomes human for a time, sometimes marrying and raising a family, before one day recovering the skin and slipping back to the realms of the ocean. There has even been an argument made relating the appearance of those seal-men (and women) to a historical period when an indigenous ethnic minority from northern Norway intermittently visited the northern and western islands in their sealskin-covered kayaks, but that is a discussion for another day.[107]

Certainly, the ocean still retains many of its mysteries which only occasionally have any impact on the continuation of the Earth's biosphere that we call 'land'. In April 2018, an Arctic Walrus probably swam past Gabhsann, although everyone on land was oblivious to its presence. We know this because the same animal was seen in Sanday in Orkney in March, and again ashore in Harris in early May. Although it made the BBC news as a minor sensation, Harvie-Brown could have told them that a Walrus had been killed in 1817 at Caolas Stocnais in Harris (and another in 1841 at Heisgeir). So too could William MacGillivray, for in 1817 he was spending a year living with his relatives in his childhood home in An Taobh Thuath, in southern Harris. At that stage he was just embarking on his illustrious career as a natural scientist, and he recorded the daily details in his field journal [31] including the special trip he made from An Taobh Thuath to Stocnais to describe and dissect the Walrus, (which became the subject of his first scientific paper in 1820.) That our ancestors would have been familiar with the Walrus is beyond question, for the famous Lewis Chessmen (made around 1150-1200 AD) were largely carved out of Walrus ivory (and some whalebone) and uncarved Walrus tusks were a trade item sought after by craft workers in northern Europe for hundreds of years.[108]

There are, of course, many other creatures in the ocean which are technically, even temporarily, part of the complex ecosystem of Gabhsann, although many of them pass us by without notice. Close to shore, the ocean shelf off the west coast of the islands is shallow and gently shelving, unlike the eastern coast which is steeply faulted to permit very deep water close to shore. This is perfect topography to view sealife (from the bridge of the research ship "Ocean Bounty" I once recorded over 350 cetaceans in the nine kilometre transect of the Minch sailing north between the lighthouse on Rubha an t-Siumpain and the point of Rubha Tholastaidh). This coast is a playground for cetaceans, and we are spoiled for choice; since 1980, at least twenty-one species of cetacean have been recorded here, including the Common Porpoise, White-beaked Dolphin, White-sided Dolphin, Minke Whales and Fin Whales, spectacular Killer Whales, even Risso's Dolphin as well as an occasional Humpback Whale. As always, it is a moot point whether this stretch of the northern Minch is a hotspot for cetaceans, or whether the regular sightings attract more whale-watchers, which in turn produces more sightings. On the coastline in Gabhsann, there have been two huge Sperm Whales washed ashore in living memory; one, three generations ago, was buried by the people near the mouth of the Abhainn Gabhsann bho Thuath (the ground is boggy to this day) and the other carcase was washed away by a high tide and later deposited by the strong longshore current on a beach in Nis. From a small boat offshore I have seen the awesome co-ordinated hunting of Orca (Killer Whales), but from the solid land of Gabhsann I count it a rare treat to catch a fleeting glimpse of a Basking Shark - the second-largest fish in the world and the largest in the Outer Hebrides - lazily floating at the surface to feed on plankton with its huge mouth; a scarcely discernible smudge of grey on a shimmering silver ocean, but a gentle and crucial component of the marine food web.

On land and sea - the Otters

I would defy anyone not to smile, at least internally, when watching a pair of Otters playing together on a river bank. Apparently, however, such people do exist, and it is little wonder that Otters have an instinctive wariness being around humans. Harvie-Brown recorded their systematic destruction in the 19th Century,

> "... a total of 95 Otters ... in the Lews, from 1876 to 1885 inclusive ... in 1884, eighteen; and in 1885, nineteen; .... A shepherd in North Uist, on his beat alone, had shot over seventy Otters during a residence of twenty-five years..."[79]

It beggars belief why any shepherd would kill even one Otter, far less indulge in such a relentless persecution, but that was characteristic of the time.

Down by the rivers in Gabhsann there are a few subtle signs for alert human walkers to indicate the presence of Otters. Although the shores of the Outer Hebrides include some of the best locations in the whole of Europe to actually see live Otters, they are still very elusive creatures. Otters here are partly marine and partly freshwater, and while they can show amazing alacrity on land when needs must, despite appearing slightly clumsy to us, in the water their movements look effortless and elegant. As they are largely nocturnal, their lifestyle is out of sync with most of the human inhabitants of the region, and despite a relatively high population density of Otter in the Outer Hebrides, their ecology means that males and females are apart for most of the year, ranging over large and overlapping territories of coastline and adjacent freshwaters. In the lower reaches of the Gabhsann rivers there are occasional Otter droppings (spraints) marking territory, and a practised eye might spot flattened areas of vegetation beside the stream where an Otter has been resting, or one of the rare mudslides which they seem to enjoy just for the sheer pleasure of it, but the animals themselves are generally harder to observe. All of this combines to make it so much more of a joy to see them when the chance occurs, particularly to see two Otters cavorting together.

As might be expected, very early morning or the twilight of dusk generally provide the best circumstances to see an Otter, and the short - almost non-existent - nights of the Hebridean summer provide the best opportunities of all. Walking by the river, very, very slowly, on a beautifully clear and calm July morning - so early that not even the occasional noise from the main road of the earliest traffic heading for the ferry is audible - my pulse gives a little jump. Not fifty metres ahead, a soft brown nose cuts the surface of the water in a wide pool, and leaves a sinuous V in its wake. Usually it is just a trailing line of bubbles that can be seen on the surface of a pool.

This is an interesting time of change to be observing Otters in Lewis, because although the clear, unpolluted Hebridean waters have historically sustained a relatively healthy population in the islands, while most other areas of the UK have been in decline, this is still a very difficult environment to enable a small carnivore to thrive. Otters don't like to be far from water, so they tend to occupy long, linear territories - stretched out along a river or loch and the adjacent coastline. They tend to hunt in the sea, but return to the freshwater to rest and wash out the salt in their fur. In the cold, aqueous environment, they need a steady intake of food in order to conserve heat-loss, and the high-energy requirements of moving around their habitat, combined with a high investment in rearing the cubs, does not leave much margin for error in the game of genetic survival. For the past fifty years or so, escaped American Mink have been a further ecological complication. The smaller-sized Mink has a more generalist diet, taking slightly different food than the Otter seeks, which is more specialised in its diet and habitat use.[109] Otters prefer fish, particularly slow-moving, easy-to-catch fish, while Mink will take fish when they are available, but also prey on small mammals and birds.[110] While this might have been welcomed by some people for keeping down the rabbit population, it has been a disaster for ground-nesting birds throughout Lewis and Harris, and in Gabhsann, more than just our own hen-house has been subjected to a rampage by Mink.[111]

In some areas of the UK, research has indicated that the larger body-mass of the Otter tends to dominate over Mink, and force the latter to exploit different, more terrestrial, sources of food. It has also been documented that a higher density of Otters has resulted in a reduced population density of Mink.[112] This is good news for most indigenous species, and there was an immediate and very positive response (both from humans and other creatures which share this environment) following the success of a 17-year campaign to eradicate American Mink as an invasive species from the Outer Hebrides. Regional naturalists and wildlife observers are already noting the return of large numbers of terns, divers, and wading birds to breed in localities which had previously been devastated by Mink. The exciting question that remains is whether this will also lead to an increase in the breeding population of Hebridean Otters, for like much of the detailed ecology of this region, there is still so much detail that we do not yet know about Otters - even simple questions, such as the interaction between individual Otters, or the precise messages of spraints and scrapes and other territorial markings, which remain largely elusive.[113] There is still a lot of work to be done to understand the relevance and importance to Otters of places like Gabhsann.

The island as a refuge

In an extraordinarily empathetic series of essays linking human perceptions to the reality of the 'wild things' living in the natural environment of his woodland farm, Aldo Leopold sensitively pondered *"who is more thoroughly acquainted with the world in which he lives?"*;[114] the human or the wild things? The questions have not been adequately answered, nor can they be, for we live parallel experiences which only share the near proximity of space. With large creatures, like the Red Deer or the Grey Seal, or even the Otter, humans can remember meaningful encounters. They can feature prominently in the landscape and they can be observed from afar (if we are lucky). With scores of smaller creatures, this opportunity is barely recognised. With stray birds, blown off-course from North America or mainland Europe, the chances of being recognised and recorded in the biological database for that location are vanishingly small. This requires a human observer being in the right place, at the right time, having the environmental interest, the ability to accurately identify rare species, and the persistence to 'officially' log the observation with the relevant biological recorder for the biological discipline. When we come to consider creatures even smaller, the almost countless species of invertebrates for instance - even the large and strikingly colourful Violet Ground Beetle found on the moor - most of us do not even notice their presence unless they flutter by brightly, or bite us. As a result, most of these creatures inhabit a world of which they have an intimate knowledge as to where they can find food, shelter, and safety, but which is hidden from us. Many species travel far away, yet return to the exact same places after many months, to nest and forage in accordance with an internal system for geographical and chronological recognition that we humans might observe, but as yet cannot fully explain nor understand. We tend to stick close to the roads and habitations, the routes to grocery stores and places of commerce which are frequented by other humans, and so our mental map of awareness of the place that we inhabit is described by a very different code of understanding to our fellow creatures. There have been many times that I have walked through parts of Gabhsann, in my back garden or up the croft, or over some distant parts of the village Common

Grazings, and my attention has been caught by a damselfly, or an orchid, or an exotic bird. When I get back into my study I discover that the species has not been recorded from this place before, and I am left wondering if the species is new to the place, or simply not noticed before. So, what else is out there unnoticed?

This place is constantly changing, just not necessarily at a rate that is perceptible to humans. Many species are in fact still adjusting to the effects of the end of the last deglaciation, still adapting to survival under climatic and environmental conditions which have taken the species an uncountable number of human generations to evolve. Geologically speaking, the last ice age ended relatively quickly, and Gabhsann (along with the rest of the UK) is at present in an interstadial - a warmer pause between ice ages - so in another 50,000 years or so it is entirely possible that much of this place will return to a more hostile, glacial environment. Then there are the unpredictable effects of climate change - anthropogenic or otherwise, which create uncertainty and instability in the assemblages of species. There have been two very cold spells in northern Europe since that last period of major glaciation (sometimes called 'little ice ages') and in those periods life for most species was pretty challenging. This constant adaptation to their external environment means that many species are pushing the boundaries of their territory. For some, Gabhsann is at, or close to, the northern limits of their species; for other species, Gabhsann represents the southern limit of their territory. Still others wrestle with the oceanic-continental margin, and show a preference for the sea or the land at different stages of their cyclic existence.

To help make sense of this intricate and interconnected world of plants and animals, geology and climate, prey and predator, the human ecologists construct a Complex Adaptive System, which is exactly what it says. This concept recognises the complex and changing inter-relationships in nature, and the fact that while separate component relationships can change and adapt to the changing conditions, they are all ultimately interconnected in a whole system.[115] Some parts of the process of adaptation can be understood through studying feedback loops which either amplify the changes (positive feedback) or attempt to keep the changes within certain, more or less stable, limits (negative feedback). Due to our very partial understanding of a great many of the interrelationships between species, it is frequently impossible to predict the knock-on effects on one species that have been caused by a change in another part of the ecosystem, perhaps apparently at quite some distance away. We only perceive the connections when we begin to observe the negative (rarely, it seems, positive) changes in the natural environment, and the physical and social impact of humans can have a disproportionately high impact on island communities.[78] If it is eventually possible to understand the totality of the complexity of the ecosystem, even locally, then I will be able to comprehend the remarkable vibrancy and variety of the natural environment of Gabhsann. Of course, no such thing will even happen, because Gabhsann does not exist in a vacuum, and changes elsewhere will also impact upon us.

For these reasons, islands are wonderful laboratories to study species interaction in intimate detail. The natural boundaries of an island present benefits as well as challenges, a measure of isolation and well-defined boundaries which are beneficial, and well as distance and isolation which exert limitations on resources and biodiversity.[116] Some species, such as American Mink and the Common Hedgehog, are perfectly suited to their native natural environment, but when they are introduced, accidentally or intentionally, - the effects are the same - into an environment where they are not native, they become an alien invasive species. The impacts of their introduction can disrupt and perhaps destroy an ecosystem which had hitherto been in a state of harmonious balance, even if that balance had been subtle, precarious, and constantly adapting to changes. The journey from regarding the natural environment as a mystical realm of supernatural changes, through the need to dominate nature, towards a greater understanding of the role of humans as an integral part of the complex adaptive system, has been slow, and is far from over.[117] Although various hues of modern 'greenism' purport to understand nature, the 'rewilding' argument is still mainly about humans attempting to manage the natural environment for the production of certain commodities. It's just that the commodities have changed from certain species of crops to certain species of wildlife.[118] One of the great differences between rural living and the city is that rural life has a cyclic periodicity rather than the one-day-following-another routine of the urbanite. Crofters will compare seasons, and the lambing successes of this year as opposed to previous years, or comment on the anticipated return of the mid-winter gales, or the timing of the first call of the Corncrake. This cyclicity of rural living is reflected in the feedback loops of the complex adaptive system of our natural environment, and while people such as Frank Fraser Darling dedicated their lives to the understanding of the interplay of humans as fellow-species in island ecosystems, [119] I, personally, delight in returning again and again to attempt to fully understand the details of Gabhsann as a microcosm of that island environment.

CHAPTER 5

From the Ice Age to the Iron Age

Muddling through the Mesolithic

Gabhsann emerged from the ice age like a landscape reborn. Many previous features of the land, and all remnants of pre-ice age life that we know of, had been scoured out, washed away, or buried, with most life-forms simply forced to retreat before the advance of the deep accumulation of ice. By one of those strange combinations of physical circumstances, Gabhsann became one of the most important sites in the whole country in order to understand the sequences of the time-period around the end of the last ice age in northwestern Scotland. Recent research indicates a slight change in the movements of the local ice in the Outer Hebrides occurred near Brebhig, towards the southern margin of Gabhsann. The end of the ice-covering was a spasmodic affair, with some melting as the climate warmed, (an interglacial) followed by a period of re-glaciation, then another period of thaw. Over about eighteen thousand years, the ice gradually retreated from the landscape, and as the meltwater entered the oceans, the sea-level rose several metres, only to drop again with the next period of freezing. These islands present a view of a drowned landscape. During the Cretaceous, 65-142 million years ago, sea-level rose to cover the Outer Hebrides completely and Gabhsann was submerged, although apparently none of that sedimentary cover remains. As the water rose to fill the bottoms of the glens and cover the low-lying land, only the hill-tops remained as scattered islands of dry land, forming the straggling archipelago of the Outer Hebrides, which was once collectively called 'The Long Island'. (MacGillivray noted the appearance of this water-inundated landscape as he sailed with his uncle in the Sound of Harris on 12 December 1817.)[120]

Critically, this intermittent rise and fall of sea-level, combined with the remaining indications of ice movement across the Gabhsann area, provide a combination of landforms unique in the UK to help with the interpretation of this period of the Pleistocene in Britain. Between Brebhig and Gabhsann bho Thuath, is a very well-developed raised beach about seven metres above current sea-level, overlain by glacial till and weathered rock. At Tobha Ghabhsainn a layer of peat, interbedded with sand, is preserved beneath the raised beach gravels, trapped by the repeated rise and fall of sea-level. The organic remains have been radiocarbon dated to an inter-glacial between 39,100 and 47,150 years ago, and pollen analysis indicates that the vegetation was in a period of change from treeless, open grasslands to a more acidic grass-and heathland mix. This was a complex and changing time in recent Earth history, and despite the detailed state of our current knowledge, there are many opportunities for future research.[121]

When that ice eventually melted, a fresh, new, natural environment appeared and the first tentative encroachment of life re-appeared. There is a saying in the science of geology that *"Absence of evidence is not evidence of absence."* This is largely applied to the stratigraphic correlation of sedimentary rocks and the use of fossil evidence to date the relationships between sequences of rock formation. Roughly translated, it means that just because *you* cannot find the evidence, it does not mean to say that it does not (or did not) exist, merely that the evidence has not so far been found. This philosophy, of course, needs to be treated carefully, for indeed the evidence might never have existed. Nevertheless, it is a good reminder not to jump to hasty conclusions. In terms of the evidence so far found in Gabhsann for life in the Mesolithic (10,000 to 4,000 BC) it is a very appropriate saying.

Despite the current lack of material evidence, there is a distinct possibility that Gabhsann was inhabited by humans during the Mesolithic. Archaeological research has provided evidence for the Isle of Rum being the earliest known human settlement in Scotland [122] with traces of habitation, tools, and other artefacts dating back 8-9000 years being found in Rum and in neighbouring islands.[123] Occasional Mesolithic finds have also been recovered in Skye, at An Taobh Thuath (Northton) in Harris, and from the famous bone caves at Inchnadamph in Sutherland. Excavations at An Taobh Thuath have dated carbonised shells of Hazel nuts to between 7060 and 6090

BC and produced evidence of long-term, continuous human settlement in the area.[124] All of these sites are within travelling distance of Lewis, and given the sensitive eye of the Mesolithic settler for sheltered, cultivable land, with easy access to the shore, there is no reason to suspect that Gabhsann, too, was not inhabited at an early stage following the retreat of the last ice age.

The fact that, in keeping with most of the rest of the Outer Hebrides, no material evidence of Mesolithic cultures has been discovered in Gabhsann is perhaps due to a number of factors. The earliest human inhabitants were light on the ground, they were hunter-gatherers and did not construct big towns. Over the thousands of years since they travelled over this part of the earth, the wood and hides that they may have used for shelter have rotted or been removed, and the stone constructions have been re-used and re-used by successive generations of builders up until relatively modern times. Sea-level rise and engulfment due to the accumulation of peat has also possibly contributed towards hiding any evidence.

Narrating the Neolithic

Although in Gabhsann, the Mesolithic appears missing, as it is in most of the rest of the Outer Hebrides, (well, perhaps not so much missing as simply lost, or obscured by later events) there are other local indications of early settlement in the vicinity. There have been Mesolithic finds in some parts of the area of Nis, and in the islands of Uist, but the discoveries have been patchy and hard to contextualise.[125] The stones of buildings were reused, settlements were removed by the sea or interred in peat, and the sites of habitation have moved geographically as people relocated for a variety of reasons, so perhaps we are simply looking for evidence in the wrong places. Local archaeologists Dr. Chris Barrowman and Dr. Rachel Barrowman explained to me that in different parts of the UK, the Late Mesolithic life overlapped with the early Neolithic (BC 4,000-2,500) settlements elsewhere, which in turn merged into Iron Age remains (beginning about BC 800), so definite distinctions are often difficult. At Àird Dhail, a few kilometres along the coast from Gabhsann, two bronze swords were accidently dug up on a croft in 1892 (under almost three metres of peat).[126] Intriguingly, one of the swords was particularly well-preserved and retained its ox-horn handle, which is common with several other Bronze Age sword which have been discovered in Ireland. Also, at Adabroc, near the furthermost north part of Nis, a spectacular hoard of Bronze Age tools (axes, chisels, razors, a hammer and whetstones) was discovered in 1910 (also under three metres of peat) along with with individual beads of gold, amber, and glass which emphasise the historical importance of this island as a link with Ireland, Scandinavia, and Central Europe.[127]

What is very clear, however, is that from the mid-Neolithic onwards, there are continuous records of successive civilisations inhabiting Gabhsann. In the human quest for a place to settle, to call home, the gentle green shallow valley of Gabhsann bho Dheas would have been a powerfully seductive attraction - especially when viewed from an immigrant ship after many days at sea.

Perhaps the greatest treasures, however, are the multiple sources of evidence which indicate the details of the life-styles of these long-departed people. There are graves on the shore which have been lined with stones to form 'long cists' (chests) for burial, dated to the 4th Century AD,[128] although there is no record of the people who were interred there. Even earlier, the Pictish settlers of the area left the remains of roundhouses and underground earth-houses (souterrains) which have been uncovered by the shifting sands over the years. There are many traces of very early human life in Gabhsann if a person is attentive to this landscape.

The enigmatic dùns

From the outset, the dùns are problematic. Archaeologists cannot even agree the terminology of their classification, let alone the origin, function, and abandonment of these circular drystane buildings.[129] Almost all that can be confirmed by everyone is that these are circular towers constructed of dry stones, sourced locally, which have diverse forms and purposes, frequently with a long, low entry passage and guard chambers, topped by higher level galleries reached by staircases built within the thick walls. Oh, and that these forms of construction are largely restricted to the Atlantic coastal fringe of Scotland. The famous dùn at Càrlabhagh is one of the best known examples, but there are many others along this coastline. Even their date of construction is debated, most researchers agreeing that they span from 400-200 BC, with a peak appearance around 100 BC, although some dùns apparently had continued habitation until around 600 AD. They have a characteristic positioning which is clearly marginal to cultivated land, good grazing, and human settlements, and they are frequently associated with the same terrain and similar sites as Iron Age round houses and Neolithic chambered tombs, so possibly are identified with a strong ancestral community in that place.

From the main road, the dùn in Mealabost appears much more intact than it actually is. Barely 200 metres away from the road-end of the village, and set on a natural high point which commands a surprisingly extensive view of the landscape, the dùn is less than a kilometre from Teampall Bhrighde but a world apart in cultural terms. The dùn was *"a heap of ruins"* by 1781, according to Captain Thomas [130] who also claimed that the dùn stood *"upon a former islet in a lake now drained "* but a consideration of the geomorphology suggests that while this is possible, it highly unlikely as the land here slopes to a natural high point. In support of this claim, it should be noted that these ruined round towers have an origin and a purpose lost in history. At various times it has been suggested that they were fortified strongholds, (but many lack defensive advantages) or temporary refuges in times of danger, (although deep accumulations of domestic waste would suggest otherwise), fortified watchtowers (for they are all within sight of the sea) or more simply, the ostentatious dry-stone mansion of a family of local importance, imposing their ego on the landscape (although this has also been challenged on account of their density and distribution throughout the region). The fact is that we don't really know for certain, but their formidable appearance is suggestive of power, political uncertainty, and the need for safety. Whatever their initial function, dùns were obviously strongly embedded within the wider social context of the earliest human culture of this region.

The one thing that remains obvious is the quality of the workmanship. The walls are built without mortar and without the benefit of modern surveying instrumentation, but the irregular blocks of local stone fit snugly together, and the curve of the perimeter walls, the stylish slant of the rising tower, are impressive to the point of generating speechless wonder. In the case of the dùn in Mealabost - Dùn Bhuirgh it is called, for it overlooks the village of Borgh to the south - there is very little left standing to admire, although much might still be intact below the current ground level. True, the northern portion of the external wall still stands about four metres high, but the southern rim is hardly chest-high, and the connecting sections are simply ridges of boulders. But stand on the thick inner wall, with your back to the northern high point and the inner circumference of the living chamber is clearly visible and quietly impressive. From the air the interior space of the floor defines an almost perfect circle built with rough stones. There are three dùns in Gabhsann, and two others flanking the township on either side, but this dùn is the only structure which gives any indication of the size or shape or dominance of the buildings when they were functional living quarters. There are three or four small rectangular niches inbuilt in the southern wall, provoking images of families storing their possessions in these rough-hewn recessess. A slightly protruding shelf about knee height, which archaeologists term a sacrement, shows where a wooden floor originally lay, and indicates that the current ground level is now at what was once the height of the second storey. Nothing else remains of the people who created this huge landmark and who must have, at least intermittently, taken shelter within its high walls, over many generations. Perhaps there is further investigative work to be done here.

Dùn Bhuirgh is typical in one aspect, in that it has been built on a location of magnificent natural advantage, selecting almost without our noticing the highest rise in the ground for many kilometres around. The views over the moor of Blàr an Dùin (the field of the dùn) are extensive, even though we are now restricted to a ground level perspective, and with a huge vista of the ocean to the west and north. Undoubtedly the view from the top of the tower in its operational heyday would have been impressive. The vegetation is probably similar to what it was when the dùns were first constructed, and Dùn Bhuirgh is now surrounded by low-lying Cross-leaved Heath and the wiry branches of wind-trimmed Tormentil with its gay scattering of small flowers of bright yellow. Apart from the natural hollows of the land, nothing obscures the views from horizon to horizon. In one aspect this dùn is unusual, because within the broken walls, which are easily three metres thick, the survey of the Royal Commission on Ancient Monuments recognised an unusually large number of cell-like enclosures, and although we can all speculate, their original purpose must remain a mystery. It's impossible to identify these 'rooms' nowadays, amid the tumble of fallen boulders, and we are only reminded of their existence by the diagram in the Ninth report on *The Inventory of Ancient Monuments and Constructions in the Outer Hebrides, Skye and the Small Isles* which was published in 1928.[131] This inventory also noted evidence of a stairway within the southern wall to an upper gallery, and thought that the dùn entrance was facing west. This is interesting because later research [132] on dùns indicates that most entrances either face due east or due west, and that the builders of the west-facing doorways were deliberately trying to demonstrate their social isolation and control over nature by facing their domestic entrances away from the prevailing direction of the rising sun at the midwinter equinox. (Significantly, the same words in Gaelic can be used to identify 'east' and 'front' or 'west' and 'back'.)

It is easy to imagine that in earlier times, with the origins of such impressive constructions lost to folk memory, there would have been a level of awe, and even respect, associated with the dùns. A local legend tells a tale of fairy people living in Dùn Bhuirgh who would occasionally help local humans with their magical powers,[133] but facts rather than magic dominate the history of Gabhsann, and the facts are even more fascinating than the fiction. There is also a local legend (mentioned first by that adventurous Skyeman Martin Martin) [134] of a secret passage from the dùn to the shore below at Brebhig, but due to the shallowness of the soil and the resilience of the underlying Lewisian Gneiss, this was probably never a reality. Although the dùns are open to the sky now, they probably had a wood-and-thatch roof and possibly internal supports to extend accommodate galleried floors above ground level.[135]

There is another intriguing aspect of this dùn. From this high knoll, and certainly from the top gallery of the original dùn in its completed state, it is possible to see the location of at least three of the other four adjacent dùns. There are the ruins of another tumbled-down dùn to the southwest, on an artificial island on the appropriately named Loch an Dùin, in the village of Siadar, built in the low ground below the standing stones of Steinacleit. (The name means 'promontory of the stones' in Old Norse, but are the stones a burial site, a stone circle, or a settlement with an enclosing wall?) The water-level zigzag causeway to this island dùn is clearly visible and navigable, but beware of the ubiquitous 'wobbly stone' which is set to pivot and throw the unwary stranger into the loch. Within Gabhsann itself, there is a clear line of sight to both the dùn below Steinacleit and to the place, north towards Dàil, where the dùn in Loch Bharabhat would have dominated the local horizon. The waters of this small lochan lap the verge of the main road as it leaves Gabhsann, but the opposite shore, barely 100 metres away, is a haven of surprising calm and stillness. The last time that I visited, there were dozens upon dozens of day-glow blue Azure Damselflies, flitting along the banks, lesser numbers of coral red Large Red Damselflies, and solitary, larger Dragonflies hunting among the mossy fringes of the loch. On this further shore, there is a short causeway of stepping stones, barely two metres long, connecting the 'mainland' to a small artificial island which formed the base of the dùn. There are actually three stone causeways radiating out into the loch, but even the archaeological experts have provided no satisfactory explanation for this.[136] Unlike many other dùns, this location would have access to fresh water during a time of siege, but the easy access from north indicates that its defensive role was probably not significantly strong. Nothing now remains except a small cairn to mark the spot, which can be seen from the road, but was most probably created by a generation of local children far removed from the original builders of the dùn.

From Dùn Bhuirgh, the location of another dùn can be identified in Gabhsann, which is at first unexpected, given the lie of the land. At the end of the village road in Gabhsann bho Thuath, now almost on the broken edge of the Atlantic shoreline, is the site of Dùn Sobhuill. There are plenty of lichen-covered boulders strewn around the site, but nothing remains to indicate the shape (which was recorded as 'circular') nor the extent of the original dùn. A moment's contemplation suggests the reason for its disappearance, for half-hidden in the rank, ungrazed grass are the outlines of the fallen walls of fanks and field boundaries, and the roofless remnants of croft houses whose construction reused the stones for building, though those houses would in turn be pulled down when the village was 'cleared'. In the middle distance to the southwest, the rising ground of Blàr an Dùin is visible, but the closer Dùn Bharabhat, scarcely two kilometres away to the east, is obscured by the bulk of Tom Lomaidean, not a high summit, but sufficient to dislocate the two dùns from each other. From the top of Dùn Bharabhat it would have been possible to see yet another dùn, on the small island in Loch Shiabhat, just over the Gabhsann 'border' on the Common Grazing of Dail bho Dheas. (Leave the car in the layby above Àsmaigearraidh and to the plaintive single-note piping of the Golden Plover, follow the line of the Gàradh Dubh (a turf dyke) out to the moor to a point just beyond the near skyline. The straight ridge of the turf wall is broken and indistinct in most places, but the sure-footed tracks of the Red Deer will find the driest line to lead you straight to the margin of the loch.) This site is difficult to access and unusual in being one of the very few island-situated dùns not to have a causeway leading to it, although this is possibly because the water-level of the lochan has risen over the years. It is an usual location for a small dùn, with the enveloping loch set in a hollow of the land, well away from any suggestion of an adjacent settlement or farmed land, although there is a wonderful view to the southwest towards Dùn Bhuirgh, with the whole of Gabhsann bho Thuath clearly exposed. What sort of people lived here?

The tantalising possibility occured to me that at the time of their popular use, this chain of dùns would have been visible to each other along the length of the Atlantic coastline. A short experiment with a drone and a high-resolution camera satisfyingly demonstrated that this is indeed the case. Although Dùn Sobhuill lies in a hollow near the river-mouth, it could probably have been seen from Dùn Bhuirgh, though it remains the most hidden of all the local monuments. Perhaps these dùns were the ostentatious dwellings of a family group, or an extended family who settled in this place? Was their purpose a temporary sanctuary in times of social tension, or an advanced warning network to alert the community against an attack from the sea? Current archaeological thinking indicates that the dùns were meant to be lived in, but that the homestead might also have seamlessly combined aspects of the practical, the ritual, and the symbolic in their social functions.[137] Like the identity of the original dùn builders, the function of these enigmatic structures and the reason why there are so many clustered around Gabhsann, is likely to remain a permanent mystery in our heritage.

Living in the land

Many of the features which make a place attractive to human settlers are re-discovered afresh time and time again by succeeding generations, and perhaps even by succeeding civilisations which replaced the earlier settlers. There may be some vital natural aspects in this recognition of re-settlement opportunities, such as a sweet-water spring, a sheltered glen and good, deep soil, or simply a convenient anchorage for the night, but other re-discoveries seem to be by chance. Many of these circumstances combine in Gabhsann. Less than a kilometre north-east of the dùn in Mealabost, huddled along a section of coast which is apparently little different from all of the rest, the bones of two distinctive civilisations are being slowly uncovered. It is common enough to find that several of these early Neolithic and Iron Age communities along the north-west coasts are within sight of one another, or in some cases their footprint of settlement overlapped as they sought to share the benefits provided by the landscape. In many locations, however, the building stones have been removed and re-used, or buried under soil or peat, or simply washed away by the relentless ocean. The site in Gabhsann owes its current visibility not just to the coastal erosion of a sand-bank, but also a chance stumble over a century ago.

This incident was recorded by Alasdair Alpin MacGregor, a Highland-born author who lived most of his adult life in London, but wrote extensively about the Hebrides and the rural north, usually mixing facts with a large helping of poetic licence. In the 1920s he spent some time living in the farmhouse in Gabhsann with the tenant of the farm at that time, Johnnie Morrison, who was a friend of MacGregor's father. In the chapter of a book written over forty years later he tells a story of Morrison, who went out for a walk with his cousin near the mouth of the Gabhsann bho Dheas river, and accidentally slipped down the sand-bank, in the process uncovering a bronze ring-headed pin, fragments of pottery, and some bone implements which suggested that they might be of some archaeological importance.[138] The account is interesting at face value, but as with other pieces of his writing, he mixes fact and fiction so that it is sometimes difficult to recognise now which is which. His romanticised perspectives of the Outer Hebrides also included a curiously disparaging attitude towards the natives. It is perhaps understandable that he should take the side of his host, but strange that he should commit his disdain to print and place himself so firmly against the current of history.

Fortunately, as he related in that chapter, the initial archaeological discoveries resulted in the arrival of Arthur Edwards, Assistant Keeper at the National Museum of Antiquities (now the National Museum of Scotland). There were no previous records of artefacts from this site, although a kitchen midden had been noticed here by the Director of Museums in 1914. In a thoroughly detailed excavation the following year, Edwards described his discovery of several stone constructions protruding from the sand, which he excavated and documented with accompanying drawings.[139] One of these structures, a long, low entrance passage was found, leading to an earth-house, or souterrain - perhaps 2000 years old – which consisted of five small chambers lined with stones, mostly buried in the sand, but probably with the roof projecting above the ground. The people who constructed and used these buildings were actually living *in* the land, rather than on top of it. At some time or other I stroll past this site almost every week of the year, eyes on the ground, alert for further evidence of my ancient neighbours in Gabhsann.

There have been numerous souterrains discovered in Lewis, always associated with early settlements and carefully built with wonderful dry-stone skills which appear almost as much an artwork as a practical building solution. One such souterrain was revealed in February 2018 in the village of An Cnoc Aird when clearing some ground for the foundations of a new house. Their precise function is still a matter of speculation, slightly different forms of the structures may have had many functions, but it seems likely that their small chambers provided storehouses for food and other commodities which were needed in the adjacent dwelling houses.[140]

Deer antler was also found in the Gabhsann souterrain, along with broken shards of pottery, bone implements, and a 'knocking stone' which was probably used as a primitive mortar for grinding grain with a stone pounder to make flour, in a similar manner to the saddle querns which were in use for several thousand years (and which were also found at the base of the slope). Further careful digging produced some loom weights, fragments of small-toothed bone combs fastened by delicate metal rivets, a weaving comb of deer-horn, and four boar tusks of indeterminate purpose. A silver coin of a much later age – from the reign of King Edgar, 957-75 AD – was found near the ring-headed bronze pin, suggesting that this site has had a lengthy period of occupation. Edwards concluded that the evidence indicated that this was not a temporary, transient settlement of early hunter-gatherers, but rather represented people who were hunters, fishermen, traders, weavers, and primitive farmers as the occasion demanded. Most of the stones of these dwellings and souterrains have now tumbled down the sand-bank and lie anonymously among the boulders of the beach, but what strikes visitors now is that the layer of shells which those people ate, then threw onto the ground in their midden-area – a layer perhaps 30cm thick, which was subsequently covered by more sand – is still starkly visible as a white band among the darker soil profile. To recognise another aspect of change and continuity in unexpected situations, I wonder how many of the locals who occasionally supplement their earning here by gathering Winkles on the lower shore are aware that they are carrying on a deep-seated tradition of this place that might stretch back over 6000 years?

A few years after Edwards visited, further excavations were conducted at this location, with a particular focus on establishing the relationship between the raised beach and the Iron Age midden.[141] What was discovered is not now considered very remarkable, but it certainly adds piece-by-piece to the evidence helping to build our understanding of the life of the early people who colonised Gabhsann. The raised beach here lies on an earlier outwash of boulder clay, with blown sand having accumulated on top of the raised beach. Onto that accumulated sand was thrown the refuse from the diet of the early settlers, forming a layer of shells, of which Winkles are the most numerous, but also including Limpets, Mussels, and the occasional Scallop, as well as fish bones, Cod being the most common. The bones of their domestic livestock – cattle, sheep, and pigs – are also among the debris, as well as countless broken fragments of a crude pottery, probably manufactured from the local boulder clay. Oddities include the possible remains of the bones of a Wildcat, and a Chough – a type of red-billed, red-footed crow that is now very rare but still found in Islay. A couple of pieces of iron slag were also found, which suggested that perhaps some primitive iron-smelting was practised. These remains were left by people on the sandy coastal grasslands, and though subsequent events buried the evidence of their activities in deep sand dunes after the site was abandoned, further evidence regularly emerges to remind us of their former presence.

By 1948 the souterrain in Gabhsann had completely disappeared back into the boulders of the beach, but with public attraction drawn to the site, several (incomplete) human skeletons were later discovered as the sand shifted, exposing graves known as 'long cists' lined by slabs of local stone.[142] Some skeletal remains were described in precise, if rather dull, clinical detail [143] but other work placed the analysis in a wider historical context and noted that of the five partial skeletons found, four were females, young adults to middle-aged, and ranging from about 150 cm (4 ft. 11 ins.) to 167 cm (5 ft. 6 ins.) in height. Interestingly, the older women displayed heavily worn teeth, undoubtedly as a result of their primitive diet and two of the women evidenced serious bone injuries indicative of a hard, physical life. The positioning of the cist graves and their depths of burial once again suggest a period of prolonged habitation at this site.[144]

In 1984 and 1985, two more long stone cists were excavated on the Gabhsann sand-bank as human bones were discovered to be appearing on the sand surface (and other, more stable, cist graves were noted but left undisturbed).[145] The care taken to line these graves with substantial rock slabs, and to place the thick horizontal slabs resting on the side walls to create the stone "cist" would have entailed substantial effort, and indicates that these earliest inhabitants of Gabhsann, although primitive in their lifestyle, were settled and sufficiently attached to this place to want to remain here after death. In these graves, which lay east-west orientation, two almost complete skeletons were recovered with their heads to the west, one female, probably in her twenties, (although there was evidence that she had given birth to at least one child) and one male who was around thirty-five to forty years old. Both were about 170cm in height and apparently in good physical condition with no sign of dietary deficiencies. The leg bones of the man were used to give a radiocarbon date of around 1710 years ago, confirming that this formed part of an Iron Age cemetery. Two further burials were recorded in 1993 and 1996, both males in their 50s, bringing the known burials at this site to a total of fourteen, although with stone structures intermittently being revealed by the shifting sands, it is likely that more graves are yet to be discovered. Unusually, a small decorated pot about 110mm high was found in the grave at the time of the 1993 discovery, with an adult male, who also exhibited a rare iron brooch at the front of his neck, probably fastening a garment which has subsequently disintegrated. This unused clay pot was probably fired in an open fire or basic kiln, and had simple markings which indicate its manufacture at a date prior to 300 AD, possibly to accompany this specific burial. This date is contemporaneous with the construction of Atlantic Roundhouses, but at this point in time, it is the only vessel known from an Iron Age burial context within the Hebrides.[146] All in all, the long cist cemetery in Gabhsann is unique in the Outer Hebrides, and some archaeologists have tentatively suggested that the combination of stone-lined and (earlier) unlined graves in the same locality, may indicate evidence of this place transitioning from pre-Christian to early-Christian forms of burial rituals, but the current information falls just short of proof. (The dated skeletons in Gabhsann overlap with the known dates associated with St. Ninian's conversion of the southern Picts (c AD 360-432) and it may well be that the spread of changing belief rituals in their wider society are evidenced in the changing style of burial ceremonies throughout the region.)

In the last few years, other stone assemblages have begun to emerge from the sand-bank, especially after a big storm from the north and a high sea pounding on the shore. Some of these structures may only be what is left of ancient boundary walls, but others will undoubtedly be more stone-lined graves, and there is one tantalising structure being uncovered which appears to be the remains of a wheelhouse. These house constructions appeared in the islands in the Middle Iron Age (BC 200 – AD 200) as the dùn began to fall into disuse. These buildings are unique to the Outer Hebrides and Shetland and gain their name from their wheel-like appearance of a central hearth supported by radial piers (which give the 'spoked' appearance) surrounded by small stone chambers.[123] In Gabhsann, the coastal erosion and sand subsidence has removed the seaward half of a house, although until recently the hearth was quite distinctly exposed, with the landward portion of the construction still covered by sand.

There have only been three or four of these wheelhouses discovered in Lewis and Harris, notably at Cnip in Uig,[147] but they appear to be more common in Uist [148] such as at Sollas.[149] Like the souterrains, the wheelhouses were semi-subterranean, set into the sand but with the roof-structure rising above the ground, and it is entirely consistent that the wheelhouses were the living quarters while the souterrains were the storage facilities for food and animals, as the two structures are often found in close association. Clearly this small location on the Atlantic edge of Gabhsann has been home to humans over a long period of transition. Spanning pagan burials to the incoming of Christianity, through different architectural preferences from simple skin-covered tents, to single-cell stone dwellings, dùns, then wheelhouses and on to other forms of residencies, the human communities here lived in constant, if slow-moving, change. They left marks of their passing, a bronze pin, or a hand-axe, an antler pick or the spoils of a rubbish dump of shells that had served their purpose. Unlike many other parts of Lewis and Harris, there are no standing stones in Gabhsann, although the stone circle at Steinacleit is clearly visible on the middle horizon to the south and there is a monolith over the horizon at Clach Stein in Nis. But rather than assume that they have never been present in this place, their absence in Gabhsann is more likely to be the result of successive generations removing or re-using the stones, or like the wheelhouses they may be buried in sand or peat, much as were the Calanais stones in 1857, simply awaiting rediscovery.

Here and Far Away

Until this time, and for a long time afterwards, as Dr Finlay MacLeod has observed,

> *"The people living in Western Isles did not use maps in their everyday lives but relied entirely on their cognitive maps which were facilitated by a wealth of first-hand experience and lit by the mnemonics of words."*[150]

These cognitive maps – essentially mental images of the place and the relationship of the individual to that place – are complex and shifting, but like the return of migrating animals, they are inbuilt to our psyche to allow us to recognise place and the utility of a place, for drinking, eating, sheltering, and living.

It is probably the most (over)used cliché when journalists refer to the Outer Hebrides to prefix the region of their description with the term 'remote' (citing *"… the remote isle of X…"* or *"… a remote beach in Y…"*); but this is also, possibly, the most pejorative perception. It is one of the curious properties about the description "remote" that it is both conditional and relative. Unlike geographical concepts which are directions (north is always north, until you reach the Pole) remoteness depends for its understanding on being at an unspecified distance from something else. Often, it seems, distant from someplace tacitly unspecified and vague, but we are expected to know *that the other place is at the centre.* More than that, it requires the primacy of ego-location - placing the self at the centre of the map, in much the same way as the ancient philosophers had a geocentric astronomical model placing the Earth at the centre of a universe which revolved around it. One of my favourite anecdotes is of when Scotland's First Minister, Donald Dewar, visited Lewis and stood overlooking the landscape of Uig with the mother of one of my friends. He is reported to have said that the view was *"…beautiful, but very remote…"* to which the old lady is said to have replied, *"Remote from what?"* In that short exchange is the clash of spatial location and politics, the juxtaposition of importance and meaning in relation to a specific place.

Remoteness is also relative; it requires a repositioning of the imagination between the place where you are, and the place where you think that you are - in your dreams, or your imagination, or your comfort zone. Remoteness assumes that there is a centrality of place, so that the other place, far away from you, is the place that is 'remote'. This insists upon the imperative of proximity and the belief that you are at the centre of the cognitive map, and everybody, everything else, is distant from you, not you from them. For this reason, we appear to make rather ambiguous distinctions between places which are 'more remote' and 'less remote' from a certain fixed place, and attempt to understand gradations of 'isolation' in different cultures; there are huge differences in the variations of scale and the logistics of life-style when we discuss 'remoteness' in central Australia as compared to central England. We often tend to think about remoteness as being far away from cities and crowds of people, but this too is relative. When you are in a place like Gabhsann, and the centrality of your existence is here, your family and friends, culture and history, then it is the cities that are remote, not you. The unthinking assumption of some radio presenters that we all live 'at the centre' and that everything further away from there has increasing levels of 'remoteness' is just that – unthinking.

There are differences too, when contemplating 'remote' and 'isolated'. The early Christian explorers who sought the quiet places of the north-west, such as Gabhsann, did so because they obtained a measure of isolation from what they perceived as the temptations of the world. They were not 'remote' from these places, because these places were the centre of their existence. Perhaps being 'remote' is only when you perceive yourself being somewhere else, or want to be somewhere far away. Maybe there is an analogy here with the sense of 'being alone in a crowd' or of participating with social media in a 'virtual space' which is not actually 'virtual'. It is quite real, but it is not in physical co-proximity. Isolation can be involuntary or self-imposed, and is equally applicable in a city as in a rural area. If everything that we want and value is around us, if the things and people of only tangential interest are far away, it is they who are remote from us.

For thousands of years, places such as Gabhsann were not 'remote' because they were settlements on the main artery of communications, not on the periphery. Before the national network of level roads was created and before the invention of wheeled vehicles, it was travel over land which was the most difficult. Travel by boat was the norm, and having a boat meant that islands were central nodes in a journey, not isolated outcrops separated by watery barriers to be overcome. When Pytheas made his circumnavigation of the island of Britain, there were hundreds, probably thousands, of local boatmen who had "discovered" the river-mouths and sea-lochs of this landscape – only they did not write down their experiences in navigation. (Or if they did, the accounts have long been lost). A historian of Scotland's western seaboard has called for a reappraisal of how we view the historical record of this region. It needs,

> "... placing into its proper setting; that of a maritime, multi-ethnic milieu. In short, the traditional perspectives need to be turned upside down: the periphery should become the core; the core should become the margin."

To generations after generations over thousands of years,

> *"these seaways defined their core; Scotland, Ireland, and England were their periphery."*[151]

Perhaps the only place on the planet that can truly be considered remote is the small hamlet called Remote in Coos County in the USA state of Oregon which is located at the confluence of Sandy Creek and the Middle Fork River. Wikipedia tells me that the main road apparently

> *"used to run through the centre of the community, but realignment of the highway has left Remote several hundred yards away, along a side road, around a bend and down below the highway, largely shielded by trees from highway view."*

The map of the world looks very different when we consider 'remoteness' as being the distance to the nearest large cities, rather than being distance from an arbitrary fixed point (where the observer happens to be at that moment).[152] Countries change their shape, and geographical boundaries are distorted almost beyond recognition. Yet Gabhsann is still here, at the edge of a large ocean, as it has been for many millions of years.

To challenge the ascendancy of this idea that large urban populations are "the only place to be" (or to put it in the negative - as a television broadcaster recently commented in Harris - that rural places are '*in the middle of nowhere*') we have a convention which defines the relative position of a place using a national system of grid references. Each detailed eight-figure grid reference of eastings and northings places every location to within one square metre of its unique point on the map of our world. It is not without some irony, therefore that the precise point at which four of the Ordnance Survey sheets of the Outer Hebrides meet has the grid reference 0000 0000, and that this point of geographical 'absolute zero' identifies the summit of a small hill on the Island of Taransaidh which is called Aird Vanish. (The name is probably actually Aird Mhànish (the height of Mànish) as there is no letter V in Gaelic, but the phonetic sound is the same).

CHAPTER 6

From Settlers to the Clearances

The servants of St Brigid

The piping, single-note whistle rises in an increasingly frenetic series of warning calls then dies away, only to start again where the Oystercatcher lands fifty metres away on a grassy patch of the neighbouring croft. Every other bird within hearing distance recognises the alarm-call and darts away in a radial direction from my approach. The Oystercatcher rises again and circles back to where it first took to the air, in a half-convincing attempt to draw me away from its nest among the cluster of grey, lichen-covered stones. Oystercatchers are conventionally birds of the shoreline, but sometimes they nest inland, and we are barely 200m from the coast among the cliff-top crofts of Mealabost, one of the three small villages which comprise the modern township of Gabhsann. From the shape of the bills, these Oystercatchers appear to be a pair who mainly feed upon shellfish for these birds have stumpy, chisel-shaped bills, ideal for prising shells off the tidal rocks.

Although the Oystercatchers are unaware of the fact (as indeed are most human observers) it is particularly appropriate that they are nesting at this precise location. The Gaelic name for the Oystercatcher is *Gille Brighde*, the servant of St Brigid. There are many unlikely miracles and myths attributed to the historical St. Brigid of Ireland (including being the midwife to the Virgin Mary) and several legends which purport to explain how the Oystercatcher came to be named *Gille Brighde*.[153] These stories often include impossible mixtures of real historical characters and the complete fantasies of muddled folk-tales, but the most believable derivation stems from a story in which St. Brigid becomes becalmed and fog-bound while sailing between the islands. In this folktale, Oystercatchers arrive and fill her sails with the beating of their wings, to guide Brigid towards the safety of the shore, and in so doing, earn their name in Gaelic.

The bird's name has a special resonance with this place because not only does it link the mythology of prehistory to the present-day common name of the bird, but with an intriguing twist of fate, the current nesting territory of this *Gille brighde* includes the site, just a few metres off the village road, of an ancient 'healing well' which has been named since before written history as Tobair Bhrìghde, (St Brigid's well). There are many freshwater wells scattered around the northwest coast of Lewis, (there are over a dozen wells in Gabhsann alone) but a special few are named after saints, and are claimed to possess miraculous healing powers, capable of curing a wide range of ailments. Tobair Bhrìghde in Mealabost was reputed to have a curative effect on jaundice and the clear water is still flowing freely today,[154] although, unfortunately, the old stonework around the wellhead has been capped with a concrete slab.

The well is not much visited these days, but at least it is recognisable as the site of a well, whereas a few tens of metres to the south-west, the rough outlines distorting the grass are only discernible with the eye of faith. To an experienced field archaeologist, these lines mark the ruins of a two-cell chapel, Teampall Bhrìghde. The age of this chapel is unknown, and although the tenacious collective memory of this community recalls the building as a temple to St Brigid, this does not help to date the structure because Brigid is one of those figures who were also popular in pre-Christian religious mythology. Many of the older wells and chapels have names which are markedly Celtic in attribution, whereas younger structures (although still very old) tend to reflect the influence of the spread of Roman Catholicism - and places such as the sites in Mealabost comfortably span both theologies without a murmur of discomfort. The veneration of St. Brigid (who may or may not be the historical St. Brigid of Ireland who is thought to have lived between 451 and 525 AD) is common along the western coasts of Ireland and Scotland. In the Outer Hebrides alone, there is another Teampall Bhrìghde at Scarasta in Harris, and two other sites of Cille Bhrìghde (St. Brigid's Church) one in the township of Cille Mhoire in South Uist and another in the isle of Sandraidh to the far south. Tantalisingly, although unmarked on standard

Ordnance Survey maps, there is a ruin named Brigid's Shieling on a rocky ridge in central Lewis,[155] separated from permanent human habitation (as shielings always were). There is unlikely to be a direct association between this shieling and the historical St. Brigid, real or imagined, but the perseverance of the name suggests both the importance of oral tradition, and a lasting cultural legacy.

In common practice with the colonisation by incoming religions across diverse global cultures, the idols and motifs of the older beliefs in the Outer Hebrides were subsumed and re-packaged by the newer, more dominant theologies. The difficult transitions of the indigenous communities into accepting the newer deities were cushioned by maintaining at least some of the key characters, and even some of the pseudo historical narratives. The controlling powers simply rearranged the old rituals to fit the moral codes of the new faith. So the boundaries between the Celtic St Brigid, her mythological predecessor, and her Christian descendant, have become indiscernible over time. An intriguing feature, however, is that one of the consistent attributes of the composite character of 'St Brigid', in addition to her concerns with the health issues of her community, was the custom of her followers to establish nunneries in close association with healing wells and the sites of the chapels erected in her name. The historical St. Brigid is considered to be especially associated as the protector of dairymaids, midwives, new-born children, and nuns, which is particularly interesting as there are tenuous folk-memories of the existence of a ruined nunnery adjacent to the chapel of St Brigid in Mealabost. There is also a record of St. Brendan returning to Ireland from one of his missionary voyages to the Hebrides, in order to consult with St Brigid and seek her advice, before resuming his missionary travels along the northwestern coasts.[156] Walking across the croft now, there is scant sign remaining of this nunnery, although, with a bit of imagination, it is possible to see rectangular disruptions in the low mid-winter shadows of the grass, so perhaps evidence of its foundations will be revealed by forensic archaeology teams of the future.

Healing Wells and Hermits

The belief in the power of the 'healing wells' continued over many centuries, even into relatively modern times, and many of the so-called cures were associated with very specific, sometimes bizarre rituals. It is recorded, for instance,[154] that the father of a girl who suffered from epilepsy (himself an elder in the church) was so persuaded of the efficacy of the traditional form of cure that between sunrise and sunset he walked five miles from Nis without speaking to a living thing, to enter the family burial ground around

8

9

10

11

12

13

14

15

16

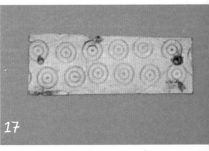

17

23

24

25

26

27

28

Captions:

1. Stripes of dark amphibolite bands in Lewisian Gneiss
2. The rounded headland of Tobha Ghabhsainn, looking towards Nis.
3. Feldspathic pegmatite (pink) intermixed with grey gneiss.
4. Golden Plover feed in many of the crofts.
5. Turnstones are regular visitors to the Gabhsann shore.
6. A watchful Grey Heron stalks by the river.
7. Dunlin paddle among the seaweed in search of food.
8. Curlew and Whimbrel are never far away from the village.
9. A Great Black-backed Gull maintains its searching gaze.
10. Greylag Geese have now become year-round residents on crofts.
11. Delicate Ringed Plover dash among the cobbles.
12. A long-legged Redshank keeps watch over its nest.
13. Fortunately, William Daniell painted this image of Teampall nan Crò Naomh.
14. The beautiful Gabhsann graveyard on the edge of the raised beach.
15. A sample of some of the Iron Age pottery from Gabhsann midden.
16. A bone comb, now in Museum nan Eilean, Steòrnabhagh.
17. A decorated box-top, also in Museum nan Eilean, Steòrnabhagh.
18. The wall of an Iron Age house slowly emerges from the sand.
19. The beautiful harness-mount, inlaid with coloured enamels. (now in Museum nan Eilean).
20. The outlines of the grain kiln in Gabhsann can be clearly seen.
21. Tobair Aonghais Ghiolais, one of the many village wells.
22. Looking into the ruins of Dùn Bhuirgh at Blàr an Dùin.
23. Marsh Marigolds delineate many of the croft drains.
24. One of the many different varieties of Orchid found in Gabhsann.
25. Ragged Robin carpets the fields in summer.
26. The mosses on Gabhsann moor are varied and extensive and worth a second glance.
27. An Azure Blue damselfly hunting among the Rushes.
28. In Autumn, Heather provides vivid colour stretching to the horizon.

33

34

35

36

37

38

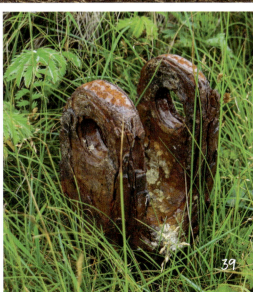

39

GALSON — LEWIS.
SMALL HOLDING SCHEME.

Scale. 6" = 1 mile.

Loch Shieved

Loch Shieved

Loch Chaurenach

Loch Rhisagere

Loch Rugleret

Strianaret

41

42

43

Captions

29. The precision of peat-cutting has its own symmetry.

30. Stacking peat for winter fuel.

31. Remnants of ancient tree-cover in the bottom of a peat bank.

32. Peat-cutting may look haphazard, but there is a sound traditional method.

33. Looking over Gabhsann bho Dheas from the moor.

34. A work in progress; gathering the intangible heritage of place.

35. Gabhsann houses, with crofts in front and behind.

36. The storm beach at Bun na h-abhainn (the river-mouth).

37. Tùlaigean, when the village boats would seek to tie up.

38. Moving sheep in Gabhsann bho Deas.

39. The stanchion for tying up the boats at Tùlaigean.

40. An image of the original map that was used to create crofts from the Galson Farm.

41. The modern Galson Farmhouse, now a croft house, (and guest house).

42. The cobbled courtyard of the old farmyard echoes its history.

43. A view over the modern farm-house, looking NE along the coast.

44. Signing Galson Estate into community ownership. (© Malcom Macleod Photography, with permission from Urras Oighreachd Ghabhsainn)

45. Unveiling the memorial plaque to commemorate the buy-out. (© Malcom Macleod Photography, with permission from Urras Oighreachd Ghabhsainn)

46. A day of celebration for Urras Oighreachd Ghabhsainn (Galson Estate Trust). (© Malcom Macleod Photography, with permission from Urras Oighreachd Ghabhsainn)

47. Looking to the future, the engraved stone records the return of the land ownership to the estate residents.

More photographs of Gabhsann can be seen online at https://bit.ly/2XbJYYv

Teampall nan Crò Naomh on the raised-beach shoreline of Gabhsann, where he dug up a human skull, filled it with water from a healing well, and gave it to his daughter to drink. Then he returned to Gabhsann to re-bury the skull before sunset. Unfortunately, the storyteller did not relate the name of the healing well, nor whether the daughter responded to the 'cure'.

In about 325 BC, Pytheas of Massalia (the Greek colony of Marseille) became the first documented Mediterranean mariner to reach and eventually circumnavigate the British Isles. The details of the precise route of his voyage are lost, and we know about his discoveries (including his description of the midnight sun) only from other authors, some of whom have uncritically repeated his stories, others who have over-critically challenged his accounts. It seems fair, however, to accept that he did sail around the perimeter of the British Isles, and in the absence of any evidence for or against, it is fun to speculate on the sight of his vessel sailing northwards along the Gabhsann coastline. A voyage following the north-eastern longshore currents along the Atlantic edge of Europe seems feasible, if only because it is surely preferable to a passage up the Minch, which though less exposed to stormy seas, would have been clearly visible from the land in all directions and much more susceptible to attack from the warlike inhabitants.

With a similar logic, I like to think that St Brendan also sailed past Gabhsann, perhaps several times, as he followed what he perceived to be his duty in seeking out the "Isle of the Blessed" in the New World across the Atlantic Ocean. According to an Irish immram (a navigational sea saga) St Brendan set off in a leather boat with some fellow monks, and over a period of years, they sailed around the northern periphery of the Atlantic, calling at the Faroes and Iceland, before eventually reaching North America and then returning to Ireland. There are several versions of the *Navigatio Sancti Brendani Abbatis* (The voyage of Saint Brendan the Abbot) which like many Medieval manuscripts is an intoxicating (and frustrating) mixture of fantasy and practical details, but the story retains an element of credibility. In his now classic re-enactment of the voyage, Tim Severin and his crew chose to sail up the Minch rather than hug the west coast of the islands, but they clearly demonstrated the feasibility of a vessel constructed according to Medieval maritime standards being able to journey across the Atlantic.[157] The details of St Brendan's voyage have been obscured by the passage of history, and most accounts were written (or re-written) hundreds of years after his lifetime, but there is a suggestion that there may have been many similar voyages by Irish monks. Again, I like to envisage Brendan and his crew just offshore from Gabhsann, perhaps nervously watching the coast for a threatening reaction from the residents ashore, or perhaps hopping from one religious community to another as they followed their vocation to spread the word of Christianity. We know from the structural remains re-discovered that these roving monks sought out small offshore islands and isolated promontories to construct their cells and chapels, and to dedicate their lives to their religious beliefs by withdrawing from the temptations of human society.

Often it seems, as with Teampall nan Crò Naomh, the chapel on the shore in Gabhsann bho Dheas, these chapels were constructed, or reconstructed, on the location of earlier pre-Christian sites. The early Christian missionaries observed a particularly rigorous form of spirituality, often escaping the concerns of the human world by isolating themselves in uninhabited, hard-to-reach places and offshore islands, and the ruins of their monastic cells are scattered the length of the western coasts of Ireland and Scotland, over to Norway and onwards to Iceland. They were, however, careful to persuade any resident communities they encountered of the perceived superiority of the new religious beliefs, and slowly, at some point in time, the sacred figures of Celtic theism became Saints in the Christian roster.

The origins of Teampall nan Crò Naomh are lost in time, as is its name, which has been variously translated as 'The church of the holy blood' and 'The church of the holy heart'. Fortunately an accurate representation of this very early chapel has been left for us through the world of art. In the early 19th Century, William Daniell set off on an ambitious tour around the coasts of the British Isles, recording the notable sights that he encountered in his wonderfully detailed watercolour paintings. He had already made a name for himself as an artist with a celebrated series of illustrations from his imperial travels in India with his uncle Thomas (also an artist) and later also from his travels in South Africa. In 1813 William Daniell set out on his massive project *A Voyage Round Great Britain*, which took him ten years to complete, initially with a commentary on the journey provided by the writer Richard Ayton, but after the first couple of trips, Ayton abandoned the project and left Daniell to complete both the paintings and the text alone. The results were published sporadically in eight volumes, containing 308 illustrations (now re-published) with the accompanying travelogue.[158] The year after William MacGillivray kept his detailed journal in Harris, Daniell was in Gabhsann. He only painted six captivating views in the Outer Hebrides, and one of these watercolours is a wonderful representation of Teampall nan Crò Naomh, with its surrounding graveyard, and with the shore of Gabhsann in the background. The Chapel was roofless and ruinous even by this date (1819) but enough of it was standing to give a clear impression of its architecture.

Although probably dilapidated before 1800 or earlier,[159] Daniell also recorded folk memories of feasts and religious celebrations which had been held at the chapel, perhaps similar to the descriptions given by Martin Martin,[134] for those religious festivals at the much larger chapel of Teampall Mholuidh in Eòropaidh to the north. He also notes, with something of the writing-style of a current-day tabloid journalist, that,

> *"At one of these merry meetings it was ascertained that a man had taken an indecorous liberty with a female: the hallowed purity of the temple was in consequence destroyed, and it has not since been resorted to."*

The site obviously continued to be of importance, however, as two other cell-like buildings were subsequently erected adjacent to the ancient chapel, and the graveyard continues to be used to the present day. Daniell apparently did not stay overnight in Gabhsann, having lodged the previous night with a Mr Morrison in Dail, and travelling onwards (stopping briefly to also paint the monolithic standing stone of Clach an Truiseil - the largest free-standing monolith in Scotland) to the village of Barabhas, where he stayed with Mr Macrae, the minister. His note-taking and powers of visual recall must have been astonishing when he finished the paintings back home in London, for the details he recorded are impressive. He was known for the accuracy of his paintings, (his watercolours of Calcutta were used to reconstruct part of the city after a great fire),[160] and his painting of the chapel in Gabhsann does not disappoint in this respect. (I am looking at the print on my wall as I write this). In addition to recording the image of the architecture of this lost chapel, Daniell captures the ambience of the building in its setting of the landscape at that time, which is extraordinary if you look at the painting carefully. Behind the chapel there is a slight rise in the land, with two small figures standing on the coast above the area now known as Cladach an Teampuill, (the beach of the chapel) and what is astonishing about this image is that none of this land now remains. The two small figures on the horizon, and Daniell's reputation for accuracy in his work, give the clear impression that in 1819 there was at least a hundred metres between the chapel and the coastline, whereas in 2020 the distance is hardly more than thirty metres. This is a historical marker of the extent of coastal erosion, inadvertently documented by a travelling artist.

Gabhsann becomes a named place

In his work of almost forensic detail, Norwegian linguist Magne Oftedal, chronicled the Old Norse place-name heritage of the villages of the Isle of Lewis and noted that *"most of these names are older than the colonization of Iceland."*[161] There are many intriguing landscape descriptions noted in his writing that have relevance to the area of Gabhsann, including Mealabost having been derived from Melbóstaðr (sand-bank farm) and Breibhig, along the shore below the village, meaning "Broad Bay" (which it is). Place-name nomenclature, with the handicap of historical reflection and factual obscurity, is not, however, an exact science. The linguistic accuracy might be fascinating to an xenologomaniac (an excessive lover of foreign words), but there is also a contradiction in attempting to bring such a level of precision to a region of human behaviour which is both subjective and idiosyncratic in its implementation. As a result, even Oftedal is forced to concede that many place-names are now obscured beyond rationalization or definition. So much is guesswork, assumptions, or supposition - trying to place a modern interrogation on name-giving processes which at the time may have been quirky and highly personalised (e.g. named after an individual person, or a local event, now long-forgotten). Nevertheless, he gives us a derivation of this place - Gabhsann - which he dissects as a combination of the Old Norse "galt" = 'hog') and "sund" which is *"a stretch of water crossed by swimming; a crossing-place in a river."* He concedes that it might also be the name of a river, or a man's name, but most logically, according to Oftedal, the original meaning of Gabhsann is very practically, if not prosaically, that this place was simply *"the crossing place of the hogs".*

Oftedal was Scandinavian, and sought to devine a particularly Norse interpretation of cartographic nomenclature, but twenty years before his writing, a Gaelic-speaking Lewisman gave a different interpretation, based more firmly on the topography of Gabhsann.[162] He suggested that the village name might have a root in the Norse *"halsendi"* meaning "the neck of land" and noted that

> *"There is a long, broad ridge, at the north -west end of which the earliest houses were situated. This word would give us "hauss-onn", with the usual Gaelic aspiration Ghauss-onn, hauss-endi, [the] end of the low ridge"* where the earliest settlement of Gabhsann began.

When the first Ordnance Survey maps were being prepared, the attention given to the local authenticity and 'voice' of the place names was less than sympathetic, and certainly less accurate than the technical efficiency given to the surveying operations (although, linguistically and culturally, perhaps no more than should be expected given the imperial arrogance of the age). Alexander Carmichael (collector and Editor of that treasured record of oral culture *Carmina Gadelica*),[163] was for a time engaged in 'sense-checking' the names collected, prior to including them on the master copy of the maps, and he wrote at one stage to express his dissatisfaction at the process.

"The system pursued by the Ordnance Survey in regard to taking up place names is altogether erroneous. Non-Gaelic speaking men go about among non-English speaking people to take down Norse-Gaelic names with their English meanings! These lists are then sent to the district office at Inverness or to the head office Southampton... and finally the lists are sent down to the 'local authority' [including, for instance, Carmichael] *who is asked but is 'not expected to do more than give his opinion' of this precious nonsense..."*[164]

This inherent inaccuracy compounded the recording of place-names from one iteration of mapping to the next,[165] although three main categories of Norse place-names can be recognised; the names of settlements; the names of major physical features; and other, more obscure names, which either merge with Gaelic, or retain fragments of Norse elements without the whole name being recognisable.

I am in Edinburgh again, standing with the ever-enthusiastic and helpful Christopher Fleet, the Map Curator, in the map library of the National Library of Scotland. In front of me is a map so old and so famous that I can hardly bring myself to breathe on it, far less touch it. The Blaeu maps, published in Amsterdam around 1654, are a collection of coloured engravings comprising the first complete atlas of Scotland. The work of mapping was actually done half a century earlier by Timothy Pont, but the maps were unpublished in his lifetime. This earliest map of the Outer Hebrides is unlike anything that we are used to seeing. To begin with, the islands are spread horizontally, with north on the right-hand side of the pages, and the southern isles to the left. The outline of the islands is also unfamiliar, with Lewis and Harris an amorphous polygon, and the islands of Uist clumpy and undifferentiated. We take for granted the modern satellite images, aerial photographs, and electronically precise triangulation, and so it is now almost impossible to imagine how Pont managed to produce his maps with even the approximate accuracy that he did achieve. What interests us on this occasion, however, is in the top right corner of this map of Lewis. I had asked when Gabhsann had first appeared on a map, and it led us to this publication. The villages of Parvas (Barabhas), Shader (Siadar), Borg (Borgh) and Eorby (Eòropaidh) are clearly labelled, and above Borg is the annotation "Gaeƒt". Although the spelling is problematic, the annotation is in the correct geographical area, and the place names on both sides are accurate, so clearly it cannot be anything else other than the earliest cartographic indication of Gabhsann as a named place. Following the (mis) translations from Old Norse, through Scottish Gaelic, then Lowland Scots to the Dutch engravers is obviously a tortuous linguistic route.

Beside the Blaeu atlas on the map-room bench, Chris Fleet had laid out another famous map, the 1750 atlas of sea charts created by the Orcadian, Murdoch MacKenzie (who was commissioned to produce the charts partly due to the failure of the Hanoverians to capture Bonnie Prince Charlie). The new regime wanted a more accurate understanding of the geography that they had now acquired. On the map of north Lewis there are several places named with the usual mangled versions of phonetic spellings, but here "Galson" is named in English for the first time. Mackenzie's charts of the Scottish islands were much valued at the time by ships masters, for they gave a much more accurate rendition of the coastline than any previous attempts at mapping the region. They were often accompanied by detailed navigational directions which could make the crucial difference between safety and disaster for vessels seeking port. Despite the later criticisms of his work (largely unfounded)[166] his draughtsmanship was based on meticulous measurements from the sea, and cross-checked from the land, which resulted in major improvements in map-making.[167] I sometimes look out of my study window over Gabhsann and wonder where MacKenzie stood (and perhaps Pont, 150 years before him?) when they were adding Gabhsann to the map of the world. By the time I left the Map Library, after immersing myself in several iterations of Ordnance Survey maps of Gabhsann spanning from 1853 to the present-day representations, I felt elated and slightly disoriented, as if I had been time-travelling at speed, which is indeed what I had been doing.

But there was one remaining question. Maps are stories in a pictorial form. The lines, the shading, the symbols, suggest features and objects which were apparent when the land was surveyed to make the map. The landscape changes, however, and so too does the naming of the land. New people arrive and rename the landscape to suit their own world view. Names fall into disuse, or have their spelling altered to fit with the new tongues. In every detailed map of Gabhsann that I have ever seen, there is small peat lochan out on the moor, roughly triangular in shape, about 3km due south-east of the village. In every map but one, this shallow, distinctive water body is called Loch Rumsagro. The name is not particularly relevant; it's derivation is lost to history, and nobody now knows if it's meaning was Gaelic, Norse, or some confused combination. By chance, while I was studying the most recent Ordnance Survey maps of the area, the 2007 Explorer Series at the scale of 1:25,000, I noticed an anomaly. Scarcely visited Loch Rumsagro had now become Loch a' Cheisteir (the loch of the Catechist). The Ordnance Survey do revise place names and features as new information becomes available, but although there is a folk memory of a catechist who went missing on the moor I knew of no reason for the name-switch, and no-one locally knew the new name. The loch is at the far edge of the Gabhsann Common Grazings, well away from any common path. The name-change intrigued me, and so I raised it with Chris Fleet at the National Library of Scotland. He was also interested, but all his maps and records could shed no light on the matter. So, Chris asked a colleague of his in the Scottish National Archive, where the Scottish log-books of the Ordnance Survey place-name records are held, but the name-change was too new, and no record existed in the National Archives either. I was then referred to an e-mail contact at the central offices of the Ordnance Survey. I got a holding reply, then another message indicating that the matter was a bit more elusive than initially thought, and finally, about a month later, a reply that they too had drawn a blank. There apparently exists no explanation of why the loch should suddenly have a dramatic change of name in recent times. Due to the lack of any supporting evidence from either local or national sources, the Ordnance Survey has decided that the name Loch Rumsagro will be reinstated on future maps, but the mystery remains unsolved.

Fashion-conscious Vikings

The sand on the shore in Gabhsann comes and goes. There is a strong current close inshore, and this longshore drift regularly picks up the white shell sand and dumps it further along the coast in Nis. One week there are several white beaches, largely devoid of humans, another week only rounded boulders intermixed with shingle. The differences are particularly notable after a big winter storm, but the cyclic process has continued throughout the seasons, year after year. In 1986, walking past an eroded sandbank, a curious regularity was caught in my peripheral vision. A small, dark, rounded outline against the pale sand looked slightly out of place, and I automatically stooped to pick it up. At first I thought that it was an old pre-decimalisation penny for it is about the same size and shape. The first few seconds in the palm of my hand, however, told me that it was something much more important, although exactly how important I didn't yet know.

The object is about 30mm in diameter, with a slightly concave back which has a central lug protruding, pierced-through like an old fashioned button. The front is flat, with what seems to be a complex Celtic design looking like three interlocking boomerangs whirling about a central circle. This all seemed sufficiently interesting to send the object to the friend of a friend who is an expert on Medieval history, and Viking material culture in particular. Dr. James Graham-Campbell worked at University College London, and immediately identified the discovery as an enameled mount of a type associated with ornamented horse harnesses. The Celtic pattern on the mount is extremely rare, but he identified two other mounts which are almost identical, one from a Viking grave-site in the Isle of Man, (dated to the period AD 850-950) and the other from a Viking grave in the Nord-Trøndelag area of Norway. The mount from Gabhsann is of a copper-alloy of Celtic workmanship, and the pattern on the front has been inlaid with coloured enamels, so old that the glasses have devitrified with burial, leaving only tiny tantalising remnants of their previous colours stuck in the sharp corners of the design. When the mount was subjected to further scrutiny in the British Museum Research Laboratory, using a combination of highly specialised x-ray fluorescence and x-ray diffraction techniques, another astonishing discovery was made.[168]

Two colours of enamel had been used in its manufacture, the innermost parts of the 'boomerang' shape had originally been a bright yellow enamel caused by pigmentation with lead-tin oxide, whereas the other parts of the design had been inlaid with a bright red enamel coloured by cuprous oxide. The metal of the mount itself was determined as being a bronze with a substantial percentage of lead. All of this points towards a high level of sophistication and skill in the workshop construction. A bridle-mount for a horse harness of this quality would have been a prized possession, and now we can only rely upon our imagination to explain how it came to be lost on the sands in Gabhsann. A trace of zinc was also found in the red enamel, but not in the metal of the mount, and this is unusual, both for the fact that the presence of zinc in ancient enamels appears to be unrecorded previously, and also because, unlike the other trace elements which have been used for colouration, there appears to be no useful function for incorporating zinc. The Norwegian mount was subsequently also found to be made of leaded bronze, with relict red enamel bearing small amounts of zinc and slightly more tentative evidence of a yellow-enamel inlay. The rarity of these finds and the striking similarity between the harness-mount from Gabhsann and the other two from Norway and the Isle of Man, suggests the stunning possibility that they may actually have been made in the same workshop, either in Scotland, Man, or Ireland, but this remains just a tantalising speculation.

The enamel harness-mount has been on permanent display in Museum nan Eilean in Steòrnabhagh since it was re-discovered by me in 1986.

What is more certain, is that these archaeological discoveries point-up the fact that the shoreline of Gabhsann lay on a major trading route between western Norway and western Ireland. For many hundreds of years, this coast was a thoroughfare for the movement of goods and people. It was the 9th and 10th Century equivalent of a motorway or autobahn. These islands were not "hidden" and they were not "remote", they were key destinations and marker-posts for critical journeys. This is a further reminder that travel by boat was the method of choice before roads were improved enough to enable wheeled vehicles to travel overland; before that, journeys were made on horseback (for the fortunate) and on foot (by most other people). Islands and coastal villages were the nodes which connected people, shared cultures, and traded goods. These were not communities which were "cut-off", rather they were the vital connection-points which provided the flexibility to spread ideas and to demonstrate an independence which was both internally sustainable, and yet outward-looking in its world-view, which enabled Norse vessels at one time to explore as far apart as North American and the Black Sea. In the 5th and 6th Centuries, Ireland was the centre of high culture in Europe, and the west-coast seaway was the mainline artery along which those cultural values were transmitted. This was no "periphery", it was at the cutting-edge of spiritual, cultural, and geographical exploration, and Gabhsann had a ringside seat.

The Norse Village

This landscape abounds with the legacy of the Norse people who lived and visited this place. From the simple rhombic iron rivet which I found on a sandy beach where their boats would have been run ashore for maintenance and mid-voyage relaxation, to the naming of the landscape features that can be seen all around. There is a preponderance of Nordic-sounding names covering this landscape – names plucked straight from Old Norse, names morphed phonetically from Norse into Gaelic spellings, and names which sound Scandinavian, for which no meaningful derivation is now recognised. The Norse legacy inhabits this landscape. We need to be careful how we think about the naming conventions that claim this place, because ethnographic investigation, "...*reminds us that settlement area and sphere of influence are not the same.*"[169] There is no doubt, however, that the Norse came to Gabhsann and stayed. They were not just "passing through".

Along the coast in both directions, there are patches of disruption on the land, sometimes splashes of extra-green vegetation, indicating locally altered drainage, and sometimes physical signs such as the curious 'combed' appearance produced by the ridge-and-furrow style of agriculture called feannagan. Although named 'lazy-beds' in English (probably by someone who had never tried to cultivate them - no irony intended, apparently) these feannagan were formed by a double thickness of earth, turned over from the adjacent furrows, which then provided the drainage. Seaweed, and perhaps animal manure, was spread on these ridges, and the crops planted on top. This form of cultivation persisted for many generations, but it must have been back-breaking work, and not unsurprisingly when methods of agricultural practice improved, the feannagan were abandoned. The vestiges of this human toil, anonymous in their origin and age, are especially visible in the low sunlight of winter, and must have been a potent reminder of the cyclic return of fertility, harvest, and fallow. Like the intricate Buddhist artwork, produced by artists who disdain to scribe their name to their creations because they consider it is both folly and egotistical to claim that the artwork is the inspiration of only one person, this land carries the evidence of the toil of hundreds of people over thousands of years. Where the shallow valley of the Allt Meagro drains the stream towards the ocean, the unattributed feannagan flank the sides of the glen. On the edge of the shore near here there are a couple of places where grave-sized rectangles of stones are protruding from the ground. Are these the graves of the people who worked the feannagan on the slopes above? Or are they the graves of strangers released from the sea at this spot? Or are they simply random clusters of stones? Look on them and provide your own story.

Between the end of the village road and the mouth of the village river, on the shore of Gabhsann bho Dheas behind the beach, and among the shells of Iron Age buildings and other remnants half-buried in the sand, lies a Norse settlement. It is unusual in that it appears to have no defensive fortifications. This fact suggests that the community had been settled in this place long enough to feel secure in the neighbourhood, perhaps as farmers and traders, perhaps even inter-married with the prior inhabitants of the land. There is evidence of early agricultural workings, as yet undated, and Thomas cites a Norse saga that claims when;

> *"The first inhabitants were sent* [to Lewis] *from Lochlin* [Norway] *by King Donmarag (?Denmark) they found only an old woman with two sheep at North Galson."*[170]

This 'folk memory' needs to be treated with care, for like many folk tales the world over, the Norse sagas are often convoluted mixtures of precise historical recollection and muddled stories which conflate events from different dates or attribute wildly different activities to the same heroic figure. None-the-less, it is fascinating that Gabhsann features at all.

This is a curious period of history, for which we are either left with a lot of information, or none at all. Many of the great events of 'the Viking age' are etched sharply in the national calendar. A succession of warring clan chiefs, owing only nominal allegiance to the strong-men of Norway, and giving no deference to the kings of Scotland, wove a complicated history of political intrigues, many of which were documented in genealogical detail, but are now of lesser importance for their significance in the grand schemes of history. As early as AD 800, Lewis became a place of major importance for the Norse, a safe haven from which to launch their early attacks on Ireland,[171] and later was colonised to create permanent settlements, but among the dramatic events of European history, places like Gabhsann are now scarcely mentioned parts of the historical backdrop. Over the next 200-300 years, there were several bursts of Viking expansion, driven, for instance, by the persecution of the megalomaniac King Haraldr inn hárfagri (the Fair-haired) of Norway which scattered Norse refugees all across the western Atlantic seaboard.[172] Some settled here in Lewis, some merely used it as a base to launch raids, including on their former neighbours in Norway, provoking bitter reprisals and local wars throughout the Atlantic region. Trondheim became an archbishopric in AD 1154, so also held the authority over the Hebridean church, and it is thought that the famous Lewis chessmen (some now exhibited in the museum in Steòrnabhagh) were carved here from Walrus-ivory and whales teeth between AD 1150 and 1200. Others have argued for an Icelandic origin of these famous chess pieces.[173] (As an aside, when the chessmen were discovered in Uig in the early nineteenth century, it was presumed that the cache was the property of a travelling trader or sailor, simply passing through, but the possibility that the chessmen were *used* here, and that they might actually *belong* in Lewis, raises interesting speculations on the complexity and sophistication of local culture at that time.)[108] Certainly the elegantly simple construction of Teampall Mholuaidh, in Eòropaidh, which some date to the twelfth century, has been compared in layout with a thirteenth century church in the Gardar region of south-west Greenland.[174] Teampall Mholuaidh would have been an outpost of the Trondheim archbishopric, and for all its modest size today, for hundreds of years it would have loomed large on the landscape, physically, spiritually, and culturally.[125] Dedicated to St Moluadh, who was a pupil of St Brendan, and an important figure in promoting the early spread of Christianity,[156] local folklore identifies this church with a protective sanctuary throughout the north of Lewis. This sanctuary extended southwards to Buaile na Crois in the village of Dail bho Dheas, the highest point in the local vicinity, and is marked with a cairn as the most southerly point from which the church of Teampall Mholuaidh can be seen. (The stream to the north, in Dail bho Thuath, is called Sruthan na Comhraich - the stream of the sanctuary – and fugitives escaping over this burn into Nis could claim to be under the protection of MacLeod of Eòropaidh).[176]

Gabhsann, lying just to the south of Buaile na Crois, would have been outside the sanctuary, but there is no doubt that the inhabitants of the whole area

would have been cognisant of the sanctuary's existence and its importance
as a temporary refuge, for there are records of fugitives fleeing to here from
Sutherland, and other parts of mainland Scotland.

On 7 July 1263, in response to complaints from the Norse settlers in the
Hebrides of harassment by the clans who owed (tentative) allegiance to
Alexander III of Scotland, the aged King Hakon of Norway set sail with a
large fleet of longships filled with warriors, intent on a showdown and the re-
establishment of his perceived right of suzerainty over the Hebrides. His fleet
reached Lewis in August,[167] and immediately began to "persuade" the local
warlords to rally in support of his cause. Undoubtedly, components of this
fleet would have been seen from shore in Gabhsann as the ships sailed south,
generating what? Fear? Excitement? Anticipation of unknowable changes?
All of those emotions, probably. On 1 October 1263, while anchored off the
Cumbraes, a big storm blew up, beaching and wrecking many boats. With the
arrival of Alexander's army, the Battle of Largs took place the following day,
and although the victors subsequently claimed a great battle, most historians
now regard the encounter as little more than a series of serious skirmishes.[151]
The result was defeat for Hakon, who retreated for Norway, but died in
Kirkwall before he reached home. With the Treaty of Perth eventually agreed
in AD 1266, the real impact of the defeat at Largs became significant, and the
Outer Hebrides changed their national identity to become part of Scotland.
This was a momentous event of nation-forming, although it would, initially,
have meant almost nothing to the ordinary people resident in Gabhsann, and
would probably only have merited comment as months-old cautious gossip
drifting around the hearth in an evening.

Like the sand that comes and goes at various places along this coastline of
Gabhsann, it is easy to imagine Viking longships regularly arriving on the
beach, not least because the gentle, green glen of Gabhsann presents such
an attractive vision from the sea. In Gabhsann, despite scant contemporary
documentary testimonials of this period in history, there are ample sources
of other evidence remaining, including a geophysical survey that effectively
maps the shape of the structures hidden in the sand.[178] Despite their ruinous
state, some of the buildings emerging from the sand along the shore
obviously have a different character from the round-houses of the Iron Age.
From the nineteenth century onwards, the domestic structures here tend
to have a rectangular shape, though those buildings are closely related to
earlier patterns of habitation, suggesting a continuity of settlement over a
long period of time, probably at least from around BC 500 to the fourteenth
century AD.[179] The apparent smoothness of this continuity, and the close
association of Norse material with the Late Iron Age occupation suggests

that, whatever the nature of the initial interactions between the Iron Age residents and the Norse incomers, over a very short time, perhaps only a couple of decades, the original raiders became settled farmers. Another significant distinction marking the beginning of 'the Viking age' has been documented by archaeologists who noted that:

> "*one of the clearest indicators of a significant change in technology and dietary preferences at the onset of the Norse settlement in the Western Isles is the radical shift in the exploited fish species and fishing methods utilised.*"[180]

Species such as Cod, Hake, and in the Outer Hebrides, Herring, become overwhelmingly dominant food items. (It seems that our rubbish tips can reveal a lot about our lifestyles, and the old midden in Gabhsann may be worthy of continued future analysis.) The pursuit of Herring, in particular, is an important behavioural change, because fishing for Herring is a communal task, involving not simply the collaborative labours of an extended family, or several families, but also a change in technology (investment in boats and nets) for the benefit of the common good. A simple difference appears to be a preponderance of offshore species in the Norse diet, compared with a tradition of mainly inshore, coastal species, at pre-Norse sites.

Probably the most common relics indicating the arrival of a different culture, however, are the hundreds of irregular sherds of pottery that are being slowly uncovered in the sand, and these pottery pieces have an interesting story to tell.

Of Pots and Bowls

I have an old fish-box in our agricultural shed, filled with hundreds of pieces of broken pottery. Most of the sherds are undistinguished and some might not at first even be easily recognised as pottery by an unpracticed eye. The pieces are rarely more than 3-4cm across, and vary in colour from a light tan, through various browns, orangey-reds, and sooty ochres to almost black. A definition of futility might be to imagine that it would be possible to reassemble these myriad sherds into anything recognisable as the parent artefact. Most of the items in the collection are battered and formless, without any decoration or indication of the shape of the original vessel, and all of the sherds have been made of coarse, local, glacial clay. Many of the pottery pieces have rough pieces of grit and quartz gravel in the clay mix – which absorb the thermal shock of putting a pot of cold water on a hot fire – and the outside of some fragments have been blackened as a result of that fire. I have picked up these sherds for more than five decades as I make my weekly stroll along a 100m stretch of our coast where the eroding sand is slowly revealing evidence of human habitation that has been left in this place for more than twenty-five centuries.

In another place, in a small bowl in our study, sitting on a shelf beside a hand-axe from the same location, I have a couple of dozen pottery sherds which are special to me, because these have a variety of simple decorations on them. They are also less commonly found, only a very small percentage of sherds recovered display any ornamentation. A few sherds have quite an elaborate zigzag vvvvvv embellishment, which may be a Middle Iron Age feature, and several show the indentations where the potter has left her fingerprints in the wet clay. I say "her" because tradition has passed down to us that most of the pottery was made by local women. I never fail to marvel, and gently rub my own fingers over these indentations which have been left for us by our predecessors. Nobody yet has meticulously drawn images of these Gabhsann patterns and shared them in the published academic literature like it has been done for the excavations at An Taobh Thuath,[181] but thanks to the collective work of many archaeologists it is almost possible to build up a chronological sequence of Hebridean pottery styles. I say "almost" because there are many issues of uncertainty, and some contested academic opinions, in their interpretations.

In the first instance, it is clear that a very similar type of local pottery has been made in the Hebrides for perhaps 5000 years, making undecorated sherds virtually impossible to date. By close comparison with other archaeological sites, some clues begin to emerge that enable specialists to ascribe approximate dates to certain styles. Dogmatic decisions need to be carefully avoided, for many factors combine to obscure almost every aspect of these broken sherds. Although they have all been manufactured from the same coarse glacial clay overlying the ubiquitous Lewisian Gneiss, local variations in mineral chemistry can sometimes create a false impression that different materials were used, resulting in a (limited) variety of clay textures. The disconformity of shape and fabric varies from vessel to vessel, so every fragment can appear slightly different. In addition, variations in the efficiency of the firing process, in a bonfire or perhaps partially buried in a clamp kiln, resulted in variable degrees of oxidation, which has produced the range of external colours. These colours can even vary across a single small sherd. It is not known if different island locations had favoured styles and patterns, although there is evidence that the early Medieval ceramic of the Outer Hebrides was substantially different from that found in the Inner Hebrides and Argyll. A further complication is that the cultural materials found in archaeological periods often cannot definitively dated; early Iron

Age grades into Middle Iron Age, and so on, and a distinctive cultural style might have occurred at various dates at different sites, as ideas spread. Large quantities of locally-produced pottery has been found throughout the Outer Hebrides, in contrast to the relative absence of such finds in most of mainland Scotland from the Bronze Age to the Medieval period.[182]

Counterintuitively, the earlier pottery usually has a primitive decoration, while the later vessels do not. A sherd in front of me on my desk has an impressed band of simple circles, such as might be made by pressing a finger-ring into wet clay. This form of ornamentation has been discovered elsewhere, such as in North Uist, where is is thought to date from the early Iron Age, around BC 500 at least.[183] Other pieces on the desk have the rim marked by a row of impressions made by a fingernail, again a common feature described from other sites and found, for example during the excavations at Dùn Èistean a few miles to the north.[184] The wavy vvvvv pattern has been recognised from Dùn Cuier at Bornais in South Uist and placed at AD 450-550 using radiocarbon dating.[181] Quite a few of the Gabhsann sherds with any decoration at all are pieces exhibiting the smooth rim of a vessel, perhaps with a slight curve or lip. The earlier forms tend to turn inwards at the rim, while later vessels turn outwards, even demonstrating a slight narrowing to form a neck.[185] By the Late Iron Age (around AD 500) the vessels are mainly undecorated, although still made from the same coarse clay.

A fact with which all archaeologists agree, is that the arrival of the Norse settlers marks an entirely new form of pottery, both in way that it was manufactured, and in its appearance. Earlier pottery was mostly bucket-shaped jars made by building-up slab coils of clay which leave 'tongue and groove' joining marks, in what has been termed 'Plain Style'. In contrast, the slightly smaller vessels created by the Norse potters were open bowls, cups, and circular platters, with flat but slightly rounded bases which were constructed by pressing together smaller coils of clay at an angle. The exterior of some of the undecorated sherds have grassmarking on the surface, another indication of a new tradition which seems to be characteristic of this period of Hebridean pottery construction.

The appearance of the small cups and open bowls substantiates the other evidence of new eating and cooking habits which arrived in Gabhsann during the Viking period, and the adaptations in the pottery, together with the construction of rectangular buildings directly on top of the earlier cellular structures adds further confirmation that this is a place with a long and continuous history of human settlement. Although not found in Gabhsann, in some adjacent areas the local skills of the women who fashioned handmade pottery from clay that was available nearby, persisted into the early twentieth century, resulting in so-called 'Barvas ware'.[186] These coarsely-fashioned 'craggans'- globular jars with narrow necks - are in some cases remarkably consistent in their appearance with earlier forms of Hebridean pottery, indicating a unique combination of functional domestic requirements and localised native skills which have coexisted for millennia.

Part of history's backdrop

For the next seven hundred years or so, details of the history of Gabhsann have been overshadowed by the bigger pictures of history.

> "... the centuries between about 1100 and 1300 in Scotland's western seaboard teeter on the abyss of obscurity. They are bathed in perennial historical twilight,at best always in danger of being outshone by the dazzling brilliance of the ages that precede and follow them...."[151]

This is not to say that Gabhsann, and the residents of Gabhsann, played no part in shaping the history of those centuries, but for the most part, the role of the village was akin to an "extra" actor in a big, long-running, feature film. The main events of those times have been documented in detail in countless volumes, not least by articulate historians from Lewis, explaining the roles played by the usual cast of those perceived to be the heroes and villains of their time. A history of the Outer Hebrides,[177] and of Lewis specifically,[187] as well as the rise and fall of royal households,[188] is recorded in detail, but Gabhsann is not specifically credited with any significant roles. The Lordship of the Isles grew in strength and prominence, then finally over-reached itself to collapse in disarray. There were continued clan tussles and political intrigues, initially along traditional divisions in the diverging roles of the Outer Hebrides in relation to Scotland, Scandinavia, Ireland, and the Isle of Man, but increasingly events focussed on Scotland only, then on the union of Scotland with with England. There is no shortage of adventurous side-stories reflecting the societal instability of those centuries, including the role of Dùn Èistean in neighbouring Nis as a fortress and a sanctuary,[189] and the growing prominence of Steòrnabhagh as a regional centre with minor parts to play in the struggle of nation-building. Steòrnabhagh saw the invasion and defeat of the Fife Adventurers and of the soldiers of Oliver Cromwell, but there appears to be no documentary information on how pervasively those events affected life in Gabhsann. If at all.

With the involvements of Lewis people in the Jacobite intrigues of the first half of the eighteenth century, there comes the reappearance of Gabhsann as a specific locus of national interest. This locus makes an appearance indirectly, and slowly, for although the main events occur elsewhere, and although the individual residents of Gabhsann are not specifically listed among the leading players, a knock-on effect soon becomes apparent locally. The decision of the 5th Earl of Seaforth to side with the Jacobite cause in the 1715 rising, and thereby also commit his loyal clansmen in his territorial stronghold of Lewis, was a calamitous error of judgement. The Battle of Sheriffmuir on 13 November 1715 between the Jacobites commanded by the Earl of Mar, and the outnumbered Government army under the Duke of Argyll, has gone down as a battle in which the left wing of each side was defeated, while the right wing of each side was able to drive their opponents back. Militarily the day might have been called a draw, but the political effect was to demoralise and disperse the Jacobean army, who subsequently lost the insurrection. The Seaforth Highlanders, who had fought in the centre of the Jacobite lines, had some other mainland skirmishes, then withdrew to their islands, but the disgraced Seaforth had his lands confiscated by the Crown and parts were later leased to tenants, who were all expected to pay rent, as well as obedience, to the new Hanoverian government.

The Forfeited Estate Papers of 1718 show in the first detailed rental records of Lewis, that Gabhsann bho Dheas had been leased to Rory Mathewson, Alexr Morrison, and Evander Morrison.[189] The saga of Tac Ghabhsainn (the Galson Farm) had begun.

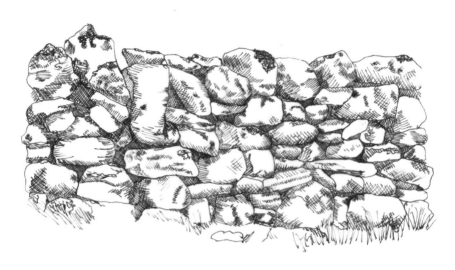

CHAPTER 7

Two hundred years of standoff

The Farm

From those earliest details recording the rental of Gabhsann bho Dheas to
Rory Mathewson, Alexander Morrison, and Evander Morrison, there follows a
long list of names spanning the next 206 years as families were shuffled in and
out of the area that, in those days, constituted the settlement of Gabhsann.
Similar to many rural areas in the Highlands and Islands, a commercial
farm operated adjacent to clusters of the subsistence agriculture that would
eventually become crofting, and it was a situation that fostered social tension.
Apart from the farm in Gabhsann bho Dheas, there were several small
villages on the land of this place. There was Old Gabhsann, mostly on the
site of the present-day Gabhsann bho Thuath, but then most of those people
were removed and made to start afresh in "New Galson", which was located
on the uncultivated moor to the east of the main road, before that too was
cleared and returned into the moor. There was also Baile Meadhanach (the
Middle Village) between Gabhsann bho Dheas and Mealabost, before that too
vanished, to all but those few local families who can still point to small piles of
stones as being the last homes of their ancestors.

The people now appear to have been moved like pawns on a Lewis
chess board. Unfortunately, the record is largely just a list of names and

approximate dates, which though carefully collated,[190] is akin to following the spoor of an animal without any knowledge of the life history or the ecological relationships of the species. Reading through the lists, matching the family names to now-vanished croft boundaries around the village, produces a strong sensation of helplessness; the realisation that those people had no real life choices. Reading between the lines of these lists of croft genealogies is fascinating, but obscure. There are records of families being moved between the half-a-dozen small parcels of ground sitting on the site now occupied by Gabhsann, but no background details on why people were moved, or how they felt about moving. The bigger picture of migration across this place is at best sporadic and most often absent. That is the way that the people who had the power wanted it to be. There are occasional records of people moving into the area from other parts of Lewis and Harris - from Riof and Bhaltos in Ùig, and from Càrlabhagh - presumably because they had somehow secured the rental of a croft in Gabhsann, but no indications remain if they had any prior familial connections to the locality. Occasionally there is a mention of individuals moving back to Gabhsann from Glasgow, or Dundee, and one striking note of Angus MacLean (mac Chaluim Iain) having returned from Ontario to take the tenancy of a croft in Borgh. Throughout it all, the village of Gabhsann bho Dheas was treated as a small farm, sometimes having croftland added to the farm, other times shifting the boundaries to create a few more crofts, largely in order to increase the potential rent from the area. Across the Highlands and Islands at this period, landowners;

> "... attempted to introduce modernisation across the estates: this commonly entailed the abolition of the semi-communal system of runrig, the institution of new enclosures, new crops, tree planting, new drainage methods, larger consolidated farms, and investment on new roads. There were also ambitious plans for new villages to accommodate the landless population to be displaced by the abolition of runrig..."[191]

From this perspective, Gabhsann was a fairly typical microcosm of the bigger regional situation.

In 1724, a new farm tenant, Angus Morrison, was added to the rental roll, and by the Judicial Rental (review) in 1754, the tacksman of Gabhsann bho Dheas is noted as being Alexander Ross. (A tacksman was essentially a middle-class land manager who rented land from a landlord, perhaps worked some of that land, and sub-let portions of his rental as smaller-scale agricultural holdings.) Twelve years later, in 1766, Alexander Ross signed a lease of Gabhsann bho Dheas at £20 rent, though by 1776, the tenant is John Morrison, who remained tenant until 1780 (although by then his rent had increased to £26). By 1786 the tenants were William Morrison and his mother (perhaps a son of John Morrison) but by 1787 the tenants were listed as William Morrison and Margaret MacKenzie. By 1807 the tacksman is John MacKenzie, paying a rental of £40 which rose to £75 by 1814. At this time it is recorded that there were twenty-nine crofting tenants in Gabhsann, together with seven cottar families (who held the fragile occupancy of a cottage, but had no land to work).

There is a feeling of tension in the quick turnover of names and the rising rental values being demanded. By 1819 - the year that William Daniell passed through and painted his iconic image of the chapel of Teampall nan Crò Naomh - the farm had been let to William MacGregor from Gairloch, although there were still eleven subtenants on the farm, rising to thirteen by 1841. At this point, Murdo Graham and his family at number ten, emigrated to the Lingwick Township in Eastern Quebec, which must have been a tremendous undertaking, a decision borne only out of desperation. Murdo MacLeod and his family, living at No. 7 Gabhsann, removed to the Winslow Township in Eastern Quebec in 1845, maintaining the genealogical connections between western Lewis and eastern Canada. Reading between the lines, there is a fragile sense of continuity here, although the paucity of detail reads like a condemnation of those people who did not matter (to the landlord) being deposited in the little-visited archives of history. The historical victims of clearances in Gabhsann may lack the recognition in the national psyche that has been eloquently documented for the Sutherland Clearances by James Hunter[192] and others, but the collateral damage of that history remains with us still. There appear to be no surviving photographs of the Gabhsann clearances, photography was in its infancy, but the engraved images from that time capture well the horror and the destitution.[193]

In 1848, the tenant farmer William MacGregor and his family, "were removed" from the farm in Gabhsann to Achonachie in Strathconon in Easter Ross - another indication of the regionally networked connections and consequence of the clearances - and Hugh MacPherson from Cumbernauld became the leaseholder of the farm of Gabhsann. His tenancy lasted nine years, and his name is still remembered with bitterness. During his tenancy, Mealabost was cleared of its sub-tenants (in 1853) and the land was added to the farm of Gabhsann, but by 1857, Hugh MacPherson also gave up the lease of the farm and it passed to Alexander MacRa for a brief period (who is remembered with respect, if not affection) until 1862. Then the whole of Lewis was bought by James Matheson, a merchant from Lairg, in Sutherland, who had made a fortune trading during the opium wars of the Far East. He bought all of Lewis from the Seaforths in 1844, for £190,000, although its annual rental then was only £9,800.[194] Although Matheson subsequently undertook one of the largest estate investment programmes in the Highlands and Islands, (even John Prebble's groundbreaking account of the clearances considered him "*a benevolent proprietor*")[195] there is a growing sense that this island was not returning enough money to meet the new landlord's aspirations. Although, why the crofters should pay anything at all for the simple privilege of scraping a bare existence on this poor and unproductive land does not appear to have been a legitimate topic of discussion by the ruling establishment. This peasant population often received no benefits at all from any landlord, yet were frequently the subjects of considerable harassment and exploitation. James Matheson was subsequently knighted in recognition of the apparent benevolence of his famine relief efforts as the potato blight of the mid-nineteenth century reduced the population of Lewis, and much of the Highlands and Islands, to famine and utter desperation. A more careful scrutiny of the estate accounts in recent years has indicated that his estate simply gave out meal to the starving families, then added the cost of the relief to their croft rents, and used the increased indebtedness as a reason for the dispossession of land and forced emigration. (During the potato famine, Matheson spent £60,000 refurbishing his Lewis residence as "Stornoway Castle" to enhance the prestige that he assumed was due to his image of himself.)[196]

Looking today, along the many kilometres of dry-stone walls that delineate the key features of Gabhsann - the margins of the village roads, the separation of the northern and southern villages of Gabhsann, the occasional field edges - it is easy to underestimate the immense labour that must have gone into their construction. To see a contemporary dyker working for several days of hard, physical graft, in order to repair a chest-high stretch of wall scarcely fifteen metres in length, begins to indicate the extent of effort required, but this is only just a hint. It does not even begin to account for the hours of toil that were necessary in order to prise the boulders from their half-buried resting places in the fields, and then to carry them to the piles of stones waiting to be built into a wall. Most of these walls were constructed during the time of the Gabhsann Farm, when labourers were cheap, and a responsive labour market was locally available among the many under-employed crofters who were handicapped at every level by the pervasive extent of their poverty. There is an anecdote that has been repeated through generations of oral history in Gabhsann that helps to illustrate the nature of that employment relationship. After a back-breaking day of work on the farm, starting probably at first light and lasting until the evening light began to fade, a crofter from the Gabhsann area (a neighbouring village?) was sent home with his day's pay from the tenant farmer - a pail of sour milk! Apparently he was glad enough to have that to feed his family.

We cannot effectively judge the past by the legal standards and the ethics or morality of the present, but it is astonishing that there seems to have been no public clamour at all that speculated on the potential improvements, to the economy, the social wellbeing, and the health of the great mass of the people, if they had been encouraged to spend what little income they had on better houses, and better crofting, rather than their 'rent'. Their 'debt' to the landlord was unrecoverable, anyway. With even a modest retention of their economic assets, their property, their diet, and their employability skills would have surely benefited. Rather than that, they had that pittance extracted from them under severe pressure to pay rent for meagre parcels of land that were otherwise almost worthless to their overseeing landlord. Instead, any improvements to the homes, steadings, or land of those tenant crofters, resulted simply in a demand for an increased rent for the "improved" property.

This was a time of social turbulence throughout the Highlands and Islands. It was not the ferocious inter-clan warfare of previous centuries, but it did lead to the dissent known as "The Crofters' War".[197] Nor was it as clear-cut as powerful Lowland Scots and English imposing their will on the indigenous population, although that was certainly a common component. Most of the tenants of the farm of Gabhsann came from outwith the Highlands and Islands. Morayshire farmer Patrick Sellar, and subsequently James Loch, those infamous architects of the Sutherland Clearances, were both Edinburgh lawyers, but Evander McIver, who became Factor for the Assynt area of Sutherland, was a Gaelic speaker from Lewis. McIver spent much of his long working life in the belief that there were too many people on the land, that crofting should be done away with and replaced by farms, and that it was in the best interest of Highlanders to be encouraged to emigrate, indeed he had said that, *"it is wonderful the extent which Emigration is taking place from Ireland."*[198] He really believed, apparently, that the best solution was for the whole population to be removed to somewhere else, preferably abroad, because the landlord would always be compelled to carry the burden of the crofting community. He (McIver) considered that his job as an estate manager was to impose a more efficient system of financial returns for his boss, the Duke of Sutherland. Patrick Sellar was eventually tried for culpable homicide, though acquitted of his actions. It was the end of his career as a Factor, but his reputation is still associated with brutality, over 200 years later.[199] We can only wonder today what Evander McIver would think to see the successes of the Assynt crofters and the dozens of other community owned land trusts, managed by the descendants of many of those same recalcitrant crofters who did not want to be removed from the land?

In Gabhsann, the equivalent personality to Evander McIver, was Sir James Matheson's 'Chamberlain', or Factor for Lewis, John Munro MacKenzie. A Gaelic-speaker from Lewis, he also became an Honorary Sheriff Substitute upon the retiral of his father, who had already served a lengthy period as the island's Sheriff. John Munro MacKenzie was a powerfully-built man, with a great white beard and side-whiskers, who took management decisions with a stern and self-confident righteousness.

It seems incredible, now, to realise the overwhelming power of the estate Factor in the mid-nineteenth century. He (and it always was a man) had a controlling influence, and frequently the ultimate authority, over almost every aspect of community life. From the setting and collection of rents for crofts and farms, to the award of employment contracts; from making legal decisions over the allocation of poor relief, to permission to cut peats for fuel, or heather for ropes and roofing, the Factor's decision was as good as law. In the adjudication of these matters, and on all land boundaries and disputes, the Factor was the representative of his boss, the landlord.[191] In the case of John Munro MacKenzie, we have a uniquely intimate window on his world. For some unexplained reason, during the year of 1851, he kept a daily diary detailing his work.[200] In those days there were no holiday entitlements from employment, even Christmas and New Year's Day were normal working days, so this diary gives a particularly insightful perspective into the life of an estate Factor during a crucial period in the history of the Highlands and Islands. Mostly, the diary is little more than a long list of general tasks - "... *wrote letters...*" or "... *met with* [so-and-so]...." that Mackenzie carried out day-to-day, with few elaborating details, but even in its brevity, many comments betray the Factor's thinking and attitudes. The stark phrase "*deprived... tenants of their land*" occurs with an ominous frequency.

Local historian, James Shaw Grant, noted that:

> "*In 1849, taking a year more or less at random, the Estate served 64 summonses of removing on crofters in Lewis. All of these were multiple summonses, affecting a number of crofters. Each crofter evicted was the head of a family. At a modest estimate, the 1849 evictions [alone] must have affected fully 10% of the population in rural Lewis.*"[201]

Like Evander McIver, the Factor in Assynt, John Murdo MacKenzie was from Lewis, and a native Gaelic speaker. Also like McIver, he was an ardent exponent of '*improvement*' and of compulsory emigration for the population of Lewis under his charge. The opening sentence of his diary on January 1,

1851 is a note recording that he went to his office and *"was engaged settling accounts with Mr McPherson Galson and arranging his rent for last year "*. As early as 23 January, he is instructing local grounds officers to make plans for clearing certain districts. By Thursday 27 February he writes of his meeting at the schoolhouse in Borgh where he *"addressed them as usual"* and recorded that from the four villages of Coig Peighinnean Bhuirgh, Baile Meadhanach, Mealabost and Gabhsann bho Thuath, he proposed to emigrate 24 families, 115 *"souls"* of whom only three families were *"willing"* to leave.

John Murdo MacKenzie was well acquainted with Gabhsann, and his diary records that during the year he visited several times. On the nights of 17 and 18 July 1851 he stayed in Gabhsann to calculate stock and collect rents for Nis (with no hesitation, he foisted himself on his hosts in the farmhouse, as travellers did in those days). On Tuesday 23 September, for instance, and the nights of 13, 14, 15 October he visited to discuss details of their rent with the people of Gabhsann, and noted that *"Angus Graham must be removed."* The following day, with the help of MacPherson from the farm in Gabhsann he attempted to confiscate sheep and cattle in Borgh in lieu of rents, but when the locals saw what he was up to, they rallied round and recovered most of their own livestock. (MacPherson supplied meat throughout the year for Sir James Matheson's household in the Lews Castle, and in any case it would repay the farmer well to be on good terms with a powerful Factor like John Munro Mackenzie.) MacKenzie again stayed with MacPherson in Gabhsann farmhouse on 3 and 4 December when he met with the remaining tenants in the area to collect whatever rent they could manage to scrape together. He was not able to raise more than fifty shillings between Gabhsann and Siadar, and issued a warning that *"it would be well if they could be got to emigrate in a body."* During Hugh MacPherson's tenure of the farm in Gabhsann, he had his sub-tenants removed to a new location, the "township" of am Baile Ùr (New Galson) on the moor side of the main road, across from Gabhsann bho Thuath.[202]

Those mid-nineteenth century inhabitants of Gabhsann have been scattered across the globe, with the other diaspora of the Highlands and Islands, and with them has disappeared many of the first-hand accounts of that persecution. The rickles of fallen-down cottages remain on the landscape, if a person is attentive to the topography of the place, or has been educated about where to look and how to interpret landscape, but little else is remembered about the people. There is one anecdote that is still mentioned, however, and although the several versions of the story differ in slight details, there is enough of a common thread to indicate that the collective folk-memory is strong. The version that holds a particularly vivid resonance for me, was told to me by a cousin-by-marriage. Roderick (Rodaigan) Martin is a crofter in Mealabost, with an incredible memory for the complex detail of local genealogy and the stories that adhere to those families. Some of those stories are snippets that have been passed down by word-of-mouth, but others also have the support of circumstantial fact, and occasionally the backing of documentary evidence.

The story of "the Gabhsann curse" is one of those undocumented stories of the Highlands and Islands the details of which, nevertheless, are well-known. During the farm tenancy of MacPherson, two old sisters, Margaret and Ciorstaidh Martin, walked back from an open-air church service in Dail to find the thatch of their cottage on fire. The farm manager had used the occasion of their absence to evict them from the land on the brae above the farmhouse. The ruins of their cottage can faintly be seen as a low lump of ground in one of the fields of my wife's croft at what is now 23 Gabhsann. The distraught women, as they left the village seeking shelter, shouted their curse as they walked past the farmhouse. In their despair and desperation, they had nothing left to lose by refusing to adopt a false subservience. In their fury, they cursed the Gabhsann farmhouse and its occupants. *"Cha bhi oighre gu bràth air Taigh Mòr Ghabhsainn"* (There will never be an heir in the Big House of Gabhsann – the farmhouse). And to this day, there never has been an heir in that house.

Some versions add that they prophesied that MacPherson's wife would not die a natural death, and this found resolution when she subsequently died aboard a ship and was buried at sea.

The two evicted sisters were taken to a shieling out at Peicir, which neighbours had quickly made habitable for them, and after that they went to live with family in Borgh. Like all the best "supernatural" stories, the evidence is combined from different sources, but the facts remain that the old women did utter a curse, and since that day to now, few children have grown up in that farmhouse. For a brief spell in the late 1880s, the tenant farmer James Paul Helm (from Closeburn, Dumfries) and his wife Margaret Fowlie (from Manor Farm, Steòrnabhagh) attempted to raise a family, but several children died in infancy, and later the entire family left Gabhsann to try their luck somewhere else. Local memories are of the children "flying around, screaming like seagulls". They left behind, apart from a few fading memories of their bad relationships with the local crofters, only one sad, tangible reminder of the fact that they were ever in Gabhsann at all. A few metres from the ruined foundations of the chapel at Teampall nan Crò Naomh, in the beautiful, windswept cemetery on the Gabhsann raised beach, there is a double-grave that is different to all the rest. The obelisk-like tombstone, with its lettering slowly disappearing after enduring decades of wind-driven sand, is enclosed entirely by an incongruously robust cast-iron fence. It's lonely isolation seems desperate to make a statement of distinction and defiance that proclaims, "I am still remembered!" for here lie the remains of Alexander Knox Helm, aged two and William Aeneas Helm, aged seven, the only sons of James Paul and Margaret Helm.

Throughout the year of 1851, John Munro MacKenzie displayed no hesitation in recording in his diary his orders forbidding a family to cut peats for their fuel until rents had been paid, or to prosecute alleged poachers, and there was scarcely a village in Lewis where he did not visit and threaten the residents with eviction and forced emigration. His diary accounts exhibit no compassion for the starving and impoverished people or for the pitiful situations of the families that he was coercing for rent arrears. On Tuesday 3 June he was confronted by crofters who had been evicted, and had waited, homeless, a month for an emigrant ship. Starving, and having disposed of their few possessions and livestock, he still threatened them that he "...*would see them punished*" if they took [back] a sheep for which they had already been paid. He seems to have had no conception about how people could be expected to pay rents when they no longer had animals or seed crops, and no prospects of employment (the kelp industry had slumped by this stage, and making whisky at home had been declared illegal). In Siabost, in September, he refused to pay cash to people who were working on a quay for the landlord, and insisted that half of their earnings would be paid in meal (because the estate had an unused stockpile of meal). On 20 May, he attempted to get some of the crofters from Gabhsann bho Thuath onto an emigrant ship at Port Nis, but the people already on board (from Ùig) refused to allow any more passengers because they had heard there was fever and smallpox in Nis.

By 16 October he is already suggesting in his diary that all the Gabhsann villages should be cleared and turned into one large farm, although on 20 December he refused an application by Hugh MacPherson for a drainage project in Gabhsann. Investment on the Lewis estate, it seems, was highly selective, although there are frequent notes of discussions with Sir James and Lady Matheson on plans for the landscaping of the gardens of the Lews Castle and the surrounding walks.

One of the most astonishing diary entries that year is also one of the most revealing. It might not be initially obvious, but 9 February is in a class of its own. Although John Munro Mackenzie had no holidays at all during 1851, and made the effort to write something about his workload every day, he did not work on Sundays, so there is an account written about every day throughout the year, but no Sundays are included in his narrative. Apart from one Sunday, that is. On Sunday 9 February he felt strongly enough about his topic to make a very unusual comment. "Bella", his pet deer hind had gone missing, but now the head and entrails had been discovered, hidden in a drain behind the laundry. Also hidden some distance away were two fore quarters of the venison, presumably for collection later, and the hind quarters were missing. Mackenzie was enraged, and promised dire consequences for the thief. There are a few other comments made on subsequent days as he searched, in vain, for the culprit. From the lack of any confirmation, we can take it that the enterprising hunter was never discovered. Dwelling on this incident for a second, we surely feel a sneaking admiration for the daring of the person who took this extreme step in order to feed a starving family. Getting caught would not only have brought down the full wrath of the law, which was in Mackenzie's pocket, but surely also would have led to immediate eviction and transportation to the New World. The Factor had previously imprisoned men for poaching wild fish, how much greater would have been the revenge sought for this very personal insult? That the force of Mackenzie's anger should have caused him to break his Sabbath observance indicates a depth of sensitivity for his pet deer that is manifestly absent for the human lives in Gabhsann, and everywhere else under his governance.

John Munro MacKenzie was of the opinion that the future economic prosperity of Lewis would come from the sea, but Sir James Matheson could not be persuaded. (He thought that the people should show some enterprise, but how this could be achieved, with Matheson owning all the land, the piers and the infrastructure, while the populace could barely afford their next meal, was never evident.) On the shore below Gabhsann bho Thuath there is a narrow inlet called Tùlaigean, where the village boats would be drawn ashore and secured - an anchoring iron ring is still visible hard against the fence line. Standing here on a day with even a moderate swell evokes bewilderment and admiration that anyone should even try to steer a boat into this shallow cleft, which can only be navigated at high tides, and barely even then.

Rodaigan also recounted to me another folk memory, retained in astonishing detail. On 6 or 7 May, 1849, two of the village fishing boats, *The Lily* and *Dun Shobhail*, left Tùlaigean for a day's fishing on the sand banks off the coast of Suainbost. The seven-metre *Dun Shobhail*, skippered by John MacLeod and a crew of five, soon sailed past *The Lily* near the rocks of Sgeir Dhail. It was the last that anyone ever saw of *The Lily*, her twenty-two year-old skipper, Roderick Morrison (Ruairidh Mhurchaidh Alastair) or any of the other five crewmen, who were all from Old Galson.

Most people were convinced that *The Lily* had sunk with all hands, but the loss remained a mystery. Three years later, Roderick Morrison's wife, Ann, who was a cook at the Gabhsann farmhouse re-married to Donald MacKenzie from Borgh, despite the advice of her employer, farm manager Hugh MacPherson, who advised her to wait for seven years. Ann and Roderick had a young daughter (also called Ann) and the remarriage was almost certainly a matter of survival, as much as anything else.

About seven years later, sometime in August or September, Angus MacKay, a crofter living at 9 New Galson, was making his way home after helping his father-in-law in Siadar Uarach with his barley harvest. At Tom na Bà, near where the offices of Urras Oighreachd Ghabhsainn (the community land trust) now stand, he met a stranger. The anecdote passed down in oral history describes precisely the appearance of this stranger, who is said to have worn shiny knee-high boots, a long jacket with brass buttons, a blue velvet muffler at his neck, and a three-cornered hat that was typically worn by mariners of that generation. MacKay greeted the stranger in Gaelic, but on being told, "*No Gaelic*" attempted to converse in broken English. He told the stranger of his surprising likeness to Roderick Morrison, who had disappeared on *The Lily*. At this point, the stranger admitted, "'*S mì a tha seo.*" (It *is* me.) The identification was confirmed by the unusual feature that both the stranger and the vanished skipper had two sets of teeth in both jaws. Angus MacKay took the stranger home with him, and his wife, Margaret, fed the stranger mutton broth while their news was exchanged. The MacKays told the newly reappeared Roderick Morrison everything that had happened to his family since the disappearance of *The Lily*. Morrison, on his part, told them of how, along with the crew of *The Lily*, he had been captured by a cruising pirate ship, and transported to the West Indies as a slave, but had managed his escape by marrying a well-off lady who had taken a fancy to him. Eventually, he had managed to find his way back to Scotland, and to Lewis. Although there is no proof, it is rumoured that he visited his young daughter, who was being raised by his sister, Catherine, but then, realising the effect that his reappearance would have on the family, immediately left Gabhsann, never to be seen again. Of course, sensational news like this became the common subject of talk in the area, and Ann Morrison, now MacKenzie, found her circumstances very difficult, and in 1863 she moved with her husband to Port Nis, then in 1877, after his death, to Dail bho Thuath. Like so many others who left Gabhsann, she never returned. Several of the descendants of Roderick and Ann Morrison continue to live in surrounding villages.

In 1862 the farm was taken into the proprietor's (Matheson) own hands until 1870, and during this time he executed the final removal of the indigenous residents of Gabhsann, including the two shepherds and their families;[190] Donald MacLeod from Carlabhagh was removed in 1855 to Huron Township in Bruce County, Ontario and Duncan MacRae from Amhuinnsuidhe left sometime in the 1860s. For the first time in over three thousand years, the green glen of Gabhsann, apart from the farmhouse, had been made devoid of human residents.

A harvest of grain

It was one of those odd surprises of life that brought the big grain-drying kiln in Gabhsann into sharp focus for me. I was in the old Science Library in the University of Aberdeen (on the site of what is now the Queen Mother Library) doing some post-graduate research. I forget what exactly I was looking for, but probably something to do with the natural history of Lewis. I certainly did not expect to discover the grainy, overexposed photograph which fell out of the pages of the journal that I was browsing. It was a piece of 12 x 17 cm photographic paper that someone had been using as a page-marker. I nearly just stuffed it back into the journal and carried on browsing, but something made me glance again at the image in the photo. It was a copy of an illustration in a book, and it was a line-drawing plan of the Gabhsann kiln. I was speechless with surprise. This ruined kiln is hardly more than three hundred metres from the top-end of our croft, so I knew the place of course, but seeing it objectively displayed in some anonymous textbook somehow gave it a celebrity status. It took me many years of intermittent searching and asking archaeologists (in vain) before a colleague at the University of the Highlands and Islands, Prof. Hugh Cheape, was able to tell me, straight away, which book the illustration originally came from.[203]

For as long as I have known it, (and long before) the Gabhsann kiln has been a ruin of stones, yet the boundary foundations are still clear, and even some of the internal details are recognisable. There is a long rectangular tunnel, or teallach, which was a flue to carry the hot air from the fire near the door, up to the rounded bowl of the sòrn at the other end and through the platform of straw to dry the grain which was spread there. From the size of this kiln – slightly larger than most others which are still identifiable – my long-term friend Dr Finlay MacLeod, who is a font of knowledge on almost every aspect of Lewis, tells me that he thinks this kiln belonged to the days of the farm in Gabhsann, rather than the smaller versions which were more common, each usually operated by a few crofters or an extended family. The age of the Gabhsann kiln is difficult to pinpoint, not least because the style of the construction has hardly varied for over four hundred years. In some villages, small family kilns were in use right up until the Second World War, but not in Gabhsann. By that time the people of Gabhsann had been forcibly removed as a resident community. Standing by the kiln, in the area known as Cùl na feans, (literally, 'behind the fence' i.e. outside the enclosed inbye land of the village crofts) is very peaceful today, just a solitary Skylark singing high above, with three or four young Meadow Pipits of the season, and (somewhat appropriately for this monument) a beautifully marked Wheatear bobbing on the tumbled stones and flashing its white tail as it flies away. Quite commonly, the kilns were built as this one is, located further away from cottages and barns of the village, so limiting the risk of accidental house fires. It must have been an important centre of seasonal activity in its heyday.

In contrast, the traditional "Norse Mills", with their ingenious horizontal turbines, were scattered through almost every village, close to the small streams from which they derived their power. Finlay has documented the Norse mills in Lewis and described the details of their operation.[204] He recorded six separate Norse Mills in Gabhsann, although you will need a good deal of luck and the eye of faith to see them now. (The river in Gabhsann bho Dheas is deceptively strong, and though the stream is rarely more than two metres wide from bank to bank, its depth can be twice that during a spate, with a correspondingly powerful flow). At a minimum, there were at least four mills in Gabhsann bho Thuath and another two or three in Gabhsann bho Dheas. Like the kilns, these mills were small-scale constructions, designed to meet the needs of a few individual families in each village. How many generations of inhabitants in Gabhsann spent countless happy hours nestled in the Norse Mills in this township, listening to the hypnotic clacking of the millstones as they ground the flour for their baking? In the early years, the grain would have been Bere, or perhaps Black Oats by the end of the nineteenth century. Unlike the kilns, which fell into disuse as social circumstances changed, many of the Norse Mills, or their millstones, were purposely destroyed by commercial mill-owners in order to force crofters to mill their harvested grain, for a price, in their newer mills with their larger, vertical turbines. Significantly, there have been no millstones discovered in association with any of the Gabhsann mills, and they are speculated to be buried, broken, or physically removed from their original locations. They are generically called "Norse Mills" because of their known connection with the early Norse settlers, but in reality their design has a much older, and wider, pedigree, and they were still in use in some parts of the island until the 1930s. To capture the ambience of these old Norse Mills and grain-drying kilns, you need only go as far as Siabost to visit the renovated mill and kiln, which together re-create a wonderful impression of the whole operation. Sadly, in Gabhsann, with the mills all gone, all that remains are the ruined foundations of the old kiln, but even this is worth a visit in order to walk around its outline and contemplate the demise of past indigenous technologies.

The Final Clearance

During the Factorship of John Munro MacKenzie, the tenants of the farmhouse in Gabhsann bho Dheas would have looked out across the ruins of a growing number of abandoned family mills and croft houses. MacKenzie was succeeded as Factor in 1854 by Donald Munro, who was already the Solicitor of the estate of Lewis, as well as Procurator Fiscal - at the summit of his career he held nearly 30 public offices in Lewis. Although MacKenzie was stern, and a firm believer in crofter clearance, there is some evidence that he occasionally tried to mitigate the effects of his actions. Not so with Donald Munro, whose legacy in Lewis was one of unremitting misery and vindictiveness.[205] It is almost a tradition in the history of the Highlands and Islands to solely blame the Factor for the misfortunes inflicted upon the populace, and to excuse his boss, the estate proprietor, as being 'unaware' of the situations on the ground. It is clear from the diary of John Munro Mackenzie, however, that Sir James Matheson was regularly informed, consulted, and kept his finger on the pulse of the Factor's actions. Donald Munro, however, as prosecutor, judge, and executioner, was in a league of his own for sheer spite. Throughout his twenty-year term of office as Chamberlain (Factor) of Lewis, Donald Munro operated with impunity, combining his contradictory public roles with a breathtaking abandonment of the law that he was supposed to uphold, and frequently including a petty malevolence that was tyrannical and sociopathic.[201] His authority was fickle but absolute, being infamous for fining crofters if they did not pay their meagre rent with enthusiasm ("*A*[n extra] *shilling for your scowl*".) His common threat was, "*Cuiridh mi às an fhearann thu*" (I'll take you from the land) and he did not hesitate to use his multiple public roles with impunity for his own advantage. It would eventually be his downfall, but not before he brought torment to an uncountable number of islanders.

In 1863 all the remaining tenants were forcibly removed from Gabhsann bho Thuath, leaving only the farm and the cottages of two shepherds. Comparing the 1:25,000 Ordnance Survey maps of Gabhsann from 1853 and 1898 (surveyed in 1895) makes extraordinary viewing. Even my colleague, who spends his life working with maps, had never seen anything quite like it before. On the 1853 map, the straggling line of houses and adjacent steadings that comprised Gabhsann bho Thuath, are stretched out in a long, linear array between the river and what is now the village road of Gabhsann bho Thuath that turns off the main Nis-Barabhas road and heads north-northwest towards the Atlantic. The line of the old village was almost parallel with the present main road. On the map of 1895, the main lines of the map appear the same, and it seems that little has changed. More careful scrutiny, however, reveals that the little rectangles on the map which represented the cottages and byres where people lived, are shaded in the 1853 version of the map, but the same locations in 1895 are sterile white boxes. There were no inhabitants remaining, for by this time, the village had been cleared.

The human anguish of the clearance of Gabhsann has only been recorded in snippets of family stories that have been recorded almost by chance. The year of 1862 had been very wet and the harvest of oats and potatoes had failed again; there was no seed for sowing, and no money for back-rent, so the Factor had earmarked the inhabitants of Gabhsann for emigration. A few years before, a long-line fisherman from Càrlabhagh had an accident at sea with an adze, and needed to be landed at Gabhsann. His sister, Mary Paterson, came to look after him, and consequently married John Graham from Gabhsann. In 1859 John and Mary were permitted to tenant a new croft, at No. 1 New Gabhsann, but in April 1863 they were evicted, along with all the remaining tenants of Gabhsann, and had to walk with three children under five to Càrlabhagh to join the ship which took the family to Ireland, then to Canada.[206] As they trudged through Siabost, some families stopped at the village crossroads, where at that time there was a shop, owned by a man named MacAulay. Cold and hungry, abject in their poverty, the tenants on their way to exile noted the tweed blankets in the shop but said that they had no money and nothing to pay for them except the manure on the crofts from which they had been evicted. The shopkeeper, in a gesture of humanity that has been remembered in oral history, gave them some salt herring to eat and agreed to accept the manure in payment for blankets, then subsequently sent carts on a 52km round-trip to Gabhsann to collect the manure. On 29 June 1863, the largest group of emigrants left Càrlabhagh en route to Ireland then Quebec. They were "seen off" from Lewis to Ireland by Donald Munro himself, (presumably to make sure that they did indeed leave the island, for it was not unheard of for people to try to evade exile).[207] It took six weeks and four days to sail on the '*Elizabeth*' from Ireland to Quebec, during which time Mary was on deck only twice, once when the captain thought that the ship was in danger of sinking.

From Quebec, they had to walk a hundred and twenty miles through the bush to the land allotted to them, and eventually they settled in the Marston Township of the Eastern Townships of Quebec,[190] along with with many other displaced islanders in the locality. Mary lived to be a hundred and one, but she and John Graham never returned to Gabhsann. John wrote a poem, in his native Gaelic, about the hardships of their clearance, but even in Canada he was to have little respite, and he was summoned to appear in court in Montreal because of what he had said in his poem. With his smattering of English, he said that he would plead guilty if the court could point out any lies in his poem. Nobody could, and he was let off with only a warning. The surviving fragments of this poem were reprinted in the Stornoway Gazette a hundred years later,[206] and you can judge for yourself who was entitled to take the moral high ground; John Graham or his accusers. (See appendix 4).

The first two verses are:

(Excerpt)

B'e siud bliadhna na h-éiginn:	That was the year of extreme difficulty:
Shil na speuran na frasan,	Rain showered down from the skies,
Bha an crodh air na stéillean	Cattle were carried on biers,
Ri dol eug leis an acras;	Dying from hunger.
Cha robh connadh ri fhaotainn	No fuel [peats] could be found
Air gach taobh do'n bhaile,	Anywhere around the village,
Is chaidh gach bruthach agus garradh	And so every hillside and dyke
Chur gu làr air son teine.	Was razed down to feed the fires.
Dhùilt an siameurlan sìol dhuinn	The Factor refused to give us seed
Air son biadh na sìol-cura;	In order to sow food crops
Is rinn na ceannaichean cumhnant	And the merchants entered an agreement
Gun làn a dùirn 'thoirt do dhuine;	Not to give a fistful of it to anyone;
Mura pàigheadh sinn sìos e	If we could not pay for it
Leis an iasg bho'n an dubhan,	With the fish from the fishing-hook,
No le crùna na Rìoghachd,	Or with British crown coins,
Cha deidheadh sgrìobag air duinte	No one would have as much as a scratch.

John Graham, formerly of No. 1 New Galson, died in Canada of homesickness, leaving Mary with six boys and one girl to look after, but the account of his experiences has stayed with us. About a week after John Graham was cleared from Gabhsann bho Thuath, a local man travelling between Borgh and Dail bho Dheas was surprised to see smoke arising from Graham's house. When he entered the empty house he found that the peat fire, banked by the departing family, had caught alight, and this, together with the cat sitting watchfully in the kitchen, created such a sense of despair at the eviction, that the memory stayed with him for the rest of his life.

Just to set a clear historical context, in 1863, the year of the final clearance of Gabhsann, Queen Victoria was already in the twenty-sixth year of her long reign, Lord Palmerston was the Prime Minister of Britain, and Abraham Lincoln was the President in America. The American Civil War was half-way through. On January 1, Lincoln had signed the Emancipation Proclamation, signalling the beginning of the end of slavery as a war objective, and the following July, the Battle of Gettysburgh took place, marking the major turning-point in that bitter war. During the intervening April, Gabhsann had been cleared of its indigenous population, who were then scattered across the surface of the Earth. Mary Graham died in Canada in 1929. There are people alive today who personally knew people who, when they were young, knew and spoke with the people who were cleared from Gabhsann. We are not contemplating ancient history here. The clearance of Gabhsann was contemporaneous with the clearances in Ireland, where peasants in places such as Donegal were being evicted and their houses unroofed in order to introduce Scottish sheep and Scottish shepherds, so perpetuating the cycle of dispossession.[191]

In contrast to the original crofting village, the footprint of the buildings of the Gabhsann farm looks almost the same on the 1853 map as they appear today. You can examine these old maps for yourself now, courtesy of digitisation and the internet, by going to https://maps.nls.uk clicking "find by place" and searching for "Galson". You can even split your computer screen to display two generations of maps side-by-side, or contrast it with a modern satellite photograph that allows the map and the image to be compared. The stout, two-storey farmhouse is delineated, facing to the northwest, with two other low steadings, one parallel, the other perpendicular, forming a boxed-in farmyard to protect the farmhouse from the worst of the Arctic winds. The small farmyard is still wonderfully cobbled with rounded stones, and though part of this has now been covered by tar, the inner area gives a good sense of the permanency of the settlement; all those rows of small stones neatly fixed in place laboriously by hand. The garden as it is today, did not exist, but there is a plan of a substantial enclosed area to the south of the farm buildings, on the ground now occupied by the croft house of 23 Gabhsann bho Dheas.

In 1853, this cluster of farm buildings was the end of the village road, and the upper windows of the farmhouse looked across the river onto the ruins of the small cottages, partly pulled down and already cleared of their inhabitants, the victims of earlier evictions. End-on to the road is a small but sturdy three-room building, which was used to house the farm servants in the later years of the farm, and in front of the farmhouse, lying parallel to each other on either side of the village road, there are two buildings. The one on the northern side of the road was used for a barn and later became an asset of croft number 37; the building nearest the farmhouse was used for storage, then the village bought the building for use in handling sheep (we still have the mortgage document for £80 in the village records). Still later, it was used as the village bothan (an unlicensed place to drink alcohol) and then converted into a shelter to dip sheep. Remember these buildings, we will come back to them later. Adjacent to these farm buildings, there is a square of grass, enclosed on three sides by a dry-stone wall. This is the farm pound, so called because it was used by successive farm tenants to temporarily contain the impounded livestock of neighbouring crofters until a fee had been paid for the release of the animal(s). There is one story in the village lore, that recounts of one tenant farmer (attributed to Helm, but in reality it could have been any of them) who spotted a white mark on the horizon, indicating a stray sheep on Tobha Ghabhsainn, fully two kilometres away, and despatched two farm labourers to capture the sheep and impound it. (Anyone who has ever tried to catch a solitary sheep, far less to then walk it over two kilometres of moorland and two rivers, will know what a labour-intensive and petty directive this was).

Maps are aggregations of information, layer upon layer of data presented in a spatial context using standardised symbols - a twisting blue line for river, a shaded polygon for a building - but those simple white rectangles of the abandoned Gabhsann are an eloquent testimony to the failure of the nineteenth century landlord system. In a perceptive analysis of the situation (although, bizarrely, he calls the book *The Crofting Problem* rather than 'The Landlord Problem') Adam Collier wrote;

> "… the problem of the Highlands really arises out of a clash of social philosophies… It is a problem for the Highlands because of the disparity in power and pervasiveness of the two cultures…"[208]

With no intended irony, the lighthouse at Rubha Robhanais (the Butt of Lewis), shone its light for the very first time in 1862, the year before Gabhsann was completely cleared to make a farm.[209] The lighthouse is built of brick from John Barr and Co. of Ardrossan, by David Stevenson, the uncle of Robert Louis Stevenson, and the light could be seen from the coast of Gabhsann, but by socio-economic indicators, these were dark times.

At the same time as Gabhsann was undergoing forced depopulation, even Factors like Evander MacIver became anxious about the persistent destitution, and wrote in 1863 that, *"It is really difficult to keep cheerful or in good humour. I could not muster courage to even think of going to the Dunrobin Ball!"*[197] Poor Factor, to have his social life upset by those unpleasant clearances that he had commanded! Nevertheless, those Factors persisted with their philosophy of 'improvement', which meant improvement for themselves and their bosses, but the destruction of a way of life for thousands of others of the dispossessed. Destruction, too, for any hope that an alternative development option might be pursued, which might benefit the whole of society. Even Collier concluded;

"The standards and values of a crofter living in a small community in a remote glen or island must necessarily differ considerably from those of a town-dweller, be he an unskilled labourer or university professor."[208]

Well into the mid-twentieth century, most economists apparently lacked any awareness of development opportunities other than full-time agriculture or rural industrialisation. The apparent possibility of a university professor also being a crofter, living in a small village such as Gabhsann, in an island community, apparently did not occur to that author.

The turning point

In June 1883, the Royal Commission of Inquiry into the Condition of Crofters and Cottars in the Highlands and Islands, which has become rooted in history simply as 'the Napier Commission' after its Chairman, passed slowly through the empty landscape of Gabhsann.

The previous day, 6 June, they had reached Barabhas, after being landed in Càrlabhagh from *HMS Lively*, and driven the twelve miles to the Free Church in Barabhas for their next public meeting in their grand tour of the Highlands and Islands.

Present in the room was the Chairman, Lord Napier and Ettrick, (a Borders landowner and retired Diplomat) along with Sir Kenneth MacKenzie of Gairloch (a Ross-shire landowner), Donald Cameron of Locheil, (Conservative MP for Inverness-shire and another Highland landowner), Charles Fraser-MacKintosh (Liberal MP for the Inverness Burghs and although another Highland landowner, an enthusiastic advocate for crofting reform), Sheriff Nicolson (a Sheriff of Kirkcudbright but a Skye-man and a Gaelic-speaker), and Professor Donald MacKinnon (the first Professor of Celtic at the Edinburgh University and another Gaelic-speaker, being originally from Colonsay). After years of public campaigning for a Royal Commission, the Commissioners appointed by Parliament drew a mixed response. Undoubtedly the driving forces in Westminster regarded them as a safe set of establishment hands, and even *The Scotsman* newspaper approved of their selection. Critics, however, noted that despite the inclusion of three Gaelic speakers, all but one of them were landlords or the sons of landlords, and land reformers had very low expectations that the disputed issues would be seriously addressed. In the end, the critics were correct, for although all the Commissioners signed the final report, all three of the landlords added personal notes to declare their dissent on certain points. Fraser-MacKintosh thought that the report did not go far enough, but the other two (MacKenzie and Locheil) were more cautious in defence of the landlords and small farmers.[210]

For all that so many people were disappointed - the establishment because the report was too radical, the crofters who risked all to give their testimony because it was not radical enough - the Napier Commission surprised everybody with its ideas on liberal reform of the land laws. The consistent demands of crofters, who echoed the cry of the Irish Land League calling for "*the three F's*" which were fair rents, fixity of tenure, and free sale (or compensation for improvements made by the crofter) were not granted immediately, but at the next General Election, in 1885, four of the five Highland MPs were committed to land reform, and these rights were subsequently established in law by the first Crofting Act of 1886 and flowed directly from the recommendations of the Napier Commission. Crucially, however, the Napier Commission did not recommend the creation of any new crofts, which would have helped to reduce overcrowding and increase agricultural productivity, and this omission resonates as a topical issue to the present day.

The oral and written evidence [211] taken in Barabhas makes powerful reading, as it does for most of the other locations on the itinerary of the Commission, not just for the precise recall of the details of generations of injustice and oppression, but for the courage and hope which was implicit between the lines of those testimonies. We can see in retrospect that this Napier Commission was a fundamental turning-point in the history of the Highlands and Islands,[212] but none of us, now, can really begin to understand the tremendous leap into the dark which these men (and they were largely men) made by raising their heads above the parapet. Ordinary people were giving open voice in a public, legally binding forum, to the catalogue of injustice to which their families had been subjected, often by landlords and their representatives who were still in positions of power to do them further harm, and occasionally were in the same room, listening to that evidence being given. The Napier Commission was remarkable in several ways. Firstly, it allowed the witnesses to give their testimony in their native Gaelic, which was subsequently translated verbatim for the Parliamentary records. Secondly, right from the start, the Commission consistently compelled the landowners and their representatives to publicly declare that the witnesses would face no repercussions, whatever the nature of their evidence, without which it is doubtful if a single crofter would have testified at all. Thirdly, although much of the evidence collected related to crofting rights and rents, or their interactions with the Factors of the landlords, the questions from the Commission ranged far and wide and documented many fascinating aspects of the everyday life and conditions of the people of the Highlands and Islands.

The honesty of those simple statements, and the explicit hope of the witnesses that if those facts were more widely known then their situations would change, and justice would be done, provided personal accounts which make reading now which is both compelling and admirable. There is considerable detail for the historian to scrutinise, for these testimonies documented individual experiences of forced clearance, the dumping of cleared families upon people in other already overcrowded villages, and the imposition of fees for activities for which they had no responsibility, such as farmers constructing field dykes and landlords planting trees to enhance the 'amenity value' of their estates, then passing the costs to the crofters. The written submission of Angus Graham from Siadar Uarach is fairly typical when he says:

> "Fifty years ago there was only about twenty-two families, who paid the rent of £90. Now there are forty-three families, eighteen of these extra ones were people who were put out of Galston [sic] for sheep and put into our township, and the rental was not made less."[211]

He goes on to complain about being made to pay for the upkeep of the farm wall, which was three miles away from him, and about his desire to get access to some land to work, before ending, "I am one of those who were evicted from Galston [sic] since about thirty-four years."

A similar plea "was unanimously agreed to at a meeting of the crofters in Borve, held 29th May 1882" and was submitted on behalf of local crofters by Murdo Grahame, who itemised their hardships, ending his statement with:

> "We are paying two shillings in the pound for hill pasture, between Murnag and Galston, [sic] which our forefathers held as common grazing between themselves. Our cattle are chased by shepherds, our women have been assaulted by gamekeepers, our men have been fined by factors and ground officers, with no better justification than the law of superior force."

The following day, 7 June 1883, after travelling through Gabhsann to the School at Lìonal in the district of Nis, the Commission re-convened to continue their journey to collect the evidence from the people in other crofting communities. Among the questions, Mr Fraser-MacKintosh asked, "Were there any places cleared within the parish in your recollection?" Yes, came the answer, Galson. "How many people were taken out of Galston [sic]?" continued Fraser-MacKintosh. "About seventy-eight families," replied delegate John MacDonald, and when he was asked "What became of the people who were removed from these places?" he was told that "Some of them came to Ness, and some were crowded in upon other townships on the west side.... Several went to America."

My favourite testimony, however, was given by John MacDonald, a 57 year-old crofter from Dail bho Dheas, but formerly from 20 Old Gabhsann, who was *"freely elected by the people"* as their representative.

In his evidence to the Napier Commission, the dialogue exchanged is succinct and poignant.

> *"Do you know about the people who were removed from Galston? – I ought to. I was born there and my ancestors lived there.*
>
> *What was the name of the town you lived in? - North Galston.*
>
> *How many families were removed from that town? - There were over sixty of them. Fifty-four paid rent.*
>
> *Were there any more townships cleared besides North Galston? - Other three.*
>
> *Name them? – Balmeanach, Melbost, and South Galston. In Balmeanach there were ten families, in Melbost twenty-five, and in South Galston thirteen."*

And later on:

> *"Was it against their will that they were put out of Galston? Yes, it was against our will, but we went away without being summoned.* [i.e. without requiring to be taken to Court].
>
> *Was it for the benefit of the Galston people that they were turned out in this way and went some to America, and some to other places? – I don't know one who benefited by it except one family.*
>
> *Would you like to go back to North Galston? – I would have some of my furniture there before I slept if I got it."*[211]

CHAPTER 8

Re-settlement to the present

Direct action

Twenty-five years after the clearance of the people of Gabhsann, the name of the village became familiar to newspaper readers through the UK. The years 1887 and 1888 were turbulent times in Lewis, and public discontent in support of land reform still simmered throughout the Highlands and Islands. The rapid population growth was causing problems of overcrowding, and the situation could not continue. In addition, the Mathesons were beginning to experience a reaction to their own actions as well as being on the receiving end of the Seaforth legacy of clearances.[187]

In November 1887 the people of Pairc, in the southeast of Lewis, took direct action against the Matheson estate to challenge the status quo that large areas of land should be kept empty of population as "deer forest" rather than portions of it being made available as new crofts. It should be emphasised that many people were starving and landless, and the creation of new crofts would require them to break in the new hill ground before cultivation could begin to provide food for the hungry families. The allocation of new holdings was not a soft option for the estate to offer. It would have meant a lot of hard work by the new entrant crofters to make the land agriculturally productive. At the same time, although small in area in comparison to the extent of the deer forest, the creation of new holdings would have increased the value of that land and brought in a small additional rent from the new tenants. Lady Matheson (Sir James had died in 1878) was no friend to the crofting population. She had previously dismissed appeals for land settlement, and sent the petitioners on their way, telling them that their poverty was their own fault. Matheson had sub-rented the agricultural rights of the sheep farm in the district of Pairc to the son of Patrick Sellar, whose father's name even at this time was infamous for his role in the Sutherland Clearances.[199] By the time of the Pairc Deer Raid, the deer forest itself was leased to an English industrialist called Joseph Platt for stalking, and although he was away on business at the time, his wife, Jessie (a member of the aristocratic Thorneycroft family) confronted the Pairc men as they entered the deer forest, demanding that they stop. The 'raiders' gave the memorable response of quiet resistance as they swept past Jessie Platt to commence their protest, "*My Lady, we have no English*".

The 'raid' was short-lived and peaceful, but it sent a frisson of excitement around the Highlands and Islands. As so often, the quality of the public impact was heavily influenced by the high calibre of the populist leadership, in this case the new schoolmaster in the village of Baile Ailean, named Donald Macrae, but the arrival of troops led to the apprehension of half a dozen of the leadership who were then 'escorted' to Edinburgh. Despite a show trial, the raiders were acquitted of mobbing and rioting on a technicality, but the trial raised the profile and the urgency of land agitation in other parts of the Highlands.[213] The drama of the Pairc Deer Raid has been described in detail,[214] and its significance examined in the context of the history of the crofting communities,[212] but historical events do not exist in isolation. The direct action of the Pairc 'raiders' was in part inspired by the resistance of crofters in the neighbouring island of Bernera, and in turn it gave encouragement to the events unfolding in Gabhsann.

In 1874, an incident occurred that became known as "The Bernera Riot". Pushed to their limit, the crofting population of the island of Bernera rose up against the arbitrary tyranny of the Matheson estate, as directed by their Factor, Donald Munro. In doing so, Bernera influenced the tide of history and set an example of popular intervention in the escalating land agitation. This first public resistance against the oppression of the estate laid the foundations for subsequent actions, including the "Battle of the Braes" in Skye in 1882, as well as in Pairc, Gabhsann, and elsewhere throughout Lewis. As was so often the case, the dispute centred on the allocation of land, and was initiated by Donald Munro, in pursuit of his own interests. Although apologists for the clearance landlords like to claim that the Factors operated without the knowledge of the estate owners, the publication of a long letter from D. MacKinlay to Hugh Matheson, the Commissioner for Sir James Matheson, makes it clear that it was otherwise. Of the proprietor's knowledge of his Factor's activities, MacKinlay wrote:

> *"... the case was the general talk of the island during the months of April, May, June, and July; and as Sir James Matheson was then resident at Stornoway he must have heard from his factor what all the hubbub was about."* Moreover, *"As soon as "this painful incident" came to Sir James's knowledge, he might have instructed his factor to cancel the decrees of removal – but he never did so..."*[215]

Elsewhere in this correspondence, the writer made clear from other comments that both Sir James and Lady Matheson paid close attention to the details of their estate, including Lady Matheson issuing an instruction to her Factor to *"...get the rabbits extirpated as soon as possible at Galson."* (although they were apparently not very numerous). On another occasion, Lady Matheson, having raised the price of milk throughout the island from fourpence a pint to sixpence, was irritated by one old lady who refused to raise the price of the milk that she sold. Her reward from Lady Matheson was to note, *"I see you have your farm too cheap."* The next term, the lady had her rent raised.

At that same time, the tenant of the farm at Gabhsann, Mr Andrew Smith, originally from Thurso and later removed with his family to the Glenelg Manse Farm, commented on the lack of schools in the district (despite Factor Munro being the Chairman of the Education Boards of all four Lewis parishes), arguing that twenty-five new schools were needed. Significantly, he also complained about the lack of investment by Matheson, and that,

> *"Without a lease the crofter has no inducement to improve or drain his land, as his doing so would only tend to a rise in his rent; and being merely a 'tenant at will'* [i.e. not having any security of tenure on the land or buildings] *he is simply dependent on the factor, or the ground officer, for a roof to cover himself and his family."*[215]

Having articulated his feelings thus, it can be no surprise to us that he was subsequently 'removed' to Glenelg.

In fact, although the Sheriff eventually removed Donald Munro from the his role of Procurator Fiscal, deeming that to be incompatible with also being the estate Factor, Sir James,

> *"... showed no intention of removing Mr. Munro from the factorship after the Bernera trial was over..."* but rather, *"... Sir James had expressed his intention of sticking to his favourite factor as long as he lived..."*[215]

As history has shown, however, the Bernera crofters were acquitted of any crimes, whereas this episode marked the beginning of the downfall of Factor Munro. If it had not been for the Bernera 'riot', actually no more than a stubborn and principled refusal to be bullied by the Factor, the crofters of that island would have likely been put aboard the emigrant ships, like so many of their fellow Hebrideans. The importance of that resistance is much, much more significant in terms of the example it set for the subsequent self-assertion of civil rights in other communities in the Highlands and Islands – right through to the present day.

The mood of Lewis continued to be unsettled towards the end of 1887, and the politicians in Westminster (always with one eye on 'the Irish Question') were also restless, so a detachment of eighty-two men and five officers of the Royal Scots had been dispatched to the island while the deer raid was in progress. It had originally been intended to send a detachment of the Seaforth Highlanders, but the Commanding Officer objected because the regiment contained so many men from the Highlands and Islands, (suggesting perhaps, as was the case thirty years later, that the soldiers might prefer to side with the protesters.) This force was supplemented in December by the gunboat *Seahorse* and a force of forty Marines.[197] In the New Year, another gunboat, *HMS Forester* arrived with more Marines.

The farm tenant in Gabhsann following Andrew Smith, was Dundas Helm, who came from Wigtonshire to live in Gabhsann, and who was later 'removed' to the Holm Farm in Steòrnabhagh, to be replaced in Gabhsann by his nephew, James Paul Helm, from Closeburn, Dumfries. On Wednesday, 21 December 1887, approximately 300 landless men from Borgh and Siadar, headed by two pipers and in military formation, marched to Gabhsann and gave warning to the younger Mr Helm to leave Gabhsann when his lease was up. A similar announcement was made relating to the farm in Aiginis, and it was this latter location that proved to be one of the most serious confrontations of the entire land agitation movement.

On New Year's Day, 1888 there was an altercation with the police as three men attempted to destroy the boundary dykes around the Aiginis farm. For days thereafter, there were raids to pull down the fences, and on 9 January, the day agreed by Land League meetings throughout the peninsula of An Ruadh, up to a thousand men and women occupied the Aiginis Farm, confronted by heavily armed Marines with fixed bayonets, Royal Scots soldiers, and police. After a tense day of stand-off, and one of the most violent confrontations in crofting history, the crowd dispersed home, but not before thirteen men had been arrested. The verdict of the subsequent trial in Edinburgh was never in any doubt. The establishment had taken fright after the incidents in Bearnaraigh and Pairc and were determined to set an example of law enforcement (when the Queen's Riot Act had been read at Aiginis Farm, there was a shout that "...*the Queen can go to Hell*"). Lord Craighill was carefully selected as the judge ("*with the reputation of being a belligerent and uncompromising hardliner*") the Lord Advocate personally led the prosecution, and the Government refused to meet the expenses for defence witnesses. The defendants were split into groups, the inference being that if the jury was too soft, another jury would be sworn in to make sure that, unlike the Pairc trial, there would be no acquittals.[214] The jury found all 16 defendants guilty, and Lord Craighill felt duty-bound to pass heavy prison sentences.

It is complicated now to make sense of the sequence of events of that time, because there were multiple activities in diverse localities. Earlier in the month, when Lady Matheson was petitioned to make the farm in Gabhsann into crofts by a delegation of three hundred men from Borgh, Barbhas, Siadar, Brù and Arnol, on 3 January 1888, she steadfastly refused even to meet with them.[187] Despite the soaken men having walked to Steòrnabhagh, on one of the wildest nights of the year, to ask that land might be made available for settlement and cultivation in order to reduce their poverty, she dismissed the idea outright, and with a characteristic lack of diplomacy (not to mention compassion) stated, "*The land under sheep and deer is my property and I can do what I like with it.*" An analysis permitted by hindsight has noted that:

> "*Never once was there an offer of help, never once was the hand of kindness or charity extended from the Matheson estate. Their only contribution to the lives of these people was to hinder progress and to extract as much possible in rent.*"[214]

Although James Matheson was made a Baronet in 1851, partly in response to his perceived benevolence in distributing (oat)meal to the population on his estate in Lewis, numerous more recent sources of evidence confirm that the meal, including the meal made available at Government expense, was dispensed by the Matheson estate, who then added the cost to the rent due from the recipients. Famine relief was also allocated to poor families as an incentive for them to provide labour on the Matheson estate at little cost to the proprietor. In his damning account of those years, MacKinlay quotes a letter that appeared in the *Glasgow Daily Mail* on 3 April 1877, in which the correspondent asked the Editor,

> "*... and is he aware that the populous township of Galson, in the parish of Ness, containing perhaps upwards of thirty families,* [we now know that it was at least twice that] *was cleared to make room for sheep? These things*

have not been done in a corner, and could not possibly be unknown to Sir James Matheson. It is quite possible that he did not take the initiatory steps towards these evictions, but he must have homologated the actions of his factors, by whom he was led too much in such matters. I need not ask for any witness to confirm the truth of what I have written above, for the very stones of the walls of the old houses in the townships I have mentioned will bear ample testimony."[215]

The stones of these old houses can still be distinguished in the landscape of Gabhsann in numerous places, fading from memory as the tumbled-down walls slowly have their stark boundaries masked by the build-up of the covering vegetation. Perhaps even this condemnation is too lenient for the Matheson family, for in the subsequent press correspondence relating to the above letter, one satirical writer noted,

"In the early part of this century Mr James Matheson, in whom benevolence was largely developed from his youth, was engaged in the holy work of bringing the blessings of Western civilisation within the reach of the Chinese.... After much reflection, he arrived at the conclusion that the blessings of Christianity and the precious fruits of Western thought would be most advantageously presented to the Chinese in the form of opium... Mr James Matheson took an active part in the importation of the drug, and did not permit either the foolish regulations of the Chinese Custom-house or the horrors of actual war to deter him from faithfully carrying out his self-imposed task."[215]

On Friday 13 January 1888, the "Special Correspondent" of the *Glasgow Herald* made a visit to the farm in Gabhsann to view the situation for himself.[216] He reported on a village meeting in the school-house in Borgh at which it was reaffirmed that the Gabhsann Farm would soon be raided. The meeting acknowledged that:

"The only steps that had yet been taken was the breaking down of the dykes, which had taken place a few days ago. Of course none of them would admit to having been present at this destruction of property.... In fact, any question put plainly on this subject was passed off with a joke, one of them remarking that the walls probably went down like the walls of Jericho."[216]

The men had no animosity towards Mr Helm, the farm tenant, *"and one of of them said he had been a good neighbour"* but they intended to occupy the farm. Mr Helm, for his part, noted the destruction of fences, which had been torn down and thrown into the sea, but said that he was *"not in any way alarmed."* In view of this, it makes the subsequent reaction of the authorities even more ridiculously overbearing.

On 18 January 1888, to great popular delight, but the consternation of the conservative establishment, the fourteen Pairc deer raiders were acquitted by an Edinburgh jury, and this gave a fresh impetus to the land agitators requests to break up the farms of Gabhsann and Aiginis. Not that much encouragement was needed, because the cessation of the Pairc raid did nothing to lessen the tension throughout the island, and notwithstanding the arrests in Aiginis, there was heightened anticipation of a raid on the Gabhsann Farm by the landless crofters of neighbouring villages.[212] Ten police constables had been posted to the farmhouse, and another half a dozen were in the manse in Barabhas.[217] For the previous few days, men of the neighbourhood had been knocking down the turf dykes around Gabhsann in order to allow crofters stock onto the farm. A routine had developed that the raiders would demolish the boundaries during the night, and the following days the tenant farmer and his employees would attempt to repair the damage. At 2.00 in the afternoon of 17 January 1888, the police stationed at Gabhsann observed a party of forty to fifty men approaching with shovels, graips, and long poles. A hand-to-hand fight then took place, *"the police using their batons, and the crofters sticks, stones and clods. After a ten minute conflict, the police retired to Galson Farm steading with some of them badly injured, while the crofters went home."*[218] This was the first serious clash at Gabhsann, and Helm, the farmer, sent a mounted messenger to Steòrnabhagh with the news (there was no telegraph to the village).

From one of those nightly raids, as they marched to pull down the farm walls, local oral history has recounted a curious story. One evening, as the raiders advanced from Borgh towards Gabhsann, in the darkness and thick mist, the police contingent could only hear the crunch of the raiders boots coming towards them in the night. Then a call rang out, *"Forward men by twos!"* Recollection is that the police then shouted, *"They have had military training! Run for it!"* Unusually the command had been called in English, so perhaps there is a foundation that the order had been learned by repetition through some having received military training. From another source I was told that, perhaps even on the same night, an order was heard, *"On the shoulder put!"* which was interpreted by the police as a command for the raiders to shoulder arms. (Though unlike the police and Helm the farmer, there is no record of the raiders having carried arms). As this was an American, rather than a British military order, it caused further consternation among the forces of the establishment. It may have been an elaborate bluff, but this was only twenty-three years after the cessation of the American Civil War. The immediate outcome was that the gunboat *Seahorse* set sail at once from Steòrnabhagh, with the Sheriff Principal and reinforcements of police and Marines. Soon afterwards, a company of the

Royal Scots and more Marines from *HMS Belleisle* marched off for Gabhsann by foot. The unfolding events were printed daily in a wide variety of newspapers throughout the UK (usually syndicated news) with the *Aberdeen Press and Journal* leading with the typical heading, *"The agitation in Lewis, Serious Moonlight Outrage. Conflict with the Police."*[219]

On 18 January, Gabhsann Farm was garrisoned by eighty Marines and Royal Scots and about twenty police. Before daybreak, Chief Constable Munro and John Ross, the Depute Fiscal, together with about fifteen constables, accompanied by Mr Helm and his two shepherds (to assist in identification) led a raid on houses in Borgh. It was a dark, frosty morning, and as they had hoped, they caught most of their intended targets in bed. They first went to the house of John Smith, a crofter and carpenter, where they arrested his son, Malcolm, aged 24, a fisherman and carpenter. They next surrounded the house of Robert Saunders, where the sons Roderick (24) and Malcolm (28) were roused from their bed and joined Malcolm Smith in handcuffs. John Nicolson (22) was treated the same way, as also was Malcolm MacIver (32) who had already been down to collect seaweed from the shore. He was carrying his creel of seaweed back to the house when Helm identified, him, and when Malcolm asked to be able to take his seaweed back to the house, it was refused, and he too was arrested. In each house they visited, the women of the house tried to reason with the police, and to allow the menfolk time to get properly dressed, but it was only in the widow MacKay's house that the daughters were able to secure any concessions. Norman MacIver (30) was sought, but his wife was feeble as she had recently given birth, and when Sheriff Fraser heard this, he ordered MacIver to be released. The whole party then reformed and marched the prisoners back to Gabhsann Farm. On 19 January, *The Scotsman* newspaper, no great friend to the crofter (a *Scotsman* correspondent had given evidence in court against the Pairc raiders) reported that, *"The raid occupied less than an hour. The affair was so quietly executed hardly any were aware of it but those concerned."*[220]

A report in the same newspaper on the same day, noted that the men of Barabhas had, *"...made an attack on the salmon river there"* with the intention of restoring the river to its previous channel, from which it had been diverted forty years previously, resulting in flooding on the crofts and people's houses.

The following day, the arrested men from Borgh were taken escorted by *"... police, Marines, and Royal Scots, close on a hundred in all..."* to Port Nis to join the *Seahorse*. At Port Nis, a crowd of fifty or sixty had gathered and cheered the men as they arrived. The prisoners were conveyed to Steòrnabhagh jail, leaving a garrison of ten Marines and six police in both Gabhsann and Barabhas. The dispatch boat, *Amelia*, arrived in Steòrnabhagh with more Marines, and the troop-ship *Resistance*, was *"...daily expected with a large force from Portsmouth."*[221] By 23 January, the Borgh men had been released on bail of £30 each, secured by Murdo MacLeod, a merchant in Steòrnabhagh and President of the local Land League, but unrest was still prevalent in numerous locations in the island. Three warships lay at anchor in Steòrnabhagh, and further disruptions in Gabhsann were expected. A report in *The Scotsman* on 21 February noted, *"The police and Marines are still at Aignish, Galson, and Barvas. The Barvas minister's glebe is expected to be attacked."* [222] A few days later, Sheriff Fraser remitted the people charged with *"mobbing and rioting"* in Gabhsann to the High Court in Edinburgh for trial on March 5.

At the trial in Edinburgh before Lord Rutherfurd Clark and a jury, James Paul Helm said that he was the tenant of Gabhsann Farm, and that early in the morning of 17 January, he had gone with the constables to near his shepherd's house, where a large group of men were pulling down boundary fences of the farm. Later, the Gabhsann shepherd, Robert Ross, admitted in evidence that, *"...he saw the crowd, but he could identify none of the prisoners as having taken part,"*[223] There were several conflicting claims of identity, with the defenders providing alibis, and there was no disputing that the confrontation had turned violent, but His Lordship, summing up, noted sardonically that,

> *"It was a remarkable thing, no doubt, that the policemen who were in search of persons engaged in the riot apprehended only those who were sleeping quietly in their bed during the commission of the riot."*

The Glasgow Herald court correspondent noted that,

> *"The jury retired at twenty minutes to six o'clock, and were absent for half-an-hour. Their verdict, by a majority, acquitted all the prisoners of the charges brought against them, and it was received in Court with loud applause."*

On March 6 1888, *The Scotsman* also reported, *"The Galson men were found not guilty of rioting and mobbing. There was applause in court after the verdict."* The report concluded rather laconically, *"The Barvas men are still hard at work on the river."*[224]

After a brief burst of exposure in the national press, the land agitation for Gabhsann Farm became quieter for a while, but the social and political unrest rumbled on. One hundred years later, the memories of *"The Battle of Galson Farm"*[225] and its aftermath,[226] were so vivid and still so relevant, that they were still referred to as a significant local series of events that influenced national history.

In October 1888, the Crofters Commissioners drove from Steòrnabhagh to Barabhas to convene a hearing in the Barvas Free Church. Most of the business concerned the levels (and arrears) of rent on the small crofts in Siadar and along the west side of Lewis, but also the clearance of the farm at Gabhsann;

> *"was spoken of by many of the witnesses whose relations had suffered at the time, but the most distinct and detailed account was given by an old man of over seventy-two who had been one of the Galson tenants. He said he had first been in South Galson, and had been removed to uncultivated land in North Galson. For the first six years after he went there he had nothing to eat but the shellfish on the shore. During the second six years the land improved, and was yielding something, when the ground officer came and pulled down the house."*

> *The Chairman asked why he had pulled down the house. "To put me out, and put me away to Shader. He put out the fire, took the roof of the house, and took the timber away in a cart to Shader, I was lying crying at the back of the house."*[227]

The underlying reasons for the disturbances remained unchanged, and would boil to the surface another twenty-five years later.

Will you give us the land?

A common feature across most areas of the Highlands and Islands, is that the aspirations of the landowners have frequently not been the same as the aspirations of the families and communities that live on that land. I have even heard it claimed that a certain landowner was a "good" landowner because s/he was largely absentee and "left the people alone" i.e. did nothing to enhance the socio-economic conditions of the local population. Taking Gabhsann, as a microcosm of the Isle of Lewis, the impact of successive private landowners has historically been more an issue of apparently satisfying personal desires and community development by neglect, rather than any proactive engagements to enhance local welfare. Francis Humberston Mackenzie of Seaforth, inherited Lewis in 1783 because the main line of the earls of Seaforth had died out. He had been born and brought up in England, but he became an enthusiastic supporter of the 'traditional' customs of his Highland clan. It has been argued that his sentimentality over what he perceived as his duties as clan chieftain was a major factor in his reluctance to force compulsory clearances ('dispeopling' in the language of contemporary land agents) and that he was slower than many of his fellow landlords to introduce single-tenant farms and large-scale sheep farming.[228]

It could also be argued that, aside from his distractions with his romanticised views of traditional customs, he had less benevolent reasons for his actions. As an enthusiastic recruiter for the army (which appealed to his sense of his national status) he needed to retain a pool of potential military recruits on his estates, and also to supply labour for the expanding kelp industry.[229] Despite this, local animosity towards enforced recruiting (sometimes described as 'men in return for land') was so intense that up to 300 Ùig men left their villages to establish an armed resistance in the hills at Cnoc a' Champ (Hill of the camp) when Mackenzie arrived in 1793 to recruit in person. At this time, forced recruitments by roving press gangs were not unknown, and local anecdote remembers that some of the pre-clearance houses in Gabhsann bho Thuath had a "hidden room" built into their walls where a young man could find shelter from the attentions of a recruiting party. The Ùig men, however, were united and, "... *vow death to any Sergeant, Drummer or Recruiter, who dares enter the parish, and also threaten with death whoever dares inlist.*"[230] The situation was serious, and Seaforth, suspecting a larger plot, wrote in a letter to Lord Adam Gordon, Commander in Chief of the army in Scotland, that posters and handbills (in support of the French Revolution, just four years earlier) and copies of the *Rights of Man* by Thomas Paine (published just two years previously) had appeared in circulation in Steòrnabhagh. He also reported to his superior that a "French privateer" had appeared off the coast of Lewis (inferring it had appeared to aid the spread of democracy in Lewis) and it was suggested that the,

> "... *dissidents in Ùig had been in contact with, if not incited by, men in Greenock and Inverness... who may have been influenced by the current democratic ideas.*"[231]

The Ùig resistance was resolved peacefully, and in return for his recruiting efforts Seaforth was rewarded with the Lord Lieutenancy of Ross-shire in 1797, and made a baron in the same year. In 1800 he became the Governor, and a plantation owner, in Berbice (now part of Guyana). He had hoped to cross-subsidise his Scottish estates with the profits from the labour of his Caribbean slaves, but like his domestic affairs, his business-sense was muddled and contradictory, and this episode was not a great financial success.[232] Although he also held land in Kintail, and later sold-off parts of it (with the prior knowledge that the new owners intended to clear the villages) he resisted selling pieces of Lewis, largely because of the profit he was making in the kelp trade. ("*The rental of Lewis rose from £4458 in 1799 to about £9000 in 1813*" largely because of the kelp industry there.)[228]

The farm and the crofting villages in Gabhsann remained largely undisturbed in his lifetime, but when the estates passed to his daughter Mary, she sold Lewis to James Matheson in 1844 for £190,000. Matheson, as we have seen, had made a fortune trading in the Far East during the Opium Wars, and was not a man to be squeamish about his personal ambitions. The crofting families of Lewis were not among his highest priorities. After Sir James died, his wife, it seems, was even less well-disposed towards enhancing the lives of her tenants, and sent the crofters delegation from Gabhsann back to their homes without giving them an audience. By 1899, Lewis had been inherited by Major Duncan Matheson, a great-nephew of Sir James, but despite the continuing unrest throughout the Highlands and Islands, he showed no inclination to release land for use by the overcrowded and hungry population. In fact, he publicly opposed the proposals of the Congested Districts Board to create new holdings on Gabhsann or the other Lewis farms.[212] In 1913 Major Matheson offered to sell Lewis to the nation to free himself from the accumulated financial liabilities of taxation and death duties. There were murmurings of revolt in numerous locations, including Gabhsann, but the intervention of the First World War placed the land reform movement temporarily on hold. Significantly,

> "The Isle of Lewis had the highest proportion of its population serving [in the armed forces] in the First World War of anywhere in the British Isles... Lewis also had the highest proportion of casualties: 17% of those serving died in the conflict; the ratio of deaths to the general population on the island was twice the national average."[233]

Per capita, the island probably suffered the highest losses than any community in the entire Commonwealth.

In 2014, amid the many acts of memorial of the First World War, there was a poignant "poppy trail" throughout the villages of the west coast from Baile an Truisel to Port Nis, with a single saucer-sized 'poppy' placed outside every house that had lost a family member. The cumulative effect of driving the trail was almost an overwhelming reminder of the tragedy of that war. In Gabhsann, alone of all the villages, there were no poppies, because Gabhsann, as a populated village, did not exist at the start of that world-changing global turmoil. After the war, the devastating loss of life sustained by communities throughout Lewis and Harris,[234] together with the tragic deaths of hundreds of demobilised servicemen in the wreck of the HMY Iolaire on 1 January 1919, [235] cast a cloud of demoralisation over the island. The demand for the breakup of the Lewis farms began to be articulated publicly again, and in 1917 the Secretary of State for Scotland, Robert Munro, (himself a Highlander), had been seriously considering a proposal that the Government should purchase Lewis on behalf of its inhabitants.[214] In 1918, Matheson sold Lewis to Lord Leverhulme for £143,000 and effectively ended the Matheson family's history with the island.

Leverhulme had first visited Steòrnabhagh as a tourist in 1884, and had been flirting with the possibility of buying the Lewis estate for almost a year before he finally secured the deal on 15 May, 1918.[236] He ushered in a period of great optimism, partly because people were war-weary (WW1 still had six months of misery before the armistice would be signed), and partly because of Leverhulme's high reputation as a successful and innovative businessman who might revive the economic fortunes of the island. Set against Leverhulme's undoubted qualities as a social reformer and as a financial achiever were the unflattering aspects of his character that liked to micro-manage every aspect that he was involved with, his inability to tolerate criticism, and his total lack of self-doubt. Consequently, people tended not to tell Leverhulme anything unpleasant or divergent to his own line of thought, and this lack of external challenge led him to be convinced by his almost uninterrupted success and his image of himself as having a unique, irreplaceable position in society.[236] For a man at the head of a multinational corporation, with extensive land holdings in West Africa and the Congo, it seems that the Isle of Lewis had become his 'pet project', and the focus of his inventive personality. In respect of his African properties, Leverhulme is quoted as saying, "... *Natives should be treated as willing children; housed, doctored and moved from place to place as required...*"[214] and it could be argued that he expected the same cooperation from the residents of his property in Lewis. Gabhsann once again comes sharply into the focus of national attention during Leverhulme's ownership, as despite his ambitious (and sometimes far-sighted) plans for the island, he only heard what he wanted to hear, which would eventually lead to his downfall. He considered (irrationally) that Gabhsann, and the other farms in the island, were absolutely necessary for the production of the milk that would be needed to support the proposed population that would labour in the factories that he was planning to build in Steòrnabhagh. Regardless of the wartime political promises of the creation of new croft holdings for returning servicemen in a "land fit for heroes",[237] Leverhulme was implacably opposed to land reform

In one contemporary account, there is an electrifying transcription of an encounter between landless protesters and Lord Leverhulme, revelling in his role as the visionary entrepreneurial landlord.[238] Colin MacDonald of the Board of Agriculture, who described the scene, was only thirty-seven at the time and a Gaelic speaker from Strathpeffer who knew many of the crofters through his work; Leverhulme was a multi-millionaire industrialist, the founder of a company which was well on its way to becoming a global corporation, and with great personal plans to "improve" the condition of people on Lewis, whether they wanted it or not. In this classic confrontation, Lord Leverhulme, the wealthy landlord, who was noted for his charm as well as his almost tangible megalomania, is addressing a large crowd of almost 1,000 disgruntled men and women who are landless, underfed, and seeking to obtain the tenancy of new crofts - strips of bare, uncultivated land on which to work and feed their families. The open-air meeting took place at the bridge in Griais at around 11.00 on the morning of 12 March 1924, but it is emblematic of the highly tense confrontations that were taking place in Lewis in several locations, including Gabhsann. Leverhulme was very persuasive, with his eloquent language, and his promises of his vision for their future. MacDonald, as an independent observer, gave us a detailed account of this meeting, and from this account, one section stands out. It is a long quotation, but I think it is worth quoting in full, for it may give you an insight into this clash of identities.[239]

Leverhulme is already addressing the assembled crowd.

> *"I have already thought out plans which will involve me in an expenditure of five million pounds! But there has been some discord between us: we have not seen eye to eye. When two sensible people have a difference of opinion they do not quarrel: they meet and discuss their differences reasonably and calmly. That is what we have met for here today – and the sun is shining! But what do I propose to do with this five million pounds? Let me tell you"....*

> *And then there appeared in the next few minutes the most graphic word picture it is possible to imagine – a great fleet of fishing boats – another great fleet of cargo boats – a large fish-canning factory (already started) – railways – an electric power station; then one could see the garden city grow – steady work, steady pay, beautiful houses for all – every modern convenience and comfort. The insecurity of their present income was referred to; the squalor of their present houses deftly compared with the conditions in the new earthly paradise. Altogether it was a masterpiece; and it produced its effect; little cheers came involuntarily from a few here and there – more cheers! - general cheers!...*

> *And just then, while the artist was still adding skillful detail, there was a dramatic interruption.*

> *One of the ringleaders managed to rouse himself from the spell, and in an impassioned voice addressed the crowd in Gaelic, and this is what he said:*

> *"So so fhiribh! Cha dean so gnothach! Bheireadh am bodach mil-bheulach sin chreidsinn oirinn gu'm bheil dubh geal 's geal dubh! Ciod e dhuinn na bruadairean briagha aige, a thig no nach tig? 'Se am fearann tha sinn ag iarraidh. Agus 'se tha mise a faighneachd [turning to face Lord Leverhulme and pointing dramatically towards him]: an toir thu dhuinn am fearann?" The effect was electrical. The crowd roared their approbation.*

149

Lord Leverhulme looked bewildered at this, to him, torrent of unintelligible sounds, but when the frenzied cheering with which it was greeted died down he spoke.

"I am sorry! It is my great misfortune that I do not understand the Gaelic language. But perhaps my interpreter will translate for me what has been said?"

Said the interpreter: "I am afraid, Lord Leverhulme, that it will be impossible for me to convey to you in English what has been so forcefully said in the older tongue; but I will do my best" - and his best was a masterpiece, not only in words but in tone and gesture and general effect:

"Come, come, men! This will not do! This honey-mouthed man would have us believe that black is white and white is black. We are not concerned with his fancy dreams that may or may not come true! What we want is the land – and the question I put to him now is: will you give us the land?"

The translation evoked a further round of cheering. A voice was heard to say:

"Not so bad for a poor language like the English!"

Lord Leverhulme's picture, so skillfully painted, was spattered in the artist's hand."

In that wonderful account, we have encapsulated both the source of the dilemma and its solution. The clash of identities between the "outsider" who thinks that s/he knows what is best for you, and the sense of identity of the person who wishes the right to self-determination, regardless of the rosy "alternative vision" of the outsider's power.

 It also encapsulates our heritage of democracy, and democratic decision-making at every level – the local, the regional and the national. Post-war, the pressure to break up the farm at Gabhsann and create new crofts was pursued by islanders with a quiet determination. The local newspaper, *The Stornoway Gazette*, in the *"Borve and Mid-Borve News"* column on 2 May 1919, reports a short note on a raid on Gabhsann on Wednesday 23 April in which *"an attempt was made by the people of Shader to seize the Galson farm and mark out small holdings for themselves."*[240] Unfortunately for them, the people of Borgh had arrived on the farm first with the same purpose in mind, and this led to some disagreement, to the obvious delight of the journalist, who was no great supporter of the crofter against Leverhulme's proposals (he reported virtually the same story to the *Highland News* later that week.[241]) This was a tense period in recent history, almost exactly three months after independence had been declared by the Republic of Ireland, and a mere ten days after the shameful imperial massacre by British troops at Amritsar - the authorities were apprehensive.

Although the media reporting of the 1919 raids was not so detailed, nor so sensationalist, as the earlier disturbances at Gabhsann, the land agitation continued, and within a few years Lord Leverhulme had departed Lewis and Harris forever. Many of the 'raiders' across Lewis eventually gained access to small plots of land, for the UK Government stepped in and responded to popular demands to create new crofts and new villages, offering opportunities for young families to settle in them. It is important to understand that the post-war land raids in Lewis were simply the vanguard of 2,331 new holdings created through Scotland between 1919 and 1927, from Shetland to the borders.[237] In the case of Gabhsann, the Board of Agriculture for Scotland finally used its powers of compulsory purchase to buy the Gabhsann Farm, in direct opposition to Leverhulme's dogmatic stance. Leverhulme was implacably opposed to land reform to the very end of his time in Lewis and Harris, and tried to contest the decision, but history was against him. Leverhulme left the island in 1924 and Gabhsann was left to its new inhabitants. There are further chapters to be written, however, and it is only really with hindsight that the huge significance and enduring legacy of the Land Settlement (Scotland) Act 1919 is coming to be appreciated for its potential as a precedent to address twenty-first century issues of depopulation and repopulation of land across the Highlands and Islands.[242]

The Auction

The squat, blocky, red-brick cube of offices at 20 Hanover Square, with its 5x4 matrix of white-rimmed windows in central London, seems an incongruous place for the future ownership of Lewis and Harris to be decided on the whim of an auctioneer, but that is what happened. In Estate Room 20, on Tuesday 4 March 1924, at the offices of Messrs Knight, Frank and Rutley, at 2.30 in the afternoon, the sale was conducted of *"The Greater Portion of the Island of Lewis in the County of Ross and Cromarty, extending to an area of about 288,479 acres, and including the well-known Sporting Estates"*... which the Sale Catalogue then went on to itemise.[243] Lot number 8 was Galson Estate - 56,008 acres, with mixed shooting. This was probably the first time that the name "Galson Estate" appears in public, along with the other estate names that we now recognise that had been created by the partitioning of Lewis by anonymous hands as a precursor to their disposal by Leverhulme.

The inventory gave further details on each Lot for prospective buyers, listing tantalising information on what are now individual island estates. Their "assets" were talked up, including noting precisely all the buildings and other property on the estates, their 'game bags' and any rents due or burdens owed on the Lot. Relating to Gabhsann, they announced that:

*"The unfurnished Lodge stands on the roadside about 21 miles from
Stornoway and 3 miles from Post Office at Borve (mails three times a week)
and contains - Sitting Room, 4 Bedrooms, Bathroom and Lavatory Basin, Gun
Room, w.c., Kitchen, Scullery, Pantry, and 2 Servants Bedrooms. Adjoining is
the Keeper's two-roomed House, Stable, Byre, Garage, Larder, Ghillie's House
and 2 Kennels."*[243]

The sale inventory went on to proclaim the attractions of the fishing,

*"several Lochs within the Shooting bounds on which Brown Trout can
be taken, and two streams on which Sea Trout and occasionally Grilse may
be obtained during a flood"*; and the shooting, which *"consists of Grouse,
of which 100 brace might be shot; Snipe, Woodcock, Plover, and a large variety
of Wildfowl."*

Only then did it occur to them to mention that *"There are 20 Crofting
Townships upon this Lot"*, indicating that "Galson Estate" included not just the
villages of Gabhsann, but almost the entirety of northern Lewis. To placate
the new would-be laird the sale schedule then itemised the rental value of
each and every property on the estate - the shooting rights, the farms, the
Glebe and the Doctor's house, and all of the twenty crofting villages. Under
"Galson (New Settlement)" it was noted that its crofting rental income was
£1,638 and its 'rate-burden' was £1,242.

Although there was a large crowd in the auction room, the bidding was
slow to non-existent. Lord Leverhulme was not present, he was rumoured
to be 'at sea', but he had placed no reserve price on the properties, leaving
the judgements on the sales to the auctioneers.[244] Lot number 1, the Pairc
Deer Forest, attracted no bids. The auctioneer began at £10,000 and lowered
his call to £6,000 but there were no offers at all. The *"excellent salmon
and sea trout fishing and mixed shooting"* of Grìomarstadh in Lot 3 drew
some desultory interest, but the bidding only reached £13,000 and it was
withdrawn from the sale. Lot 4 for Soval and Lot 5 for Càrlabhagh, similarly,
attracted no bids at all. Lot 8, for the Gabhsann Estate raised a flutter of
excitement when Mr Edward Valpy, who gave his address as 'the Oxford and
Cambridge Club' offered £500, (two-and-a-half pence per acre) and this was
immediately accepted by the auctioneer. Mr Valpy, a friend of Leverhulme,
later indicated that he had been an occasional visitor to Lewis and simply
wished to use Gabhsann for its shooting and fishing. Despite the heightened
anticipation, the auction for the sale of Lewis closed, after barely fifteen
minutes of anticlimax. When he later claimed purely philanthropic reasons
for 'giving away' the component parts of Lewis that led to the formation of
the present island estates, Leverhulme was clearly presenting only a partial
view of reality.

With the culmination of this sale, Lord Leverhulme largely ceased to have any involvement in the economic or social development of the Isle of Lewis, and active crofting villages such as the newly established holdings in Gabhsann have remained as prominent reminders of the failure of his grandiose plans. In some ways he was well-intentioned, innovative, benevolent, even inspired, but ultimately wrong-headed. His inability to accept guidance or to moderate his unrealistic enthusiasms, his insistence on total control and his inability to listen to contrary opinions made him a deeply flawed character. Leverhulme's tenacious insistence on control of the island farms, including in Gabhsann, remained unabated. After his passionate speech at the bridge at Griais, he privately discussed it with Colin MacDonald, the representative from the Board of Agriculture.

> *"My agricultural expert advises me that I must have farms. In this matter I must be guided by him."*

> *"I do not question the ability of your agricultural expert to advise you - in England. But - with respect - Lewis is not England."*

> *"But I must have control of my factory hands! How can I have that in the case of men who are in the independent position of crofters?"*[239]

Leverhulme's ambitious plans needed a workforce who would be dependent on him for their livelihood, and his dislike of crofting stemmed from his apparent inability to comprehend that many islanders preferred to have a say in their own life choices, rather than be regimented to suit the eccentricities of a manufacturer. Had he tried to show a bit of understanding of the perceived reality of the local people, and demonstrated as much energy and innovation as he had already proved in his other business interests, we can only speculate on the alternative vision of Gabhsann, and of the island as a whole, that may have resulted.

In purchasing what now became known as the 'Galson Estate', for the purposes of shooting and fishing, Mr Valpy had justifiable expectations. The area of Gabhsann had been a 'sporting estate' since the resident crofting community had been cleared by Sir James Matheson in 1863 with the explicit intention of maximising Matheson's sheep farming and sporting incomes. In the early years, the shooting rights were bundled in with the Gress Shootings, but by the early 1870s Gabhsann had become a free-standing sporting estate, although as access to the estate was by foot or horseback, and there was no shooting lodge, the property proved difficult to lease to sporting tenants.

In 1880, a Yorkshire woollen manufacturer, Claude Greenburg, had rented the Gabhsann sporting rights for a season, at a cost of £280, arriving on his own steam yacht at Port Nis with his servants and provisions. Over the summer, Greenburg and his guests between them are recorded as having shot 1,000 pairs of grouse, 80 pairs of Snipe, 145 Woodcock, and 14 Ptarmigan.[245] Today, you might consider yourself lucky if you saw 14 grouse on the entire moor. Greenburg had erected a corrugated iron bungalow for the duration of his stay, but the following year Gabhsann was leased by Ernest Palmer-Moreson, a Derbyshire landowner, who stayed in the Barabhas inn and also rented the fishing rights for Barabhas and Arnol. He, apparently, killed 689 pairs of grouse in Gabhsann and 75 pairs of Snipe, along with 5 Salmon, 40 Sea Trout, and 100 Brown Trout.

In 1890, Lady Matheson had ordered a shooting lodge to be built in Gabhsann (it remains in the hollow down beside the river in Gabhsann bho Thuath) in order to make the rental more attractive to prospective tenants, and there was a small succession of shooting tenants until the start of the First World War. Mr Radclyffe Walters, a London solicitor who lived in Surrey, took the property in 1890 for six years, and in 1891 took 572 pairs of grouse, 109 pairs of Snipe, 121 plover, 109 Woodcock, 62 wildfowl, 17 Hares, 65 Rabbits, 3 Salmon, 25 Sea Trout, and 38 Brown Trout. Among Mr Walters shooting guests during his lease of the lodge at Gabhsann was Sir Henry Rider Haggard, the author of *King Solomon's Mines*. Perhaps unsurprisingly, after this time, the shooting bag appears to become lower and lower each year, until the sporting interest was abandoned during the First World War, after which time the need for a gamekeeper was dispensed with and the shooting and fishing was pursued mainly by local tenants. At this stage, after decades of exploitation by the paying guests, it is easy to see why the avian wildlife of the Gabhsann estate had diminished, and the renewed focus on improving the crofting land then shifted to view the landscape of Gabhsann from other, longer-term perspectives.

The map

In 1924, Gabhsann Farm had finally been broken up, divided into 52 new crofts, and re-settled by young families, eager to make Gabhsann their home. The lines of the new crofts were now clearly delineated on the future maps of Gabhsann, although on the ground, as yet only big marker stones and an occasional wall of the old farm divided the lots.

I have perhaps a dozen different maps of Gabhsann, all at various scales of representation and all diverse in what they purport to depict. I have maps that portray Gabhsann from the geological perspective, ones that show soil type, vegetational covering, place-names, as well as numerous standard topographical maps, intermittently produced over several hundred years, and drawn to the highest contemporary standards of accuracy. All these maps fascinate me to some extent, but my favourite three have a particular significance, not just for me, but for their general ability, at least conceptually, to define and understand this place called Gabhsann. If we want to move from 'space' to 'place' then the lines and icons on a map, even a rough sketch map, are the symbols that begin to fill in the blank spaces with features that we can interpret, or at least learn to recognise. Spaces are everywhere, but places are socially constructed by people. To give a name to a place is to locate it geographically in relation to other named places, to create directions, and in doing so, simultaneously begin to edge out the unnamed spaces, and to add clarity and depth to the places that we recognise. Contemporary memory identifies nearly two hundred distinct places in the landscape of Gabhsann (see Appendix 1) but surely many more named features have been lost through age and changing relationships with this land. The perspectives from which we view each place, the depths of our comprehension, and our emotional intelligence of the place, will differ for every one of us. The indigenous resident will see and feel it differently from the visitor who perceives it from afar; the young will regard it differently from the old. Sometimes these realities will be polarised, sometimes they will overlap, or even coexist simultaneously. On other occasions the maps simply speak for themselves, although the power of what symbolism should be included, and what is left out, ultimately lies with the (usually anonymous) map-maker.

The first of my favourite maps of the Gabhsann area makes clear at first glance that there is a different, if shared, history between these west coast villages that sets Gabhsann apart. Even a casual glance at the contemporary 1:25,000 Ordnance Survey map will indicate the unique construction of Gabhsann. The long, thin, almost plastically-stretched croft boundaries in the neighbouring villages of Borgh to the south and Dail Bho Dheas to the north, are absent in Gabhsann. The lines of the croft boundary fences are like a net laid across the landscape, fastening down the land to prevent it from blowing away. It is easy for the eye to be drawn towards those geometric lines of attachment, imbuing them with an importance that they do not deserve, while neglecting the fact that the important things - the people, the houses, the crops, the animals - are in the polygonal interstices between those geometric lines. The shapes of the crofts in the adjacent villages indicate an intergenerational legacy of habitation, the long, thin strips of land being split between siblings, to become thinner still over the years. Each thin strip providing pieces of land giving access to the coastline and to the edge of the moor - a piece of the good land and a piece of the bad. The patterns of this land were created by dispossession and conflict, by survival and reclamation.

In Gabhsann, the crofts are well-proportioned and more chunkily rectangular than the neighbouring villages - the product of careful consideration and planning by a now forgotten team of agriculturalists in the Board of Agriculture for Scotland. On a wall in my own croft house we have an original copy of the map, drawn at six inches to the mile, that was created to present the "Galson - Lewis: Small Holding Scheme". This is the second of my favourite maps. It was created to confirm that the breakup of Gabhsann Farm was finally about to happen, and to guide its dismemberment. It is a large, elegantly drawn map, hand-tinted in light blue watercolour to indicate the extent of the proposed Common Grazing, and with the boundaries of 52 new crofts (the first 16 being in Mealabost, then moving to Gabhsann bho Dheas, then Gabhsann bho Thuath) marked out starkly in red ink, as if to emphasise that this map is about to become a reality. The date on this map, neatly inscribed in small, black hand-lettering, in a box-inset in the bottom left hand corner, is 10.4.23. In the top left is an elongate table of statistics, giving the detailed extent of every new croft to be created.

The croft sizes vary widely, from 25 acres, 1 roods 25 poles (croft number 8) to 8 acres, 0 roods 32 poles (number 35) based on the perception (at that time) on the quality of the land available and its ability to be worked by horses for ploughing. The total area of the new village was to be 6,129 acres, 0 rods, 2 poles, of which 5,433 acres were Common Pasture plus (for some obtuse and now irrelevant reason) the allocation of 31 acres, 3 roods, 23 poles in the vicinity of Loidse Ghabhsainn (Galson Lodge) which was to be "reserved for the estate". The extreme specificity of the measurements is bewildering by today's standards, and seems to illustrate a way of thinking that was more arcane than should be expected even by a government grounds officer in the 1920s. My father-in-law recollected that when he was a young man in Gabhsann, another of the newly-arrived crofters, Alan 'An Candal' Gillies (who lived at croft number 28) still had the actual chains which had been used to measure out and individually compartmentalise the farm into the separate crofts that would eventually welcome a whole community of families. An Candal had been hired to help with the measuring of the new crofts, probably because he had worked at the farm in Dail bho Thuath, then owned and run by the MacFarquhar family. If you look carefully along the line of the present fences, there can still be located innocuous pieces of gneiss, standing alone and partially buried under a hundred years of grass, that mark the exact line of the boundary between two adjacent crofts. These are markers of physical and social divisions that have come from the land itself and are slowly returning there.

When enough time is allowed for careful observance and familiarity, the landscape features stand out, and there is a slowly dawning realisation that the map, for all its cartographic accuracy, is only a schematic representation of the changing reality. The boulder-beach changes its shape during a big storm, a rock pool is exposed in the river-bed during a dry spell of weather, and the specific details of those broken outlines of the coastal rocks are more intricate than depicted, and indeed frequently carry specific names of identification to indicate platforms for rock fishing, or their association with local wildlife. None of these subtle changes is recorded on any map. On a small island, each of those boulders and sea-cut geos are singular landmarks in themselves. In Gabhsann, the sharply marked features of the coast are partly blanketed further inland, and give way to a softer topography, draped with soil, vegetation, and peat, to fashion other forms of landscape architecture. In his absorbing account of the island of Árainn, off the west coast of Ireland, Tim Robinson produced a different kind of map, which step-by-step, catalogues, describes, and contextualises the boundaries of the island. The book is a tour de force that explores the human connection with every feature of that insular location, and by doing so, he is able to, *"... produce the sort of focussing of the landscape that is one of the ways in which mere location is intensified into place."*[246] The map becomes more than an artistic representation, it becomes an intangible expression, almost mystic but nonetheless very grounded, that characterises the uniqueness of the locale.

The return of people to inhabit the cognitive map of Gabhsann was the activity that reconnected the present inhabitants with the thread of thousands of years during which people gave meaning, and drew meaning, from this place.

Coming home

The first public confirmation that the years of petitioning, civil disobedience, and land agitation had at last borne fruit, was the acknowledgement in the *Stornoway Gazette* on 5 April 1923 that the Board of Agriculture proposed a new land settlement on the farm in Gabhsann, noting that *"... preference will be given to suitable ex-Service men who made application for smallholdings prior to March 1, 1921"*.[247] Subsequently, the same newspaper on 22 November reported, *"Galson Farm to be broken up"* and noted that, *"On Wednesday and Thursday of last week the Board of Agriculture held a sale of the remaining portion of the sheep stock, cattle and horses on this farm."*[248] There was then a lengthy process to identify, interview, and select the successful candidates from the many applications, from both locally and further afield, that sought a croft in Gabhsann.

Eventually, in the *Stornoway Gazette* of 28 August 1924 a notice appeared on page five, which despite its simplicity, sent a wave of expectation throughout the island. Headed *"Galson Crofting Settlement: The new tenants"* the notice listed fifty-two names of new settlers and their current addresses, matched against the number of the newly-created crofts in Gabhsann.[249] Against number 23 Gabhsann is listed Murdo MacDonald, the name of the father of my wife's mother, who moved with his young family from 25 Siadar Iarach, a crofting village four miles to the south of Gabhsann. They were lucky, in the competition to select the successful applicants for the new crofts, they were allocated one of the only three standing buildings in Gabhsann, the three-room steading which had previously been occupied by the farm labourers and for which the family paid a mortgage of £10 pounds a year for forty years. The other steading went to croft 37, and the farm-house itself is now a croft house.

In an extract from a much longer interview which was broadcast on BBC radio between Agnes, my wife, and her grandmother, Seònaid Ruairidh 'an Màrtainn, the latter described the first tentative return of the community to Gabhsann. You can detect the controlled excitement.

(Translation)

> *"One day Sgodaidh's wife and I came down to Gabhsann. We walked from Siadar. Walking down and walking back up again. The village was empty at that time. There was nothing here but the Big House* [the Farm House]. *When we got home everyone was asking if we liked the place. "Oh, yes, we liked it. Yes, we liked it." It was lovely right enough. It was green and clean. Nothing was ploughed except for the land around the tack.* [the farm] ... *We came down again in the Spring. Tuesday after the Barvas Communions - February 1924. We came down then. Then my husband's mother and his sister, Mòr, came down with us when we got a bit settled. We had a cow and some sheep and a little horse. My father-in-law came down with the cart and my own father came with another cart - one cart had peat in it and the other with what little we owned. We did not have much, just a bit of every kind of thing although it would not have been much at that time. It was a lovely day. I had Iain beag* [young John, later to die in the battle of El Alamein] *in my lap and Seonag* [my own mother-in-law] *- she would have been around two. It was a lovely day right enough.*[190]

The list of new settlers had been drawn from far and wide, though the names and addresses of the successful applicants strongly reflect the local connections to Gabhsann. They were mainly from the adjacent villages of Dail bho Dheas to the north, and Siadar to the south, but there were representatives from other westside villages such as Barabhas, Bragar, Càrlabhagh, with a couple from Steòrnabhagh and one family who returned from Greenock. With a bittersweet irony, one family moved to Gabhsann from Gearrannan, which is now an abandoned village of blackhouses which have been renovated in recent years to create a 'heritage village'.

The new settler on croft 25 - where our family continues to live, and where I am writing this book - is listed as Angus Gillies, the father of my wife's father, who moved from 20 Dail bho Dheas to begin crofting in Gabhsann. His family, like all the other new residents of the three newly-created villages, had first to build their own houses from the rocks and boulders that were scattered around the small crofts that they began to plough and cultivate. Listening to the story told by Seònaid, a tale of coming into an empty village and starting to clear the fields, it is almost impossible now to imagine the amount of work that was involved. She had been one of the "Herring Girls" - *Clann nighean an sgadain* - touring the circuit of the UK coastline to clean and pack Herring, so she knew what hard work was, and she accepted this new start in Gabhsann as a wonderful opportunity, not a chore to be resented.

For many people in the Highlands and Islands, this familial and cultural relationship with the land is at the heart of the indigenous, almost visceral, attachment to land and place in the Gaidhealtachd. I have argued that it affects every element of our society, from the names that we give to identify and celebrate places, (see Appendix 2) to the way that we earn money, to the way that we feel about environmental issues, even to our basic civil rights as humans.[250] In places like Gabhsann, there are local names for places known by the names of people long gone but remembered in collective memory. Outside my study window just now I can see the site of Tobair Aonghais Ghiolais (The well of Angus Gillies, who came from 20 Dail bho Dheas to resettle Gabhsann, and died in 1947. This sense of 'belongingness' is not a purely Gaelic association of course. Over the years I have watched many visitors to Lewis, and to Gabhsann, who can be crudely classified into three types; there are the casual visitors who are interested to see the place, but are just passing through; then there are the people who visit, but think they have arrived in some sort of pre-hell because they cannot get access to 24-hour takeaways and need to queue to get off the island; then there are the visitors who come, and return again and again, some actually never leave. I have been told that the Finns have a special word for this sensation - *'sielunmaisema'* - meaning literally a 'soul-landscape', a particular place that a person carries deep in their affections and returns to often, even if only in memory.

It's a 'love-it-or-hate-it' kind of place, and if you love it, you never want to live anywhere else. There is not much 'Dreamtime' here. Even on a good day there is usually a gentle sea breeze. Throughout the year, in any season, curved grey curtains of rain can be seen for many miles away, stippled on the sky, as they advance across the landscape. There is little trouble in predicting the weather for the next few hours, it can be observed all around you. In the midst of a dark winter, it is not uncommon for one or two hurricanes to pass through, and storm after storm will sweep in, so that the wind seems to come from every direction at once. Walking along the village road towards the sea during a gale, a fully-grown man might be leaning towards the oncoming wind at thirty degrees from the vertical simply in order to keep moving. Along the length of this coastline, a 200 metre white band of tumultuous surf testifies to the ferocity of the convergence of ocean and shore. The wind has a language of its own, if you have an ear to understand its vocabulary. There are not many trees in Gabhsann, so the sound of wind in the branches is not a common tune, but a slight swishing sound is almost background music, as the air rushes like a projectile over walls and around the corners of buildings. The explosive noise of sudden gusts can be dramatic, but their impact is mostly in sound effects rather than actual physical threat. However, the soft, understated, throaty growl in a storm-force blast is the signal that makes savvy locals stop mid-action, half in expectation of follow-up damage, and half considering the night ahead. All the same, I would rather spend a night in the rural landscape during a high wind than be in the city where random items of urban jetsam are blown unpredictably. In places like Gabhsann, there is normally little damage from the regular storms, because anything loose is fixed down, taken inside, or has blown away during the previous storm.

In the absolute and total stillness that remains after a big winter gale is over, the utter calm that prevails is itself so sublime that it seems it could almost be in a dream. It is easy to see at a time like this, how so many of the 'gentlemen travellers' of history, having stepped out of their own social circles and of their city environment, thought that they had found 'magic' in the Outer Hebridean landscape. The few trees, acknowledging the superior power of the wind, point their scraggy branches in the opposite direction, as if they are complicit in pointing-out to the wind the correct direction for it to take to get out of this place as fast as possible, and so to restore the calm that the storm had replaced. Sometimes we have felt that when this calm returns in winter, or on a tranquil summer's evening with a luminescent sky and twenty-four hour daylight, the air is so fresh, so clear, so serene, that it takes little imagination to believe that this environment is newly created just for you.

Even in the earliest days of the Gabhsann Farm, there had been scattered settlements of people in the surrounding landscape, particularly Gabhsann bho Thuath and Mealabost (the land now occupied by Gabhsann bho Dheas was largely covered by the farm). The nature of this surrounding settlement was transitory, with individual cottages, and small clusters of buildings, which were used and then abandoned as the centres of habitation drifted around. There was no fixed pattern of pre-crofting settlement in the Outer Hebrides,[251] with some villages being nucleated, while others were scattered, and despite some academic attempts at recognising a standardised style, the individual uniqueness of many crofting townships has remained in the succeeding years. It appears that functional practicalities and landforms have had a greater importance than the tidy lines beloved by the planning officials. In Gabhsann, the general pattern seems to have been the common one of the living quarters and any steadings on the in-bye agricultural land, with a wall surrounding the entire landward margin of the villages to keep the animals out on the moor during the spring and summer months. In the long-drawn, tortuous process of moving from clan chiefs to landlords, the changes in the human landscape were as much economic as they were social, and though those changes were sometimes slow and other times sudden, the cumulative effect was dramatic and disempowering for the majority of the population.[252] In the aftermath of the First World War, the socio-economic changes impacted upon all of the population, throughout the country, and although its effects differed widely, in Gabhsann it resulted in a rejuvenated township, with an upsurge in agricultural activity and a minor population boom.

Over the next ninety-six years since resettlement, a substantial number of changes can be observed in the land use and distribution of the resident population. There have been changes in agricultural activity, from the fields of a single farm to a mosaic of independently managed crofts. As with the re-settlement of other crofting townships, the new tenants of Gabhsann established their own field patterns on the inbye land that are substantially different from the previous landuse patterns that were based on wider resource-use issues than simply agriculture.[253] The modern map contrasts with the farm pattern, and also with the old pre-clearance village which was characterised by small unfenced units, managed in run-rig style, lying north-east of the river and west of the current main road. Across the village area the even older pre-crofting vestiges of landuse are sometimes visible in a certain light. There are also a few localities around the township where the earlier landforms of the so-called lazy beds (feannagan) are still in evidence, though these were gradually abandoned as land management skills improved and Gabhsann became a permanently settled place. In addition to the legacy of dry-stone walls marking field boundaries, an intricate system of stone-built field drains of the old farm, leading downhill to the river is occasionally uncovered. These linked drains are intricate miniature works of architecture, constructed with an awesome elegance, about a metre below the land surface. One flattish stone is laid below, and another on top, with two intervening lines of smaller stones marking a precise rectangular culvert running underground many hundreds of metres to remove excess water. This is a hydric land, there is seldom a time when these drains are completely dry, and their contents brings life as surely as the hidden arteries in a body.

Little else remains of the earlier field patterns or land use. The resettled village did not initially separate the individual crofts, but maintained an 'open village' system which was enclosed from the outrun of the common grazings. Subsequent to the Second World War, the introduction of fencing between and within crofts has enabled greater flexibility in the cultivation of crops, as well as a greater individual control of livestock. In recent years, the increasing demands of non-crofting employment, has resulted in less attention to subsistence agriculture and encouraged a smaller headage of livestock to be retained within the village for a longer period of the year, resulting in overgrazing of the inbye and under-use of the common.

Aerial photographs of Gabhsann taken by the RAF in 1946 and 1966, clearly show that the inbye area of Gabhsann township was intensively cultivated for agricultural activity at this period. There is at least one dwelling house on each croft, usually with some additional steadings, and the photographs evidence the intensive cultivation of the arable land adjacent to the village roads. A complex patchwork of narrow, linear strips demarcate ploughed land, potatoes, turnips, oats, forage grassland, and small kitchen-gardens. It seems from the photographs that almost every square metre of these small fields had been pressed into cultivation. The patchwork effect is particularly impressive in Gabhsann bho Dheas, where it spans both sides of the village road and runs down to the coastal fringe of the north-facing raised beach. Close scrutiny can detect substantial haystacks, corn ricks, and peat stacks beside many of the houses. This mosaic of intensive, small-scale cultivation is remarkable and imposing, and in stark contrast to non-crofting landuse on the west coast of the Scottish mainland, areas from which people were cleared and the land never effectively resettled. Since the maximum agricultural activity immediately after the Second World War, there has been a continuous decline in the intensity of cultivation, as the demands of subsistence survival becomes less of an issue, and the convenience of supermarkets responds to the requirement to put food on the table. The discontinuation of the Cropping Grant in 1972, due to changes in European agricultural policy, removed a major financial incentive for small-scale arable production and was a critical turning point in the agricultural abandonment of many areas of inbye croft land.

These changes are small on the individual scale, but cumulatively they have a dramatic and fundamental impact upon the landscape and ecology of the area, and upon low-intensity farming systems in general.[254] The complex mosaic of habitats produced by the extensification of agriculture that was such a feature of the early crofting system, and contributed to its high value in nature conservation,[89] has often been replaced by poorly managed in-bye land used only for grazing sheep, and in many instances not even for that. In most cases the field sizes and configurations are unchanged since the mid-nineteen-twenties, but within each croft, the diversity of habitats that were created by small patches of oats (a total of 86.2 acres in small patches in 1959), potatoes (23.7 acres), turnips (4.7 acres) has been diminished. Cultivation still continues on several crofts, but on a much reduced scale, and mainly as small garden units (a geographical study recorded 47 acres of 'garden' in Gabhsann in 1959).[255] The evolution of these changes was noted in a land use assessment in 1988 that recorded the lack of oats, the decline in the production of hay, and the switch by some crofters to silage or haylage (both more convenient to harvest than hay), as well as an increase in the prevalence of rough grazing on the inbye land.[256]

In addition to the land allocated by the creation of the individual croft holdings, each croft has an entitlement to a share of the township Common Grazing. In the case of Gabhsann this amounts to a fifty-third share of nearly 2,210 hectares, a nominal forty hectares per holding. This allocation is largely notional as the grazing itself is generally unfenced between the village and the neighbouring townships and there is unrestricted mobility between the Gabhsann Common Grazing and the rest of the Ness General covering northern Lewis. There are three discrete areas of Common Grazing available, an enclosed area (Druim bho Thuath) between the main road, the shore, and the boundary with Dail; a second enclosure between Gabhsann bho Dheas and Mealabost (A' Phàirc Churs); and the third being the huge extent of the open moor east and south of the main road. To fully appreciate the full extent of the Gabhsann moor, it is necessary to walk - laboriously, for the ground is broken and filled with small lochans – a couple of hours due east, to the unmarked open boundary near the middle of the north Lewis moor. Looking back to the villages, the huge scope of the moor dwarfs the minimalist human constructions of space and place.

These areas of Common Grazing are recognised by villagers to have a multiplicity of functions for different land uses and ownership relationships, including grazing, peat cutting, and hunting. In some areas of the Common Grazing, individual crofters have applied for permission to enclose a portion of their nominal share for their own exclusive use. These 'apportionments', as they are termed, are small, fenced areas of moorland, to which shell-sand is applied (in order to reduce the acidity of the peat) fertilised, then the area seeded with grass to produce seasonal grazing for livestock. There are also two areas of around fifty hectares each in Gabhsann bho Thuath which are termed 'village apportionments'. These were created on a cooperative basis by thirty-five tenant crofters of the village in the mid 1960s as part of a 'minority scheme' (i.e. not the whole village) in order to improve the quality of grazing land available to the village.

Taken together, the decline in sheep and cattle, the withdrawal of the remaining grazing animals mostly to the inbye land of the crofts, and the cessation of the regular use of the open moor for seasonal grazing, has meant a significant change in land management, and consequent habitat modification. The removal of grazing pressure from the moorland has resulted in an unrestricted growth of Heathers as this vegetation is no longer pruned by livestock nor burned by crofters or gamekeepers to generate new growth. On the minority scheme apportionments, as with other areas of reseeded grassland, rushes and other invasive species, such as Sheep's sorrel have colonised the ground as it has become more acidic with progressive leaching of the lime. With the reduction in grazing by sheep, and visits from attendant shepherds, the Red Deer have begun to come right in to the edge of the villages, creating a regular hazard for driving in conditions of reduced visibility.

There have also been changes in relation to peat cutting. Under the terms of crofting tenure, each croft is normally allocated a traditional area for the extraction of peat for domestic fuel.[257] Normally this would have been cut by hand, in teams of two, although now the village Common Grazings Committee, elected by the tenant crofters of the township, permits mechanical cutting of 'sausage peats' in certain areas of the moor. The transportation of the peats from the moor to the stack at the back door of the owner's house is traditionally a collective activity, with families and neighbours operating an informal, mutual self-help system. As a result, parts of the Common Grazing are a complex pattern of inter-linking peat banks, which have strong family associations, though to the outsider there is seldom anything to distinguish one peat bank from another, far less any indication of ownership and management.

In 2007 Gabhsann was once again the focus of attention in national and international newspapers when the wider community of the old Galson Estate joined together and collectively bought the land that their villages sit upon.

There is a particular word in the indigenous Gaelic language of the Highlands and Islands for which it is difficult to give a direct translation into English. '*Buntanas*' expresses the concept of a person or community of people having a deep association with a specific area of land, a communal sense of embeddedness, and rootedness through family lineage and history of a community who belong to a certain place. This is in contradistinction to the more usual Western concept of the land belonging to an individual person, or people owning the land in its entirety.

In the poetry of the late Norman MacCaig, he asks in his long poem *A Man from Assynt*,[258]

> *Who possesses this landscape? –*
>
> *The man who bought it or*
>
> *I who am possessed by it?*

This, I feel, goes to the heart of the ingenous relationship with land and place, in creating what is, literally and metaphorically, a rooted society.[259]

The latest iteration in the story of the changing Outer Hebrides is a resilient tale of community resurgence, hope, and not an insignificant sense of historic restitution for the historical iniquities of landuse in this region. In response to an initiative by the Scottish Government, which led to the 2003 Land Reform Act, communities across Scotland were enabled to initiate legal proceedings to purchase the land on which they reside. Several crofting estates in the Highlands and Islands were quick to take advantage of this legislation to acquire the land, including the villages of the Galson Estate. Although the village of Gabhsann is in the centre of the area, it is just one of 22 villages on the 55,800-acre (22,600 hectare) linear strip of land stretching along the northwest coast of the Isle of Lewis. The boundaries of the estate are essentially what was parcelled out by the agents of Lord Leverhulme when he left Lewis and divided up the island landscape in his attempt to sell it off piecemeal in London.

Initially the Galson Estate purchase began as a so-called "hostile" buy-out (a legal description - the owners had not at first intended to sell) but in the course of subsequent negotiations, this became an "amicable" settlement. In 2004, a local steering group organised a ballot throughout the community, open to the electorate over sixteen years of age. In this public ballot, there was a 72% turnout and an 85% majority vote in favour of acquiring the land under community ownership. A non-profit -distributing company with charitable status – (officially known as Urras Oighreachd Ghabhsainn) (UOG) was then set-up, and a working group was formed to steer the negotiations to secure the land for the community. Over the next three years, the working group negotiated grant and loan funding – usually through contractual agreements with public agencies and charities – towards purchasing the land, at a cost of £600,000 (more than a thousand times what was paid by Edward Valpy eighty years earlier). A second public ballot was then held, with a 76% voter turnout, resulting in a Board of ten Trustees being elected from thirty nominees to manage the business of the company.

Although it was apparent from an early stage that simply the existing income from croft rents and wayleaves would enable UOG to remain solvent as a business, it was also clear that additional finance would be required to facilitate new rural development activities which would be beneficial to the area. A number of public meetings were held, and a community consultation study was prepared to outline local development aspirations.[260] It quickly became evident that local residents had long-term aspirations to encourage social, economic, and environmental activities on the estate, rather than simply seek the short-term profits historically characterised by the majority of private landowners. This in turn has had a profound effect on local perceptions of "sustainability", prompting a long-term vision with a wide agenda beyond solely land management. For example, in the twelve years since its creation, UOG has made land available to build social housing, has contracted with the Local Authority to manage a local waste disposal site, has provided environmental education for schools and tourists, initiated a scheme to improve old houses and increase energy efficiency, and has worked to relieve the fuel poverty of residents on the estate. The production and efficient management of energy locally is therefore of prime concern for this community

Internationally, the islands are an important area for the generation of renewable energy - wind, hydro, tidal, solar - and the Gabhsann area had been the target of a huge and controversial wind farm development which was subsequently refused planning permission by the Scottish Government.[261] Although majority local opinion was opposed to the inappropriately large scale of the commercial wind farm proposal, there was considerable local support for a small, community-owned initiative, with the result that the UOG erected three 900-kilowatt wind turbines on the estate.

These three turbines earned the community over one million pounds sterling in 2017-18. Most of this income has gone towards repaying the costs of the turbine installation and towards building financial reserves for UOG, but the Trust has now established a Community Investment Fund which can award grants of £1,000, £5,000, and £10,000 to support local groups with their plans to enhance the social, economic, and environmental amenities of the community area.[262] Although all Trusts are governed through volunteer participation, a number of Trusts, including UOG have employed an estate manager to co-ordinate the day-to-day business. Under private ownership, Galson Estate provided no jobs in the community; UOG now employs fourteen staff in various community-focused tasks.

Whereas previously, many landed estates in the Highlands and Islands were viewed primarily as providing sport (shooting and fishing) for external guests, or for simply collecting land rents from tenant crofters, the new community-owned estates have based their business plans on the planned benefits and improvements for the whole of the local resident community. In the Outer Hebrides, it is calculated that currently around 75% of all land is community owned and around 85% of the population now live on land that is owned by their own community. The main significance in legal terms is that the land-owning rights are transferred from a private owner to a non-profit-distributing company, owned by the community and managed through the democratic election by the members of that community. Land reform, as currently practiced in Scotland, is an attempt to create a more equal distribution of land ownership, and in effect, it *"implies changes in the balance of power between the individual property owners, communities, and the state."*[263] This shift from private ownership of land to community ownership is more than just semantics, for the new Land Trusts can have fundamentally different objectives than a private company created to maximize individual financial gain.[264] The adherence to social, environmental, as well as economic objectives means that local Land Trusts, managed by local people, have a different and longer-term perception of what "sustainable development" might actually mean. For added significance, the Community Land Trust of which Gabhsann is a part, is now collaborating with other island land Trusts, such as in Càrlabhagh, on a growing and ongoing basis to maximise the benefits to the people living on these estates.

The offices of Urras Oighreachd Ghabhsainn are located in Gabhsann, and the cumulative effects of democratic ownership of the land are now beginning to be felt, not just in crofting and land management activities, but also in the fields of art, education, heritage, tourism, housing, and even modest initiatives to mitigate the local effects of global climate change. It is as far as can be imagined from the visions of the future that Sir James Matheson and Lord Leverhulme intended for Gabhsann.

CHAPTER 9

Human ecology in a crofting township

Perspectives

What is the demonym of a person who belongs to Gabhsann?

Gabhsannach? Galsonian? Both plausible but cumbersome possibilities, but never used.

In Gaelic, the phrase to ask where you are from is "*cò às a tha thu?*", literally "who do you come out of?" The concept of belonging to a particular place is conspecific with an explicit assumption that your forebearers/ancestors are hefted to a locality, in much the same way as other animals return to a specific place to feed, to breed, and to shelter. There is an expectation that a person's history, their whole being, in fact, is a continuous and inseparable part of their physical environment. Time, and place, and being are seamlessly interconnected. This environment is more than just a space that we occupy on the surface of the Earth, it is a named place, with a heritage of interaction with humans that has created a relationship of belonging. This too is part of the meaning of *buntanas*. A wonderful glimpse of this is explored by Neil Gunn in his perceptive and profound novel *The Drinking Well* in which the lead character, Iain Cattanach, wrestles with the

168

tensions of music, culture, heritage, and place as he matures into a young man.[265] Incidentally, the book also introduces an extraordinarily prescient understanding of the potential of community land ownership, half a century before radical Scottish land reform enabled this to become a reality. This sense of place is woven in to the legacy of the Norse sagas, the Irish imramha (sea sagas) and the Icelandic stories of how their men originated from Norway while their women frequently came from the western coasts of Scotland and Ireland (which recent DNA studies have largely substantiated). There was no satnav or phone app or marinetraffic.com to identify offshore shipping in those days, so the stories of history and identity, of the movements of people, were bound up with the memory of places and the links between places. As has come to be appreciated by archaeologists, anthropologists, psychologists, and geographers,

> "… places are always far more than points or locations, because they have distinctive meanings and values for persons. Personal and cultural identity is bound up with place…"[266]

and later…

> "The naming and identification of particular topographical features, such as sand dunes, bays and inlets, mountain peaks, etc., settlements and sites is crucial for the establishment and management of their identity."[266]

Being able to lie in bed in the morning and hear the soundscape of this place called Gabhsann, is an integral part of the identity of this place. The calls of the Curlew, the Oystercatcher, and the Corncrake reflect the nature of the habitat outside, and even simply listening to the direction of the wind or rain on the window, is to be at the edge of immersion in this place. Though there may be a storm outside, there is a security based on familiarity that is comforting and almost tangible. "*Cuin a thànaig thu dhachaigh?*" ("When did you come home?") is the question that is put to almost every returned ex-patriate and frequently even to complete strangers on their first visit to the hefted homeland, for there is an implicit perception that this is where you belong, no matter where you happen by chance to live now.

The causal creation of 'place' through repetitive human interaction is so pervasive that it has been said that,

> "a place is not a place until people have been born in it, have grown up in it, lived in it, known it, died in it - have both experienced and shaped it, as individuals, families, neighbourhoods, and communities, over more than one generation. Some are born in their place, some find it, some realize after long searching that the place they left is the one they have been searching for. But whatever their relation to it, it is made a place only by slow accrual, like a coral reef."[267]

There are three basic types of human relationships with this land. There is the detached perspective, where the observer passes through and merely looks at the land. This can be every gradation of scrutiny from the urbanite who finds the moor 'bleak' and terrifying, through to ramblers who delight in the mountains and the open spaces. Secondly, the person who lives with this land and can intimately identify with landforms and events that do not appear on any map, is a more profound iteration of scrutiny. Then there is a form of symbiotic relationship which develops with the use of the land. It manifests itself not simply in filling supermarket shelves with the produce of the farms and the forests but as a deep association and cognizance of the richness of a place, which is itself a shibboleth to an even deeper understanding of the mosaic of landscape. Ultimately, there is an empathy with place which is almost immersive, and which, at its most pervasive, blurs the boundaries between the self and the place. A simple example of that can be expressed this way: if you lived abroad and you planned a visit home, you would never consider saying, "I am going to visit a friend on Scotland...". That would be unnatural, because we are cognizant of place being more than just the surface of the earth that we stand upon. It is not an infallible guide, but a useful approximation to distinguish an island perspective from a non-island one is the differentiation between, "I live *on* Lewis." and "I live *in* Lewis". The latter phrase acknowledges, almost subliminally, that a place is much more than just a GPS number which pinpoints a location on the surface of the globe, but rather it is something greater than the sum of the components of soil, air, water, sky, climate, people, and the intimate interaction with fellow living species in that biotic community.

There are times when there is pleasure simply to *be* in a place. No thoughts of the past or the future, simply revelling in being alive in the present, not unlike the Buddhist tradition of mindfulness. Approached from this perspective, the settlements chosen by the old Celtic clerics for their chapels, monasteries, and spiritual retreats all along this western coast, in places such as Gabhsann, becomes intimately and acutely understandable.

On the landscape

So, what is Gabhsann? On the surface, it is the physical manifestation of the various landforms that define the topographical shape of this place. A detailed description of the two small rivers in the two shallow glens, bounded by the length of coastline and the extent of the moor, with the three gentle rises of well-drained land on which the crofts are located, is simply an inventory of geography. Obviously Gabhsann is much more than that, not least because almost every element of this landscape has been created, modified, or imposed upon by many generations of human inhabitants, as well as other local species. There is ample evidence, if you seek it, of human impact in this countryside. This is true even in some of the most distant parts of the township, at the furthest edges of the moor where almost no-one now goes, or in the currently uninhabited spaces between the village settlements. In these places the only signs of humans may be the archaeological remains, but that is enough to indicate centuries of human interaction with the land. This is a significant reason why careless talk of "rewilding" this landscape can be so derisive and offensive to local feelings and local heritage. This land can only be considered "wild" because the people who once inhabited it, who lived in it and travelled through it, were forcibly removed by the power of stronger forces, and were subsequently dispersed around the world. In this country, most of the supposedly "wild" land is a manufactured landscape, created and maintained by the predominant societal values of the time. In consideration of this,

> "*The irony for those who feel that more human activity necessarily means a greater threat,* [to 'perceived naturalness'] *is that greater human presence in the past created a more productive and diverse environment than what we are striving to protect today.*"[268]

Historically, it suited the early travel writers to magnify the landscape differences of the Highlands and Islands and accentuate their risks in order to romanticise their own adventures. The more recent emphasis on managing landscape for environmental gain is a laudable iteration of the process, but in the end it is also simply about humans attempting to control the land to produce a different sort of product. The commoditization of the countryside has moved from purely food products to include landscape views and "space to breathe" for town dwellers.[269]

On any map, Gabhsann has always been at the edge of someone's geographical perceptions. It is puzzling, and sometimes irritating, for me to listen to the radio and hear the British Broadcasting Corporation comment on some news item occurring "in the north" only to discover that they actually mean Birmingham, or perhaps Manchester. Take a look at a map of the UK, even Edinburgh is barely halfway down the country. By any geographical standards of "Britishness", Birmingham lies in the south. I do not even feel like I am "in the north" sometimes, for there is even more of the country further north than me. In a more local context, Gabhsann might still be considered to be at the edge of someone's map, because as a re-settled crofting village all its current inhabitants beyond two generations back, came from somewhere else. They may only have moved from an adjacent village, but they moved to Gabhsann, (thereby creating Gabhsann as the centre of their attention). I read in a geography textbook long ago that county boundaries in the middle states of the USA were delimited almost through self-selection by noting the direction in which the ruts of cartwheels turned when a farm track met a main road. When the ruts began to turn in the other direction, you had passed a boundary; you were focused on the market town in a different direction. In Gabhsann, the tyre-tracks turn in both directions; north towards Nis, or south towards Barabhas and Steòrnabhagh, depending on familial roots or the nature of your business in hand.

In a perceptive collection of essays on land and community, the 'rootlessness' of many people in the USA is explored in the context of alienation, disaffection, and even disdain for the land.[270] This analysis relates the lack of 'belonging' to the commoditization of land in that country, and the resulting divorce of any sense of personal responsibility to place. In another collection of writing, it is noted that "*many western* [USA] *towns never lasted a single human lifetime...*" and suggested that it is time to "*acquire the sense not of ownership* [of the land] *but of belonging.*"[267] This equates closely with the Gaelic sense of buntanas, that cultural association with every aspect of a place, which when deprived of it, has led to *cianalas*, an extreme form of homesickness that can lead to psychological debilitation and the lack of will to continue living. (Such as the malaise that affected John Graham when he was cleared from Gabhsann to re-settle in Canada).

In contrast to those transient towns, it is unmistakable that for several thousand years, the land of Gabhsann has been a very desirable territory in which to live. Regardless of whether the residents were Neolithic hunter-gatherers or contemporary commuters, there is an identifiable affinity with this place. In an age when practically everyone can almost immediately locate their precise position on the planet by using the GPS on their smart-phone, surely it is passed the time to stop saying "*in the middle of nowhere*". If it ever had any value, the phrase has now become nonsensical, pejorative, and (perhaps unintentionally) offensive. As Spike Milligan once said, "*Everybody's got to be somewhere.*"

The trees have an even more tenuous hold in Gabhsann than the humans. There is a small shelter-belt in the re-seeded apportionment in Gabhsann bho Thuath, a remainder from 1960s crofting developments, and there is a small, struggling plantation between Meagro and Blàr an Dùin which was planted by the township, partly in an effort to dry the land and also to prevent livestock from getting bogged down and lost. Both of these areas are composed of introduced conifers, but there are small clusters and individual native trees in gardens and on crofts throughout Gabhsann. There are Hawthorn, Hazel, Alder, Rowan, Downy Birch, and Silver Birch, and of course several species of willow, including Grey Willow, Eared Willow, and Dark-leaved Willow. This distinction between introduced and native trees is important not simply for aesthetic appeal, but mostly because of the indigenous communities of wildlife which different tree species nurture and support beneath their leaves. Over millions of years, natural selection has allowed plants and animal life evolve to develop specific preferences, so now willows might support 450 different species of insects, and the Downy Birch can provide food and habitat for more than 300 insect species, whereas the insect species diversity in most introduced trees can often be counted in single figures.[271] The availability of small insects is reflected in the abundance of small birds.

The contemporary landscape of Gabhsann is largely free of trees and shrubs, but we know from the evidence of those broken branches and stumps in the peat banks that this was not always so. Earlier inhabitants of Gabhsann would have been much more familiar with tree species than most UK inhabitants are today. As a gentle reminder of the intimate association between the indigenous human and botanical inhabitants, we need look no further than the Gaelic language. While children today learn in English classes that "A is for Apple, E is for Elephant" etc. the eighteen-letter Gaelic alphabet is based upon the native trees of the Highlands and Islands. In Gaelic tradition, A is for *Ailm*, the Elm, B is for *Beith*, the Birch, C for *Coll*, the Hazel and so on, through to U for *Ùr* representing the Yew tree.[272] The natural history of the landscape was quite literally used to construct the language of the people who lived in that landscape, and who needed to know the variation and gradation of the biodiversity that surrounded them. The anthropologist, Hugh Brody, investigated the links between land, language, and indigenous culture in several parts of the world, and once concluded that the key terminology of terms relating to a full understanding of the land is untranslatable.[273] But what if it transpires that these terms are only discongruent with the mainstream languages of the historically relatively recent urban settlements? What if there is a direct similarity of perception - both in meaning and in idiom - between culturally distinct indigenous languages, who share a common understanding of the meaningness of place, despite their separate geographical locations?

Trees have a difficult lifetime in the habitats that Gabhsann can currently provide. Between the desiccating winds, the salty air, the nutrient-poor soils that inhibit growth, and the almost unbreakable layer of the hard iron-pan which frequently lies about 30cm below the surface - a sort of impervious shadow soil surface that limits the downwards extension of roots - it is hardly surprising that many trees are dramatically shaped by the prevailing winds. The Gaelic names of these trees are a legacy of memory, a sort of etymological fossil, a record of different habitats, and a different way of understanding what is on the land, that once enveloped human travellers and residents. The ground-litter of tree branches in the bottom layer of our peat banks suggests that the very earliest visitors to Gabhsann would have walked through a rather different habitat.

Another fossil landscape which we pass so frequently that we take it for granted, is the assemblage of dry-stone walls throughout Gabhsann. Many areas of the country can be readily identified by the functional local geology of their field boundaries - the upright table-top slabs of Caithness slate, or the blocky limestone boulders of Assynt - but the dykes of Gabhsann are formed of solid and irregular lumps of Lewisian Gneiss, which never split easily. There are more than 10 kilometres of walls throughout this small township, some dating back to the days of the Galson Farm. Other walls are a product created by the field-clearance which was a necessity when the farm was broken up and the crofting structure re-established. All of these boundaries are a long-term testimony to the almost unbelievable amount of labour-hours that were required to build and maintain these walls. Like hedgerows in other parts of the country, the static patterns of the field boundaries of Gabhsann may appear definitive, but they represent a mental map of dispossession and conflict. The outer boundary wall of the farm was erected to assert possession and exclusion, as well to assist stock management; little wonder that it was an obvious target for destruction by the "raiders".

From the landscape

The top end of the dog-leg village road in Gabhsann bho Dheas is almost the highest point in the village, and the views northeastward along the line of the coast are some of my favourite panoramas of landscape. On a calm day, there is a white margin of surf, and after a wild storm the margin might be more than a kilometre-wide band of restless ocean, marking-out the wave-cut platform just offshore and underwater. At any time and in any season, the wind-blown spray from the breakers might leap 30 or 50 metres up the shear, blank cliff face of An Tobha Mhor - An Tobha Ghabhsainn - that round-topped headland in the middle distance. A loose definition of 'tobha' is 'a prominent headland sticking out into the sea', and from the summit of An Tobha, the absence of towering land horizons in any direction and the wide sea horizon of more than 180° of angular spread, showcases an immensity of sea and sky that sometimes gives you the feeling of being suspended in space. From the top of An Tobha, an observer is looking across more than 100 square miles, (more than 26,000 hectares) of open ocean surface and an almost incalculable hemisphere of sky. When an acquaintance of mine, a professional photographer, was asked by his city clients why he lived here, he replied simply, after a moment's pause: *"Because of the quality of the light."* In certain angles of light, especially when the ocean is relatively calm, there are distinct trails of different colourations in the cold, clear waters, defining individual currents of such constant regularity that they are almost 'sea roads' and the local inshore fishermen have traditional names for them, just like the counterpoised rivers on the land.

At such moments of calm and tranquility it is easy to appreciate, even in the face of modern science and contemporary political cynicism, how the earliest human settlers in this region attributed universal wonder and mysticism to their landscape. It is even possible, perhaps, to understand the Victorian waywardness with the 'other-worldness' and the "magical " obsessions that they evoked at every hillock and hollow. The depth of perception and decoding of place which is explicit in Neil Gunn's *"other landscape"* is on the boundary between deep ecology and mysticism, but in the end has its true basis not in the supernatural, but in the recognition of subtle layers of meaning and personal interaction with the land. Even someone such as Barry Lopez, accustomed to using words eloquently to describe and explain the technical ecological relationships of natural science, can note that;

> *"occasionally one sees something fleeting in the land, a moment when line, color, and movement intensify and something sacred is revealed, leading one to believe that there is another realm of reality corresponding to the physical one but different".*[48]

For the early settlers, however, and indeed far into the last century in some cases, the human links with this landscape, and with the natural world, were not just abstract concepts to be viewed from afar, but very tangible, very necessary, and occasionally life-saving imperatives for community survival.[274] They knew the value of local plants in traditional medicine; for instance that the soft, pink-flowered cushions of Wild Thyme found at the Druim bho Thuath, and at Tom an Ime, can be used to relieve fainting and general fatigue. Or that the Wild Mint, which grows easily in Gabhsann and scents the air after a light shower of rain, was used for the treatment of upset stomachs, nausea, and diarrhoea, as well as to make a pleasant tea.[275] Bogbean, that apparently undistinguished plant that we find in the shallow, peaty lochans on the great moor of Gabhsann, was boiled and applied to relieve a persistent cough. Its leaves were good for drawing out pus, and sometimes it was made into a form of beer which was used as a general tonic and as a remedy for stomach pains, constipation, or ulcers. Dandelion roots could be dried and powdered to make a sort of coffee, and the common Nettle, in addition to providing a tasty vegetable, is good for urinary complaints, and a cloth could be woven from its fibres. Even in the presentation of this botanical menu, however, Gabhsann maintains its own ecological agenda, with at least one major isanther – a time gradient for the blooming of flowers - separating the east and the west coasts of Lewis. The blooming of flowers and the summer growth spurt of trees and grass is usually a couple of weeks later in the saltier, windier, environment of Gabhsann than on the eastern side of the island.

Not much attention is paid to these natural remedies nowadays, except perhaps when supplied in expensive little bottles of extract in health and wellbeing shops, but many of the raw ingredients lie all around us in this landscape. True, some of those 'remedies', like the 'healing wells', may be placebos, or at best be only moderately effective, but other treatments are still valid and valued, even if we cannot currently definitely pinpoint the active ingredient or why it seems to work. Other plants had non-medical uses, such as the hardy survivor, Tormentil; at Cùl na feans or on Tom Lomaidean, and at other sites on the Gabhsann moor, how many people who crush that delicate yellow flower under their walking boots know that its roots were once sought after to tan leather? As well as traditional areas for cutting peats, it was common in many crofting communities to identify particular localities for the harvesting of rushes to thatch the roofs of buildings, or for Heather roots to twist into strong, pliable ropes, and until recently there were residents in Gabhsann who could indicate where those traditional areas were, though the actual practices had long since ceased. The Sphagnum moss, so abundant on the moor, was dried and used as a field dressing for soldiers, from the Napoleonic War right up to and including the Second World War, as it is highly absorbent and mildly antiseptic. To this day, it is common for a chef living in Gabhsann to pick the edible flowers and mosses that grow in different parts of the village, to garnish his culinary creations.

In this respect, a study on land occupancy and local identity in the Gabhsann area would have similarities with the work of Hugh Brody, when he lived with the Beaver Indians in British Columbia and helped them to document their traditional attachment to the land through the construction of community-created maps. In *Maps and Dreams* [276] he recorded the obvious in addition to the more intangible connections of the indigenous people with their hinterland, identifying the ancient hunting territories and the places where people went to gather other natural resources. He made associations between land that is used now, and that which has been used in the past for certain purposes, often retaining a traditional link to particular individuals, families, or times of the year for visitation. Elsewhere, living with the Inuit, Brody has reflected on the production of *"maps as a statement of existence"*.[277] In the case of Gabhsann, these mapped associations might equate with the inherent right of crofters who still have exclusive access to areas of the moor for cutting peats to fuel their fires and stoves. It may also include knowledge of the places on the foreshore for the seasonal collection of seafood like the Edible Periwinkle or the Edible Whelk. Although it is now a comparatively rare sight to see anyone hunched over, picking winkles on the strand line at Reidheadal, it still happens now and again, and I have a quiet sense of amazement looking at those soil profiles in the Iron Age midden that show horizons of discarded seashells; a reminder that people have included these shellfish in their diet for thousands of years.

This, then, is the third of my three favourite maps of Gabhsann, a schematic representation of the multiple layers of human ecology in this small township that indicate the ongoing associations between the people who live here and their natural environment.[278]

The oceanic edge of Gabhsann has also provided a ready supply of other seafood for the human residents over the centuries. All along this rocky shore the favourite sites for sea-fishing have long ago been identified and named. There are particularly productive stances on individual slabs and geos, the twists of rock outcrops called An t-srùp, and Stipistean, and Gob an Eòin, which are best visited at different phases of the tide. The catch will vary with the season, and the state of the ocean, as well as the skill of the fishermen, but, within limits, the ocean rarely fails to provide. Saithe, Lythe, and Mackerel have all been hauled ashore by local rock-fishers, and have contributed to the diet of generations of villagers. My mother-in-law would occasionally make a delicious blancmange-type pudding from the delicate, red-coloured seaweed Carrageen which is found on the rocks of lower shore. On the middle and lower shores is also found Dulse, a reddish-brown seaweed that had many uses. It was considered good for the digestion of both humans and livestock, and it was traditionally consumed with oatmeal as a broth, or boiled and pulverised as a treatment to expel intestinal worms, or as a general fever remedy, but also as a general pick-me-up after a long winter. In some areas of the Hebrides, Dulse was considered good to help expel the afterbirth of a labouring mother. Externally, as a poultice, it was applied to soothe burns or sprains. On top of this wide application, Dulse was fairly commonly used throughout the eighteenth century, dried and rolled into a wad, for chewing - before men discovered the addiction of chewing tobacco.[274]

At Tùlaigean, a narrow inlet of the sea just to the north of where the river running through Gabhsann bho Thuath meets the ocean, the village boat used to come ashore and land its catch. The metal stanchion used to secure the boat high above the surf can still be found, half-covered by grass, along the line of the croft boundary fence. When I look down on this geo, I can never be sure which is greater, my admiration for the seamanship required to be able to dock in such a treacherous spot, or my horror at the foolhardiness of such an attempt.

Historically, the primary renewable marine natural resource was seaweed, which was taken from the shore and applied to the crofts as fertiliser to improve the organic-poor soil for cultivation, and while this practice has largely discontinued, there is still a little harvesting by householders for use on domestic vegetable gardens. At various times in the past birds' eggs (particularly gulls, but also plovers) have been harvested from specific sites for home consumption, and local anecdote suggests it was common until the late 1950s. Apart from the evidence emerging over the years from the Iron Age midden on the shore, there is little remaining to document the traditions of hunting birds to augment the diet in Gabhsann, but there is no reason to suppose that it differed significantly here from other parts of the Hebrides.[279] Indeed, the archaeological recoveries throughout the Outer Hebrides, Orkney, and Shetland indicate thousands of years of island fowling traditions.[280] It was a natural part of life on the western fringes of Europe.[281] Seabirds were the most common resource targeted, especially gulls and Gannets (the latter of which are still an important cultural legacy)[282] but also wildfowl and a small assortment of landbirds.[283]

In terms of products *from* the landscape, there can be fewer examples that are more potent indicators of land use than in the harvesting of peats for household fuel. Every possible item involved in this annual activity has its own record in the nomenclature of the moorland.[284] From the topmost part of the peat bank to be cut (an ceap) to the first-cut layer (a' chiad fàd), through the second layer (fàd a' ghàrraidh) to the lowest level of the bank (an caoran), each individual layer of peat is described relative to every other. There are further specific practices and names for how the peats are laid out to dry, and for the shape, consistency, and construction of the final peat stack outside the house. Even the gaps between the peats are named, such as the narrow space along the top of a bank between the low wall of drying peats and the cutting-face of the peat bank, which is called "rathad an isein" (literally, "the bird's road"). These are not random names constructed by plodding etymologists, but rather functional essentials of common practice, ways of relating to the necessities of existence throughout the generations.

The rituals of peat-cutting are part of a cultural system of laying claim to the land and identifying a place of possession, a place of passion. When people in Gabhsann talk about having "a day in the peats" they are *literally* in among the fabric of the land in every sense.

In the landscape

Moving southeast from the villages to stand on the near horizon of the great moorland of Gabhsann, the view over the three contemporary villages is spread out for inspection. What you see constitutes this place, quite literally, for much of the surface vegetation turns into peat, fibre by fibre, layer by layer, and builds these landforms. The underlying skeleton of Lewisian gneiss protrudes through to the surface in only a few scattered localities.

Concepts of sustainability vary with time, with the physical conditions of geographical localities, and with the prevailing cultures and attitudes of individuals within society. Activities that were once thought to be 'sustainable' may eventually prove otherwise, perhaps due to the loss of cheap labour, or because external costs which had previously been written off (such as the dumping of polluted waste into the natural environment to save on clean-up costs) have now become real costs to the business. In the case of Gabhsann, the changes in sustainability are much more labyrinthine to quantify. In one of the very few detailed studies of what sustainability might mean at a very local level, Gabhsann was compared with neighbouring Dail bho Dheas in terms of their specific economy, natural environment, society, and social equity.[285] Both villages came out favourably, but as the author confirmed, the issues are complex. Judgements on the measurements of sustainability are heavily based upon practical matters, such as the choice of indicators, the comparative time frame ("more sustainable than what?") and the ability to gather data at an appropriate scale. Conceptual matters are important too, such as balancing economic gains against environmental losses, or vice versa. Nothing is fixed in perpetuity. Everything changes, and everything is relative to some other reference point or time frame.

We need a cypher for this landscape, for it does not trouble to explain itself easily. Only those who make the effort to attempt to interpret the curves and the protuberances will come close to any awareness of the hidden meanings, the hollows and the events which are part and parcel of this land, but which are its intangible assets. Is there a particular Hebridean epistemology - a way of thinking, a system of inter-linking knowledge that co-evolves with this location? Perhaps.

There *is* an idiom of the land, however, in the way that people speak about it, and how the land relates to this language. In Gabhsann we go *out* to the moor and *in* to the shore. The cultural emphasis is not to look inwards on the island, but to view it as part of a bigger world-view and to look towards the ocean as the way to enter into that cosmos. In a similar manner, we speak, in both Gaelic and English, about going *down* to Nis - and *down north* - rather than up the map. Perhaps this is a vestigial idiom of the Scandinavian heritage of this place, for when the heartland and the homeland is in the far north, directions of travel to other places are seen in this context. (Turn your Ordnance Survey map 180° then try navigating a familiar journey with the map in that orientation to get some idea of travelling back towards yourself by going '*down north*').

There is a suggestion, nothing more, that indigenous people often pay more attention to patterns in the land - the sounds, smells, colours, wind direction - in addition to the physical attributes of that land surface that others see. The specific features that outsiders use for navigation are only background components in a cognitive map that, for the indigenous local person, does not separate geology and topography from places of culture and of wellbeing. It is a natural step to claim this landscape, not simply by giving names to familiar objects or landforms, but by capturing the intrinsic links between places that define patterns of meaning for human interaction with those places.[286] The naming might link the Gabhsann topography with fellow species, such as at Blàr nan Steàrnag (the Field of the Terns) or at Sgeir nan Sgarbh (the Reef of the Shag) or it might have an association with a particular individual, such as my grandfather-in-law Angus Gillies at the well named after him - Tobair Aonghais Ghiolais. Other appellations have been lost to recollection or might commemorate relationships with the landscape that are now only historical, such as at Tom na Bà (The Hillock of the Cattle) or at Tom an ime (The hillock of the butter – which would have been made at the summer sheilings under the old transhumance system). Still other named places are prosaically descriptive, such as A' Chlach Ghorm (The Blue Stone) or the small stream near Barabhas which links two small lochs and is named Allt edar dha loch (The Burn Between Two Lochs). The patterns are not just of the solid land and its vegetation; the places and the distribution of water throughout the land are just as important to know as the drier areas.

There are stories, anecdotes, and mythic events that combine to give a long-term view of this land, and together with the lived experiences of generation after generation of people in Gabhsann, they demonstrate the inadequacy of the creation legends. That is why each new wave of settlers in Gabhsann, whether they came as conquerors or as friends who subsequently intermarried and stayed, have altered and added layers of complexity to the nomenclature of this place. Naming and re-naming the land has created a web of meaning that transcends banal personal descriptions of place to construct a communal understanding. In Gabhsann, there are places named in English, in Gaelic, in Old Norse, and every orthographic or phonetic combination of all three, together with place names that defy linguistic attribution and whose derivation or meaning is lost in time. This is the lexicon of the cultural landscape that we pass to the next generation.

It is for this reason that Barry Lopez writes eloquently on the realisation of being *in* the landscape, not merely standing on the surface trying to observe it dispassionately and thereby attempting to understand it through an over-early or only partial analysis of the information that the senses are gathering.[287] Attempting to stand apart from the landscape will obtain only a superficial understanding at best. In order to get the best from this land, it is necessary to encounter it as an immersive experience. Even to adopt the stance of a 'neutral observer' is to adopt a particular point of view, a particular philosophical perspective of where you feel that you belong in relation to the vastness of this environment.

To spend a night on the moor, watching meteor showers so bright and apparently so close that you fear they might hit you, or to stand in the middle of the night watching the aurora borealis shake its multi-coloured charged particles like shimmering curtains of light, is to be left in no doubt about the totality of being *in* the environment of Gabhsann. No longer merely standing on a patch of earth, the totality and connectedness of the environment becomes self-evident. The clarity and the calmness of a walk in the midnight sun of summer contrasts so perfectly with the cloistered darkness of a midwinter evening, or the intensity of a March storm, that the two different encounters form part of a perfect whole. There is no doubt that the winter gale can be intimidating - Frank Fraser Darling described the ferocity of a storm on North Rona in which he watched the wind rip up the turf and carry it away - but the gales have their place. One time, I was struggling to work in my study and decided to go for a walk in the dying aftermath of a big storm; I reversed my normal route and dropped down to the river to follow it towards the shore. In the comparative shelter of the narrow glen I was shielded from the worst of the blast, but when I popped up onto the boulder beach at Bun na h-abhainn (the Mouth of the River), the effect was almost paralysing. The sudden exposure to the maelstrom of the sea, whipped up by a trans-Atlantic hurricane into a truly terrifying cauldron of foaming surf, and the roar of buffeting winds swirling from every direction in succession, could easily be the stuff of nightmares, yet it serves to remind an individual of the minisculely small role they have in the physical environment of a place like this.

The sounds of Gabhsann are also part of this totality of environment, this immersion of the self in the place. The year 2019 was a good summer for Curlew, and there was hardly a time that I walked the crofts of Gabhsann that I did not hear the mellifluous, almost fluid sound of the cry of one of those birds. Similarly, it was impossible to present a human profile anywhere along the shore without being greeted by the alarm call of an Oystercatcher. The waves, the river, the ubiquitous wind, and the communicating noises made by the various species in Gabhsann, whether resident or simply passing through, form a distinctive sonic landscape which, though sharing a similarity with many other island villages, is unique in itself. A toponymic audio of Gabhsann would include 'surround-sound' that includes the screeching of the Lesser Black-backed Gulls beyond Loch Leiseabhat, the almost apologetic solitary piping of the Golden Plover at the top end of the crofts towards Meagro, and the contrasting, slightly panicky, single note of the Snipe in the damp areas around Bun na h-abhainn. At one time, in the middle of the twentieth century, the sounds pervading the calm air in Gabhsann would also have included the rhythmic, almost hypnotic sound of the clackety-clack of the Hattersley loom, enabling the weaving of Harris Tweed. There is a pattern to this audio profile which changes, season to season, year to year, retaining most of the key aural phrases, but in fact, never repeating exactly the same combination.

In addition to descriptive Gaelic place names, many landforms are known by familiar epithets, describing some characteristic or association of the place, such as 'the misty isle' or 'the isle of barley'. Gabhsann is frequently referred to as "*Gabhsann gorm an fheoir*" (Gabhsann of the blue grass) for like its namesake in the Bluegrass of Kentucky, the braes of Gabhsann have long been regarded as fertile and desirable. It is easy to imagine the colourful splash of lush grass attracting the eye of passing Norse explorers, as well as the envious eyes of the landless families in the overcrowded villages either side of the old Gabhsann Farm. Like the ever-changing colours of the sea and the sky, and the subtly fluctuating colour patterns of the landscape, the sounds of Gabhsann combine with the visual to pervade all of the senses. Few artists have captured the essence of these views as well as Donald 'Dòmhnall Safety' Smith who, with a few lines and emotive dashes of colour, embodied the feeling of this landscape and its inhabitants.[289] Colours and textures, each playing their roles, delineate crofts and landscape slopes, the hollows, hillocks, and habitats, so it should come as no surprise that the patterns of the native cloth, Harris Tweed, find their reflection in the landscape, and the artistic but almost documentary photography of Ian Lawson chronicles these reflections.[290]

Above all, Gabhsann is a place that has to be understood by walking. This is a landscape touched with riches, and the need for harmony with the natural environment, the sights and sounds - the books of mica glistening on the shore, the vivid green of guano-enhanced moorland vegetation - need to be appreciated slowly at close hand, not just from the window of a passing car. As William MacGillivray wrote in his journal as 1817 drew to a close,

"Almost every object in nature may afford pleasure to a mind adapted to receive it from the contemplation of her phenomena." [120]

So, I wonder again, is there a distinctive epistemology of the Outer Hebrides - a system of knowledge, of understanding this place, that differentiates between evidence-based belief and subjective opinion? Certainly, there is a long association that acknowledges a deep spiritual affiliation between the place and its landscape, but is that simply another delusion of the rural idyll, or is there something more to it? Our perceptions of a place, of a landscape (or a city-scape) are conditioned in part by our already established beliefs and desires, as well as by the lived experiences of actually being in that place. To a large extent, we generally see what we want to see, but those perspectives depend on where we are when we view the place. Do we walk *within* the place, or merely on top of it? Aerial views of these islands give a different dimension to the view on the ground, throwing into thought-provoking detail the ruined foundations of cleared settlements that are hard to see on foot.[291] Similarly, the views preserved in the memory of a tourist or an exiled islander are likely to be different from the reality of a permanent resident. The American author and farmer Wendell Berry writes about the synergy between local culture and local memory.[292] Both of these forms of memes accumulate through history, but to be truly meaningful it needs to be a *lived* history and culture, one that enables the knowledge of that place to be handed down and shared, generation to generation. With this pattern of sharing, an understanding, then an affection, then respect, can develop for the place, and then - if we are lucky - a realisation of the intangible grace of being in that place - even during adversity. This constitutes a form of grace which is distinct from any religious associations, but none-the-less can imbue us with a higher order of realisation. This, perhaps, is one aspect of what Neil Gunn called *"the atom of delight"*.

If by saying "sustainable" we mean the long-term ability to survive in a place, then Gabhsann has been a sustainable place for more than five thousand years, with each generation and dominant culture handing over to their successors. The inevitability of change compels us to recognise that, over time, radical change is not the exception, it is the rule. The ability of the human community to cope with change, to have a resilient response to changing social and environmental circumstances, such as overcoming traditional orthodoxies of superstition, religious rituals, or inherited systems of outdated agricultural practices, is what drives a community forward and sustains it. It is what defines our longitudinal relationship with place.

In a total immersive experience of the environment of Gabhsann - the geology and landforms, the history and cultural legacy, the sounds, colours, and weather, the fauna and the flora - there is a combination of realisation that recognises much more than mere scenery. The pellucid awareness of, and attachment to, that "*other landscape*" is analogous to the love between two people, intangible, sometimes unfathomable, but evident and influencing by its cumulative impact. With the DNA of *buntanas* - the cumulative awareness of belonging to a place, such as Gabhsann - comes the responsibility of trust and respect for that place. This belies the myth that rural communities are backwards looking. It simply reiterates a different vision for the future, in which the legacy of past human interactivity with place can suggest alternative means for securing the resilience of future communities.

CHAPTER 10

The distant shore

What next?

When I stand in one of my favourite places in Gabhsann, looking at a BIG seascape, and an even bigger sky, I feel that here, right here, there is enough room to breathe properly, but for how long? On the opening page of his classic and groundbreaking account of living among wild nature on a small island, *A Naturalist on Rona*, (subtitled *Essays of a biologist in isolation*) Frank Fraser Darling wrote:

> "*We speak sometimes of barren coasts because our mind is apt to think in terms of soil and foliage, but they are hardly ever that. To the seeing eye the stark cliffs of the north are as rich and vivid in their own way as that natural fairyland of the pools on the Great Barrier Reef of Australia.*"[106]

Now we are seeing the Great Barrier Reef threatened with despoliation and perhaps destruction, is a similar fate awaiting the "stark cliffs of the north"?

Among the geometric grid lines of places like central Kansas, the houses, the rooms, the beds, the roads, and the lifestyles of the people are aligned unswervingly to the cardinal directions of the compass.[293] In a place like Gabhsann, the houses, the roads, and the people huddle higgledy-piggledy against the prevailing wind and sea, and along the moulded contours of this ancient landscape in a gloriously strident declaration of independent thought. The field shapes of many of the crofts may seem strange but there were solid, practical reasons in their creation and use. It is wise, however, not to over-romanticise. Despite being able to see the iconic, round-topped landform of Tobha Ghabhsainn from her back door, almost exactly two kilometres distant as the crow flies, my mother-in-law had never stood there. She was familiar with the land of the crofts, and had been many times to the moor, to work the peats and to move livestock, but there was a practical purpose behind those tasks. There was no immediate practical need to walk laboriously to the Tobha just to appreciate a different view of the same landscape. Life was often compartmentalised into very functional units of necessity. Making "*good use*" of time included more than simply manual labour and drudgery, but it did require a sensible economy of physical effort when inhabitants were required to learn the art not simply of surviving, but of thriving despite adversity.

Some people seem to wander perpetually across the globe, in search of themselves, looking for something which is obscure but also, to themselves, instantly recognisable. Gabhsann is a place where a similar result can be achieved simply by staying here in perpetuity.

Perpetuity does not mean changeless, however, and although many of these changes remain matters of conjecture, there is plenty that we can say with certainty, without lapsing into science fiction. The future of Gabhsann looks to be equally as fascinating as its past. Let's begin where I started this book, with the fundamental geological structure of Gabhsann. The tectonic movements within the Earth that have driven landmasses across the surface of the planet to create, destroy, and re-create continents, are incredibly slow but inexorable. Just as we know that Gabhsann was once somewhere near the South Pole, we also know that the current latitude and longitude of Gabhsann is not the final destination of this place. The tectonic movements that have shifted continents will continue for many millions of years after the end of our human life span. We know for certain that some oceans will close while other areas will open to create new seas; land will sink under the pressure of subduction, and other regions will collide and buckle to form new mountain ranges. The general process is known, but not the specific details of the future geography, though it is fun to compile the currently available evidence into the animated internet videos that can give us a 'fast-forward' impression of the next 250 million years.[294] Based on what we know about Earth history, we can predict that by that time it is likely that Gabhsann will occupy a location further north on the planet, somewhere near the current North Pole. In the changing environmental conditions that Gabhsann will experience over that huge span of time, the current maritime climate of the oceanic edge will be subjected to many and diverse climatic influences. Sixty million years ago, after the north Atlantic had opened, the climate shifted from a humid, subtropical environment, to a warm, temperate regime. There were swamps off the coast of Harris about thirty million years ago, and these changes were reflected in the geological landscapes of their time.

It is not just the solid geology that is changing, so too is our deeper understanding of the surface processes and the interpretation of the stratigraphic evidence. In early March 2019 I gave a lecture in Edinburgh on the geology of the Isle of Lewis. Soon after I returned to Gabhsann I was contacted by Dr Adrian Hall who had been present at the lecture. Adrian is a physical geographer who has undertaken considerable research on the past glaciations of northern Scotland. He knows the field evidence of the geomorphology of the Gabhsann coast from first-hand experience. He suggested to me that there may be another way of looking at the glacial features of Gabhsann.[295] The conventional theory is that, unlike most of the surrounding area, the land in the vicinity of Gabhsann was relatively ice-free, which could account for the preservation of the raised beach. Now that more recent evidence proves that the mainland ice mass ground its way across Lewis and continued out into the Atlantic, leaving no ice-free enclaves, how is it that the beach gravels in Gabhsann alone escaped destruction? Why have they not been scraped away like similar structures along the west coast of the island, and deposited in the Atlantic Ocean when the ice began to melt? The problem is this: as a result of the advances in new methods of geological dating, together with the use of satellite imagery and improved computer modelling, the current stratigraphic evidence is inconsistent with the idea of an ice-free region around Gabhsann. A month or so afterward, Adrian and I met on a soggy evening to walk along the coastline together.

To be fair, he had suggested this inconsistency over twenty years previously[18] but gathering the conclusive evidence for an alternative interpretation has been slow work. Adrian took me to a small cliff facing Sgarbh Sgeir and we peered closely at the exposed coastal edge of gravel and sand. As along so much of this coastline, there is a rock step in the cliff at about six metres above present sea level. This step, which is seen in Gabhsann as a flat surface about 200 metres wide on the margins of the coast, is covered by sediment, and is clearly an old landscape feature, probably relating to higher sea-levels around the time of the last interglacial 125,000 years ago. Uniquely to the Gabhsann area, a little digging demonstrates that the rock step is overlain by thin, distorted stringers of peat in sand. Pollen trapped in the peat indicates a grassland vegetation with patches of willow and juniper scrub.[296] Immediately above this organic layer is a thin grit bed similar to the spray-thrown sheets seen on our modern cliff edges, and then several metres of beds of brown sand and white rounded gneiss gravel. These are classic beach deposits, which must be younger than the rock step.

Walking along the coastal edge, I was reminded that erratics (rocks of a different type, moved and dumped by ice) such as Torridonian sandstone and Cambrian quartzite from the Scottish mainland, have been found in the till that underlies the Gabhsann beach.[297] The presence of those erratics indicates that moving ice from the mainland of Scotland travelled at least as far as the west coast of Lewis, and more recent evidence shows that at its maximum size, the Scottish ice reached far out to sea, beyond Hiort (St Kilda), to the edge of the continental shelf.

With a quiet conviction, Adrian tried to demonstrate to me as we walked from one exposure to another, that the ice did move across this area, but that the movement was largely within the ice itself. This happens when a glacier is frozen to its bed. The overlying ice sheet then might have little or no underlying effect, even on the soft sediment on its bed. Large parts of Scotland were covered by cold-base ice during the last glaciation, including the lowlands of Buchan and the high tops of the Cairngorms, but the survival of raised beach deposits through a glaciation is unusual. The configuration of the land, the slight rise inland from the shore, encouraged the development of this unusual phenomenon in which the Lewis ice cap, moving towards the northwest, disturbed the sediments of the raised beach only slightly. Instead, the base of the ice, frozen to gravel below, hardly moved, and most of the ice mass rode over the top of the raised beach, slipping due to internal fissures, and continued out to sea.

Pulling all the available evidence together, Adrian's conjecture is that the beach gravel has been deformed by moving ice, and that, in places, there is a thin till resting on the gravel. The evidence is fragmentary and hard to interpret, not least because the gravels have been disturbed by intense frost action under permafrost conditions and surface materials have in places slipped down the slope. The new proposition does account for the evidence, but Adrian is the first to admit that further detailed research would help to clarify the model. He is confident that if the recent research is correct that the last ice sheet extended almost to St Kilda, we cannot have had an ice-free enclave on Lewis. Despite, or perhaps because of, the changing interpretation, the surface geology of the Gabhsann coast remains a crucial locality to aid an understanding of the Late Pleistocene environment of northern Scotland.

There are many other facts about the likely changes in the Outer Hebrides that we can be certain about without any deep scientific knowledge or indulging in the fantasies of crystal-ball gazing. The topography of Gabhsann will continue to change. We can see over a relatively short space of time that the coastline is changing. The ravages of the sea and winter storms erode the soft, unconsolidated sediments, and the constant churn of boulders slowly grinds away at solid rock. In other parts of the Gabhsann shore, great quantities of white shell sand are washed ashore to create a temporary beach, and a few months later the sand will disappear again to be relocated further along the coast. It is clear from aerial photographs, as well as from period drawings by artists like William Daniell, that the present day shoreline is not the same as the historical oceanic margin. The rates of erosion vary at different points, depending on the substrate, the weather, and the sea, but I can confidently remember the loss of five or six metres over the last thirty years from the coastal end of the crofts in Gabhsann bho Dheas on the stretch between the road to the shore and the graveyard. The boulder beach at Bun na h-abhainn changes shape constantly and noisily during every big storm. We can be sure that the configurations of the Gabhsann shore that are described in the classic work on *The Coastline of Scotland*[298] will not be the same one that our children, or their grandchildren, will look at. The indentations of the coast are constantly changing. Geologically speaking, we are living in an interglacial period – the span of time separating two ice ages. It is certain that the combination of coastal erosion and the rise or fall of the sea level, as global ice accumulates or melts, will ensure that the coastline of Gabhsann, and the shape of Lewis, will look very different in the millennia to come.

Global and regional climate change will vary the local effect of sea level rise in different situations but change itself is certain. Global sea level rose between 16 and 21 cm between 1900 and 2016, with the rate of rise accelerating, and expected to accelerate further during this century.[299] The current trend is approximately 30 cm rise per century,[300] which is perhaps not much in the geological context, but would certainly increase current rates of coastal erosion and would further destabilise contemporary sand dunes and machair landscapes. New research that assesses the risks of future climate change upon world-class heritage sites in other island communities, such as Orkney is worrying. [301] Coastal locations are especially vulnerable, of course, and there has been talk about preparing contingency plans to dismantle and reconstruct further inland sites such as Skara Brae in order to avoid losing the heritage legacy entirely. For Gabhsann, a short-term rise in sea level of 30 cm would encourage increased removal of the soft gravels and sands of the raised beach and would threaten the destruction of the ancient cemetery, including the chapel whose image was painted by William Daniell. Over the course of the next three-and-a-half thousand years we can expect the sea to rise ten metres and flood the lower edge of the raised beach platform, sending exploratory tongues of sea inlets up the mouths of the two rivers in Gabhsann. Gone will be the Iron Age midden and the ocean will cover the site of the ruined Dùn Sabhuill. Ten thousand years from now, still well within the anticipated duration of the present interglacial, we might anticipate a thirty metre sea level rise, raising the coastline above the height of several of the village roads and covering with seawater substantial parts of the three current villages of Gabhsann bho Dheas, Gabhsann bho Thuath, and Mealabost. The two Gabhsann river valleys would become small sea-lochs, breaching the main A857 road in two places and spilling tentatively into the moor. The remains of the Viking settlement will be underwater, and of the currently known archaeological sites, only those on the high ground, such as at Dùn Bhuirgh and Dùn Bharabhat, will be on dry land.

Both the changes to the surface geomorphology of the Gabhsann landscape and the vectors which mark the shape of the coastline will, to some extent, be determined by the regional climate and the prevailing weather. Over coffees with my colleague at the University of the Highlands and Islands, Dr Edward (Eddy) Graham, we have tried to understand the changing nature of the climate of the Outer Hebrides. Climatic changes in recent decades can be accurately documented, and although there can be considerable regional variation, there has been a well-documented 40-60% increase in rainfall since the 1970s. Both seasons of the relatively warm (but not hot) summers and mild (but not generally freezing) Outer Hebridean winters have been getting warmer. There are so many variable factors that affect climate-change that the only thing absolutely certain about future climate changes is their uncertainty.[303] Over the short-term, (by the end of this century) the climate migration accompanying global warming will probably result in Gabhsann having a maritime climatic regime somewhat similar to present-day Killarney, in the southwest of Ireland. The disruption by thermal warming and expansion of oceanic temperatures, however, and the likelihood of further melting of the Greenland icecap, will result in an acceleration of the current trend for several winter storms to become stronger in intensity. (A retired ferry Captain described to me that, during his career, the frequency of the severe storms normally encountered in the north Atlantic between Scotland and Iceland, has moved south to the latitude of Lewis, and the storms historically affecting the northern Hebrides are now occurring in the north of Ireland.)

Disturbingly, the damaging effect of human activities is not simply what we can observe on the land and in the atmosphere: the seas around Gabhsann are being affected too. Thirty or forty years ago it was mostly driftwood that was washed up by the sea, which we would sometimes gather and use in summer for the occasional beach bonfire with campfire food. Now the waste washed up is a constant detritus of plastic, no matter how many beach clean-up days we organise. It also affects us in other ways that we can rarely observe directly. At the end of August 2018 two large carcasses were washed ashore on the shingle beach near Gob an Eòin. They were about seven metres long, and mostly skeletal, with a strong backbone as thick as the thigh of a large man. Samples of the remaining flesh and blubber were taken for examination by the Scottish Marine Animal Stranding Scheme, and they were identified as Cuvier's Beaked Whales, the marine mammals that dive deepest and for the longest duration. For this species to be cast ashore in Gabhsann is worrying, and joins the unsolved case notes of several other rare whales that have been found cast ashore on the western coasts of the UK. One suggestion for the deaths is that it is the result of military operations seeking hidden submarines, as some post-mortems show evidence of sonic shock, and information from other parts of the world indicates that mid-frequency sonar disrupts the whales' behaviour.[302] All species will be affected to some extent, of course. Less sea-ice will mean a loss of habitat for Polar Bears and greater potential for Grey Seals to expand their range, but the habitat available for humans at this latitude is a little more uncertain. In some regions, the 2020 global 'lockdown' has resulted in reduced environmental pollution and human disturbance, but how long will this continue?

Regardless of the extent of forthcoming climate changes, the prediction of and responses to any climate change are a key concern for the ecology of the future. Landscapes are neither primitive nor permanent; they evolve. Differential weathering breaks down rock to soil, which varies in chemistry with the geology of the rock. Changes in soil type, such as a faster rate of accumulation of peat as rainfall and humidity increase, or the recycling of machair sandscapes, will continue to influence the vegetational covering of the landscape. Over millennia, the physical effects of climate, weather, and soil chemistry have influenced the manner in which the species of the plants and animals in Gabhsann fit together, even though the abundance, distribution, and inter-relationships of these species are constantly changing. Pollen analysis indicates that the late glacial landscapes of this area supported a discontinuous vegetative cover of dwarf-shrubs and herbs until about 4400 years ago when ecosystem changes encouraged replacement by blanket peat, possibly changing substantially over less than 100 years.[304] Some plant species are currently living at the northern, or southern, limits of their natural range, and any changes in climate might result in local extinctions or the expansion of territory by colonisation. For this reason, some scientists think that, particularly in challenging ocean environments, the ecosystem health, rather than the wealth of biodiversity, might be a better predictor of ecological change.[305]

With future changes in climate and in the utilisation of the moor for livestock grazing, there may be a localised recolonisation by some tree species. Crofting as part-time subsistence agriculture has evolved because of a specific combination of cultural, political, and environmental factors. It has survived despite, and possibly because of, its unorthodoxy. If earlier inhabitants of places like Gabhsann had listened to the 'voices of reason' propounding fundamentalist capitalist and centralist philosophies of 'improvement' there would have been a very different history of the dispossessed to read about.[306] The more empathetic of contemporary historians recognise that the history of the Clearances, and the contemporary crofting community, are only single aspects in a continuum of change that may yet see the repopulation and revitalisation of currently uninhabited landscapes.[192] Crofting in the future may not depend upon sheep and cattle any more than it did upon kelp harvesting, perhaps low volume-high value crops like herbs will be exported, for thriving at the edge of agriculture requires innovation. Throughout its history, Gabhsann has provided a measure of survival for a population who worked lazy beds, or collective run-rig, moving from subsistence crofting to a farm and back to a re-settled crofting village. The structure of land occupation has gone from communal clan territory, through a process of internal colonization which, *"was a major contribution to a historical process of social and cultural disintegration"* to the creation of estates run in a different system, almost like colonial fiefdoms.[307] The most recent development, in which the land is owned by the whole community, currently seems to be exceptionally promising as the most resilient and the most exciting of the historical iterations of land management of the Gabhsann area.

It has long been understood that having a heightened 'sense of place' about a particular locality tends to create a feeling of personal attachment to that locality, however vague or indefinite it has been to measure that strength of that awareness. What is comparatively new, however, is the growing understanding of specific connections between the 'belongingness' that a sense of place encourages – the *buntanas* of the Gael – and the motivation to take responsibility for the environmental and social health of that place. Researchers are clear that:

> *"Sense of place has been shown to be a key factor in adaptation to ecosystem changes, and transformations, as well as playing an important role in people's motivation to act on behalf of local environments... The connections between people, place, and nature also help us to understand the social motivations and identify and develop pathways towards sustainability."* [308]

In other words, greater community awareness of a sense of place encourages a deeper appreciation of the value of that place. With the community ability to own and manage such places, a perspective is favoured which encourages long-term sustainability rather than management for short-term environmental exploitation. A sense of place can contribute to environmental stewardship and to the priorities for ecosystem management. There is a recognisable association between property rights which govern the use of natural resources - thereby influencing sustainable or unsustainable landuse – and the resilience of communities to adapt to changes in their physical, economic, or social environments. There is a clear link between social and ecological resilience.[309]

Islands and island communities make a disproportionately large contribution to the total biodiversity of the Earth, due in part to the occurrence of unique species of plants and animals found only on certain islands.[78] Island communities, however, are not isolated nor totally exempt from the changes affecting other parts of the world. It has been argued that we are entering a new geological age, the Anthropocene, marking the recognition of human-induced changes to our planet. Although it is tempting to point to features such as the strata of shells among the layers of sand in the Gabhsann Iron Age midden, or the use of fire to clear forests for farming, or even the possible role of humans in the formation of the Hebridean machair,[310] these are local events, not global. For this reason, many scientists prefer the identification of the world-wide, synchronous appearance of post-Second World War nuclear fallout as a specific marker for the start of the Anthropocene.[311] In the Anthropocene, island ecosystems and communities cannot be considered to be isolated from global changes such as sea-level rise, climatic alterations, or atmospheric and oceanic pollution. Rather than islands being simple models of human ecology, they are becoming recognised as complex systems whose complexity is endangered.[312] With the changing understanding of this complexity, there has been a revaluation of the importance of local knowledge in managing and protecting island environments and communities.[116] It hardly needs revpeating that the relatively recent appearance of cities and the speed of their growth are the polar opposite of the rural sense of place that has collective experience in adapting to, and implementing, local changes over millennia. It seems that the imperative of place-based knowledge and community-based resources management might have come a full historical circle.

We tend to think of time as a constant, but in fact our perceptions are fickle and relativistic. The duration of isotopic decay to form new elements in the Precambrian rocks of Gabhsann is measured against a different scale of events from the chronology of the social history of human society, which is different again from the milestones in the lifespan of an individual human. The place called Gabhsann has experienced successive waves of human settlement, and this is likely to continue. At one time Gabhsann was dominated by the influence of Irish culture; later it 'belonged' to Norway, with a corresponding cultural realignment, and still later it became a part of Scotland and then of the UK. At the present moment, it appears that there may be further European cultural shifts imminent. Gabhsann, and Lewis as a whole, are more culturally and linguistically diverse than at any time in history. What language did the earliest settlers speak? Was there a distinctive Hebridean Norse dialect? The changes from the first-used languages, to Norse, then to Scottish Gaelic, were accompanied by changing circumstances of power and influence, economically, culturally, and politically. At one time in history there was at least one immediately recognisable isogloss - a line on the map that marked the boundary of an area having a distinct linguistic feature - but now gradations in the sense of place are much more varied and much more intangible.

The myth of the timeless countryside has been shown to be just that - a myth - but the illusion of rurality as 'remote', 'backwards' and having a leisurely lifestyle, persists as a pejorative construction, despite evidence to the contrary. Throughout history, rural places have essentially been viewed as places for extractive exploitation by urban populations - for food, timber, and minerals.[313] The relationships are never simple, however, and even in a land area as small as Gabhsann, human settlements have appeared and disappeared. There have been at least half a dozen separate villages in the landscape of Gabhsann. In recent years, Tom na Ba has begun to emerge as a new extension, and this subtopian landscape perhaps begins to challenge the nature of suburbia itself. Do we take on the characteristics of the landscape where we choose to settle, or are we drawn to a landscape because of those characteristics? (There are apocryphal tales in North America of plains dwellers who became terrified by the enveloping claustrophobia of the mountains, and correspondingly mountain dwellers who got overcome by the apparently limitless boundaries of space in the plains.)

Changes in the symbols on a map reflect changing representations of time, but also of our relationships with the land. Although the turf dyke of the Gàradh Dubh, marking the moorland boundary of Gabhsann, has been visible for perhaps two hundred years, it is easy to understand that it is slowly losing its distinctive lines as the soil crumbles and the vegetation grows differentially to cover it. Apart from the re-use of stones for new buildings, it is more difficult to understand why some buildings (such as a dùn) can survive and another, contemporaneous, building falls into a ruin of stones and returns into the landscape. It is easy, also, to appreciate how traditional tools of the land might become obsolete, such as the tairisgean for cutting peat for fuel, or the sùist (flail) for hand-threshing corn, but less easy to perceive the changing habitats that wildlife will utilise. Even with the careful monitoring of Red Deer movements, or observing the behaviour of Skuas, Fulmars, or Corncrake as they expand or contract their breeding territories in response to the stimuli of their natural environment, the speed and subtlety of the changes are often only obvious in retrospect. At present we can only speculate on how bird migration will be affected by alterations to the landscape (both naturally-occurring and anthropogenic) or by the influences of future climate change. I have recorded more than seventy species of birds in Gabhsann so far, (Appendix 3) and we know from historical records that once common species such as Red Grouse are now comparatively scarce, but we do not yet know the numbers, distribution, or identification of the birds that will in future regard Gabhsann as 'their' territory. We only know that it will be a different combination from that which can be recorded at the present. It is not without significance that the largest contiguous area that returned no records at all in the 2018 Biological Recording report for the Outer Hebrides are the six 10km grid squares that cover the moor of Gabhsann and the adjacent larger area of northern Lewis.[314] There is still a huge potential to know the environment of this landscape better.

The past three hundred years have witnessed a sequence of changing attitudes of successive visitors to the Highlands and Islands, from a macabre fascination, through curiosity, to the discovery of pleasure and spiritual renewal in the natural environment.[117] Have we arrived at the stage where we cannot reconcile the seemingly contradictory acts of valuing heritage, while simultaneously threatening to destroy it by drawing attention to its distinctiveness? Will the uniqueness of a place such as Gabhsann be able to capitalise on the unique assets of its sense of place - perhaps renewable energy from winds and waves, non-extractive tourist attractions such as Dark Sky stellar appreciation, or the distinctive oral and musical culture - or will these too become commoditized solely for the benefit of others? Intimacy with the natural environment of island life has been cherished as a test of the individual ego [119] and the resilient island response to economic uncertainty has historically encouraged multiple job-holding.[315] Is this an intuitive response to the rural lifestyle, or like the old farmers in Gabhsann who impounded the straying livestock of neighbouring crofters until a fine had been paid, is this merely economic opportunism? The Scottish 'right to roam' the countryside and the growth in popularity (and success) of community-owned land enterprises promise opportunities for a meaningful reconnection of both rural and urban dwellers with the real spirit of a place, but awareness without the acceptance of responsibility is ultimately a devaluing and a diminution of both the sense of a place and of the worth of an individual. This country, and this place, are in constant change, which is carefully and consistently documented and analysed.[316] How we respond to that change is as much a response to our awareness of the history of this place as it is the result of our future actions.

Neurologists tell us that one of the 'purposes' of our memory is to enable humans to make predictive decisions on our future actions which are based on our recollection of past experiences.[317] Without our recourse to the memory of things past, it would be difficult, if not impossible, to imagine the results of future actions. This being the case, it is intriguing to contemplate what a future inhabitant of Gabhsann, 5000 years in the future, will consider to be the highlights of the collective memory of the previous 10,000 years of this place. Imagine that future inhabitant of Gabhsann sitting beside the white surf on a rock that once an Iron Age resident has sat upon, or standing on Beinn Dail looking over the moor of north Lewis, in all likelihood the only human in an area of more than 200 square kilometres, (an area significantly larger than Glasgow, or Manchester, or Dublin). Will they have an informed recollection from the collective memory of previous generations, or simply an ephemeral knowledge of this place as obscure as our mental image of the ancient sagas? When everyone has their own high resolution camera, they are perhaps at risk of reducing the impact of their direct experience to a series of digital snapshots that are never again looked at, and will remain disconnected in memory from the actual events. The sense of place becomes a disposable emotion, localised in the individual, not in a specific location. Will that future inhabitant of Gabhsann share a fate in common with Dark Mairi of the Shore, the key character in Neil Gunn's tragic novel of the Clearances, *Butcher's Broom,* who is the mystical embodiment of her land, and who at the end is conveyed to '*the distant shore*'? [318] Or will the sense of place felt by that inhabitant be more akin to Mary MacLeod, Màiri nighean Alasdair Ruaidh, from Rodel in Harris, the seventeenth century poetess of the MacLeods who chose credibility over gullibility by allegedly demanding that she should be buried face-down because she preferred to spend eternity looking towards the good soil of Harris rather than the promises of a Heaven in the sky?[319]

In the sixth century BC, the Greek philosopher Heraclitus propounded his ideas around his belief that the only thing in the universe that is constant, is change - that everything that seems to be fixed and eternal is actually in a process of constant change. His philosophy might have been based upon more abstract and esoteric ponderings, but 2600 years later, we can appreciate his logic when it is applied to the epistemology of the totality of knowledge of a place such as Gabhsann. Taking a lesson from the Scottish geographer Patrick Geddes, who encouraged people to "Think globally, act locally", we now recognise that the more we know, the more we realise what we do not know, and this makes the study of Gabhsann even more enthralling.

Although an argument can effectively be made that every place is unique because each place is socially as well as physically constructed, some places are undoubtedly much more distinctive than others. To take a diameter from one surface of our planet, passing through the core of the Earth, to its opposite antipodean location, is an intriguing but sometimes frustrating geographical game. A polar diameter from say just north of Timbuktu will emerge somewhere in the middle of Fiji, and a diameter from a spot between Madrid and Salamanca will have its antipodean partner in the vicinity of Wellington, New Zealand. The antipodean site of Gabhsann, however, has no known terrestrial equivalent, emerging at a watery location in the southern Pacific, midway between New Zealand and the coast of the Ross Dependency in Antarctica. Some places, it seems, are destined to possess a singular sense of place. Gabhsann is such a place.

Endnotes

1. The first 3 billion years

On the rocks

1. Cocks, L. R. M. and Torsvik, T. H. (2002). Earth geography from 500 to 400 million years ago: a faunal and palaeomagnetic review. J. of the Geol. Soc. Lond. 159 pp 631-644. https://doi.org/10.1144/0016-764901-118

2. Miyashiro, A. (2013). Metamorphism and metamorphic belts. London: Springer. ISBN 0-04-550026-6.

3. Smith, D. I. And Fettes, D. J. (1979). The geological framework of the Outer Hebrides. Proc. Roy. Soc. Edinb. 77B, pp 75-83.

4. Watson, J. (1977). The Outer Hebrides: a geological perspective. Proc. Geol. Assoc. Lond. 88, pp 1-14.

5. Smythe, D. K. (1987). Deep seismic reflection profiling of the Lewisian foreland. From: Park, R. G. and Tarney, J. (Eds.) Evolution of the Lewisian and Comparable Precambrian High Grade Terrains, Geological Society Special Publication No. 27, pp 193-203.

The nuclear clock

6. Whitehouse, M. J. (1990). An early Proterozoic age of the Ness anorthosite, Lewis, Outer Hebrides. Scott. J. Geol. 26 (2), pp 131-136.

7. Friend, C. R. L. and Kinny, P. D. (2001). A reappraisal of the Lewisian Gneiss Complex: geochronological evidence for its tectonic assembly from disparate terranes in the Proterozoic. Contrib. Mineral. Petrol. 142, pp 198-218. https://doi.org/10.1007/s004100100283

8. Sobel, D. (1996). Longitude. London: Fourth Estate. ISBN 1-85702-502-4.

9.Cocks, L. R. M. and Torsvik, T. H. (2005). Baltica from the late Precambrian to mid-Palaeozoic times: The gain and loss of a terrane's identity. Earth-Science Reviews 72, pp 39-66. https://doi.org/10.1016/j.earscirev.2005.04.001

10. Torsvik, T. H. (1998). Palaeozoic palaeogeography: A North Atlantic viewpoint, GFF 120 (2), pp 109-118.

11. McKirdy, A. (2018). The Outer Hebrides: Landscapes in stone. Edinburgh: Birlinn. ISBN 978-1-78027-509-3.

12. Torsvik, T. H. and Trench, A. (1991). The Ordovician history of the Iapetus Ocean in Britain: new palaeomagnetic constraints. Journal of the Geological Society 148, pp 423-425.

13. Trench, A., Torsvik, T. H. and McKerrow, W. S. (1992). The palaeogeographic evolution of Southern Britain during early Palaeozoic times: a reconciliation of palaeomagnetic and biogeographic evidence. Tectonophysics 201, pp 75-82.

Wearing down and raising up

14. Steel, R. J. (1971). New Red Sandstone movement on the Minch Fault. Nature, Physical Science 234, pp 158-9.

15. Steel, R. J. and Wilson, A. C. (1975). Sedimentation and tectonism (?Permo-Triassic) on the margin of the North Minch Basin, Lewis. J. Geol. Soc. Lond. 131, pp 183-202.

16. Von Weymarn, J. A. (1974). Coastline development in Lewis and Harris, Outer Hebrides, with particular reference to the effects of glaciation. Unpublished PhD thesis, Univ. of Aberdeen.

17. Von Weymarn, J. A. (1979). A new concept of glaciation in Lewis and Harris, Outer Hebrides. Proc. Roy. Soc. Edinb. 77B, pp 97-105.

2. The living blanket of the land

The dirt beneath my nails

18. Hall, A.M. (1995). Was North-west Lewis glaciated during the Late Devensian? Quaternary Newsletter 76 pp 1-7.

19. Glentworth, R. (1979). Observations on the soils of the Outer Hebrides. Proc. Roy. Soc. Edinburgh 77B pp 123-137.

20. Hudson, G. (1991). Geomorphology and Soils of the Outer Hebrides. pp 19-27 in Pankhurst, R.J. and Mullin, J.M., Flora of the Outer Hebrides. London: HMSO. ISBN 0-11-310047-7.

21. Fossitt, J.A. (1996). Late Quaternary vegetation history of the Western Isles of Scotland. New Phytol. 132 pp 171-196.

22. Tipping, R. (1994). The form and fate of Scotland's woodlands. Proc. Soc. Antiq. Scot. 124 pp 1-54.

23. Wilkins, D.A. (1984). The Flandrian woods of Lewis (Scotland). J. of Ecology 72 pp 251-258.

24. Angus, S. (2001). The Outer Hebrides: Moor and Machair. Cambridge: The White Horse Press. ISBN 1-874267-48-0.

Perceptions of place

25.Black, W. (1892). A Princes of Thule. London.

26. Hunter, J. (1995). On the other side of sorrow: Nature and People in the Scottish Highlands. Edinburgh: Mainstream. ISBN 1-85158-765-9.

27. Pankhurst, R. J. and Mullin, J. M. (1991). The flora of the Outer Hebrides. London: HMSO. ISBN 0-11-310047-7.

28. Birks, H.J.B. (1991). Floristic and Vegetational History of the Outer Hebrides. pp 32-37 in Pankhurst, R.J. and Mullin, J.M., Flora of the Outer Hebrides. London: HMSO. ISBN 0-11-310047-7.

29. Chambers, R. (1983). Rural Development: Putting the Last First. London: Longman. ISBN 0-582-64443-7.

30. Currie, A. (1979). The vegetation of the Outer Hebrides. In Proc. of the Royal Soc. of Edinburgh 77B, pp 219-265

31. Darling, F. F. And Boyd, J.M. (1964). Natural History in the Highlands and Islands. London: Collins.

32. MacGillivray, W. (1830). Account of the series of islands usually denominated the Outer Hebrides. Edinburg J. Nat. Geog. Sci 1 pp 245-250, 401-411; 2 pp 87-95, 160-165, 321-334.

33. Sabbagh, K. (2016). A Rum affair. Edinburgh: Birlinn. ISBN 978-1-78027-386-0.

The Moor

34. Manley, G. (1979). The climatic environment of the Outer Hebrides. Proc. Roy. Soc. Edinburgh 77B pp 47-59.

35. Vögler, A., Venugopal, V. and Armstrong, D. (2015). Wave sensor observations during a severe storm event at a marine energy development site. Proc. 11th European Wave and Tidal Energy Conference, Nantes, 6-11 September 2015 www.uhi.ac.uk/en/merika/events/previous-events/ewtec-2015

36. Seager, R. Battisti, D.S., Yin, J., Gordon, N., Naik, N., Clement, A.C. and Cane, M.A. (2002). Is the Gulf Stream responsible for Europe's mild winters? Quart. J. of the Roy. Metrological Soc., 128 (No. 586 October, Part B) pp 2563-2586. https://doi.org/10.1256/qj.01.128

A square metre of discovery

38. Goode, D.A. and Lindsay, R.A. (1979). The peatland vegetation of Lewis. Proc. Roy. Soc. Edinburgh 77B pp 279-293.

Carnivorous plants and other delights

39. Thum, M. (1986). Segregation of habitat and prey in two sympatric carnivorous plant species, Drosera rotundifolia and Drosera intermedia. Oecologia, 70 pp 601-605.

40. Schulze, W. and Schulze, E.-D. (1990). Insect capture and growth of the insectivorous Drosera rotundifolia L. Oecologia, 82 pp 427-429.

41.Ellison, A.M. And Gotelli, N.J. (2001). Evolutionary ecology of carnivorous plants. Trends in Ecology and Evolution, 16 (11) pp 623-629. https://doi.org/10.1016/S0169-5347(01)02269-8

42. Pavlovič, A., Krausko, M. and Adamec, L. (2016). A carnivorous sundew plant prefers protein over chitin as a source of nitrogen from its traps. Plant Physiology and Biochemistry, 104 pp 11-16. doi: http://dx.doi.org/10.1016/j.plaphy.2016.03.008

43. Gunn, N. M. (1988). The other landscape. Glasgow: Richard Drew Publishing. ISBN 0-86267-227-9.

44. Chatwin, B. (1987). The Songlines. London: Pan Books. ISBN 0-330-30082-2.

45. Callicott, J.B. and Nelson, M.P. (Eds.) (1998). The great new wilderness debate. London: University of Georgia Press. ISBN 0-8203-1984-8.

46. Darling, F.F. (Ed.) (1955). West Highland Survey: An essay in Human Ecology. London: Oxford University Press.

47. Darling, F.F. (1970). Wilderness and Plenty: The Reith Lectures 1969. London: Ballantine Books. SBN 345-02159-2.

48. Lopez, B. (1986). Arctic Dreams. London: Picador. ISBN 0-330-29538-1.

3. A metropolis of birds

The first residents

49. Worthy, T. H. (2011). Descriptions and phylogenetic relationships of a new genus and two new species of Oligo-Miocene cormorants (Aves: Phalacrocoracidae) from Australia. Zoological J. of the Linnean Soc. of London 163 (1) pp 277-314. https://doi.org/10.1111/j.1096-3642.2011.00693.x

50. Kennedy, M. and Spencer, H. G. (2014). Classification of the cormorants of the world. Molecular Phylogenetics and Evolution, 79 pp 249-257. http://dx.doi.org/10.1016/j.ympev.2014.06.020

51. Fortin, M., Bost, C-A., Maes, P. and Barbraud, C. (2013). The demography and ecology of the European shag Phalacrocorax aristotelis in Mor Braz, France. Aquatic Living Resources, 26 pp 179-185. https://doi.org/10.1051/alr/2012041

52. Cramp, S., Bourne, W. R. P., and Saunders, D. (1976) The seabirds of Britain and Ireland. London: Collins.

53. Egevang, C., Stenhouse, I. J., Phillips, R. A., Petersen, A., Fox, J. W., and Silk, J.R.D. (2010). Tracking of Arctic terns Sterna paradisaea reveals longest animal migration. Proc. Nat. Acad. Of Sciences of the USA, 107 (5) pp 2078-2081. doi: www.pnas.org/cgi/doi/10.1073/pnas.0909493107

54. Smith, M., Bolton, M., Okill, D. J., Summers, R. W., Ellis, P., Liechti, F., and Wilson, J. D. (2014). Geolocator tagging reveals Pacific migration of Red-necked Phalarope Phalaropus lobatus breeding in Scotland. Ibis, 156 pp 870-873. https://doi.org/10.1111/ibi.12196

The ubiquitous gulls

55. Klaassen, R. H. G., Ens, B. J., Shamoun-Baranes, J., Exi, K-L. and Bairlein, F. (2011). Migration strategy of a flight generalist, the Lesser Black-backed Gull Larus fuscus. Behavioral Ecology 23 (1), pp 58-68. https://doi.org/10.1093/beheco/arr150

56. Nicolson, A. (2017). The seabird's cry: The lives and loves of Puffins, Gannets and other ocean voyagers. London: William Collins. ISBN 978-0-00-816569-7.

57. Currie, A. (1979). The vegetation of the Outer Hebrides. In Proc. of the Royal Soc. of Edinburgh 77B, pp 219-265.

58. Rennie, F. W. (1988). The status and distribution of the Great Skua in the Western Isles. Scottish Birds, 15 pp 80-82.

59. Furness, R.W. (1987). The skuas. Calton: Poyser. ISBN 0-85661-046-1.

60. Nelson, B. (1980). Seabirds: Their biology and ecology. London: Hamlyn. ISBN 0-600-38227-3.

61. Milwright, R. D. P. (2002). Redwing Turdus iliacus migration and wintering areas as shown by recoveries of birds ringed in the breeding season in Fennoscandia, Poland, the Baltic Republics, Russia, Siberia and Iceland. Ringing and Migration, 21 pp 5-15. https://doi.org/10.1080/03078698.2002.9674271

The visitors

62. Wotton, S. R., Eaton, M., Ewing, S. R., and Green, R. E. (2015). The increase in the Corncrake Crex crex population of the United Kingdom has slowed. Bird Study, 62 pp 486-497. doi: http://dx.doi.org/10.1080/00063657.2015.1089837

63. Green, R. and Riley, H. (1999). Corncrakes. Battleby: SNH Publications. ISBN 1-85397-049-2.

64. Walther, B. A., Taylor, P. B., Schäffer, N., Robinson, S.., and Jiguet, F. (2012). The African wintering distribution and ecology of the Corncrake Crex crex. Bird Conservation International, 23, pp 309-322. https://doi.org/10.1017/S0959270912000159

65. Swennen, C., De Bruijn, L.L.M., Duiven, P., Leopold, M.F. and Marteijn, E.C.L. (1983). Differences in bill form of the Oystercatcher Haematopus ostralegus: A dynamic adaptation to specific foraging techniques. Netherlands J. of Sea Research, 17 (1) pp 57-83.

66. Skúlason, S. and Smith, T.B. (1995). Resource polymorphism in vertebrates. Trends in Ecology and Evolution 10 (9) pp 366-370.

67. Goss-Custard, J.D. and Sutherland, W.J. (1984). Feeding specializations in Oystercatchers Haematopus ostralegus. Animal Behaviour 32 (1) pp 299-301.

Belonging to place

68. Coombs, F. (1978). The Crows. London: Batsford. ISBN 0-7134-1327-1

69. Brown, L. (1976). British Birds of Prey. Collins New Naturalist Series (No. 60): Collins: London. ISBN 0-00-219405-8.

70. Love, J.A. (1983). The return of the Sea Eagle. Cambridge: Cambridge University Press. ISBN 0-521-25513-9.

71. Shannon, T.J., McGowan, R.Y., Zonfrillo, B., Piertney, S. and Collinson, J.M. (2014). A genetic screen of the island races of Wren Troglodytes troglodytes in the North-east Atlantic. Bird Study 61 pp 135-142. http://dx.doi.org/10.1080/00063657.2014.894493

72. Armstrong, E.A. (1953). The behaviour and breeding biology of the Hebridean Wren. British Birds 46 (2) (Feb.) pp 37-50.

73. Jakubas, D. and Manikowska, B. (2011). The response of Grey Herons Ardea cinerea to changes in prey abundance. Bird Study 58 (4) pp 487-494. https://doi.org/10.1080/00063657.2011.608423

74. Thom, V. M. (1986). Birds in Scotland. Calton: Poyser. ISBN 0-85661-040-2.

75. Vaughan, R. (1980). Plovers. Lavenham: Terence Dalton Ltd. ISBN 0-900963-36-0.

76. Parr, R. (1980). Population study of Golden Plover Pluvialis apricaria, using marked birds. Ornis Scandinavica 11 pp 179-189.

77. Delingat, J., Bairlein, F. and Hedenström, A. (2008). Obligatory barrier crossing and adaptive fuel management in migratory birds: the case of the Atlantic crossing in Northern Wheatears (Oenanthe oenanthe). Behav. Ecol. Sociobiol 62 pp 1069-1078. https://doi.org/10.1007/s00265-007-0534-8

78. Kueffer, C. and Kinney, K. (2017). What is the importance of islands to environmental conservation? Environmental Conservation 44 (4) pp 311-322. https://doi.org/10.1017/S0376892917000479

4. Animals come (and go)

The Ark in the Archive

79. Harvie-Brown, J. A. and Buckley, T. E. (1888). A vertebrate fauna of the Outer Hebrides. Edinburgh: D. Douglas.

80. Hurrell, H.G. (1968). Pine Martens. Forestry Commission Record No. 64. London: HMSO. ISBN 0-11-710085-4.

81. Clegg, S. M. and Owens, I. P. F. (2002). The 'island rule' in birds: medium body size and its ecological explanation. Proc. Roy. Soc. Lond. 269 B, pp 1359-1365. https://doi.org/10.1098/rspb.2002.2024

82. Lomolino, M. V. (2005). Body size evolution in insular vertebrates: generality of the island rule. J. of Biogeography 32 pp 1683-1699. https://doi.org/10.1111/j.1365-2699.2005.01314.x

83. Serjeantson, D. (1990). The introduction of mammals to the Outer Hebrides and the role of boats in stock management. Anthropozoologica 13 pp 7-18.

84. Edwards, K. J. and Ralston, I. B. M. (Eds.) (1997). Scotland after the Ice Age: Environment, Archaeology and History, 8000 BC – AD 1000. Edinburgh: Edinburgh University Press. ISBN 0-7486-1736-1.

85. Berry, R.J. (1979). The Outer Hebrides: where genes and geography meet. Proc. Roy. Soc. Edinburgh 77B pp 21-43.

86. Waters, J., Darvill, B., Lye, G. C., and Goulson, D. (2011). Niche differentiation of a cryptic bumblebee complex in the Western Isles of Scotland. Insect Conservation and Diversity 4 pp 46-52. https://doi.org/10.1111/j.1752-4598.2010.00101.x

87. Redpath, N., Osgathorpe, L. M., Park, K., Goulson, D. (2010). Crofting and

bumblebee conservation: The impact of land management practices on bumblebee populations in northwest Scotland. Biological Conservation 143 pp 492-500. https://doi.org/10.1016/j.biocon.2009.11.019

88. Gammans, N., Comont, R., Morgan, S. C., and Perkins, G. (Eds.) (2018). Bumblebees: An introduction. Eastleigh: Bumblebee Conservation Trust. ISBN 978-0-9957739-0-5.

89. Rennie, F. (1997). The way of crofting. Chapter 9, pp 123-132 in The Nature of Scotland: Landscape, Wildlife and People. Magnusson, M and White, L. (Eds.) Edinburgh: Canongate. ISBN 0-86241-674-4.

90. Osgathorpe, L. M., Park, K., Goulson, D., Acs, S., and Hanley, N. (2011). The trade-off between agriculture and biodiversity in marginal areas: Can crofting and bumblebee conservation be reconciled? Ecological Economics 70 pp 1162-1169. https://doi.org/10.1016/j.ecolecon.2011.01.010

On land - Red Deer

91. Darling, F. F. (1937). A Herd of Red Deer. Oxford: Oxford University Press.

92. Darling, F.F. (1947). Natural History in the Highlands and Islands. London: Collins.

93. Angus, S. (1977). The Outer Hebrides: Shaping the islands. Cambridge: The White Horse Press. ISBN 1-874267-33-2.

94. Fairnell, E. H. and Barrett, J. H. (2007). Fur-bearing species and Scottish islands. J. of Archaeological Science 34 pp 463-484.. https://doi.org/10.1016/j.jas.2006.09.005

95. Stanton, D.W.G., Mulville, J.A., and Bruford, M.W. (2016). Colonization of the Scottish islands via long-distance Neolithic transport of red deer (Cervus elaphus). Proc. R. Soc. B. 283 20160095. http://dx.doi.org/10.1098/rspb.2016.0095

96. Mitchell, B., Staines, B.W., and Welch, D. (1977). Ecology of Red Deer: A research review relevant to their management in Scotland. Banchory: Institute of Terrestrial Ecology. ISBN 0-904282-090.

97. Putman, R. (1988). The natural history of Red Deer. London: Christopher Helm. ISBN 0-7470-2603-3.

98. Clutton-Brock, T.H. And Albon, S.D. (1989). Red Deer in the Highlands. Oxford: BSP Professional Books. ISBN 0-632-02244-2.

At sea - An Ròn Mor

99.Atkinson, R. (1980). Shillay and the seals. Collins and Harvill Press: London. ISBN 0-00-262763-9.

100. Summers, C. F. and Harwood, J. (1979). The Grey Seal 'problem' in the Outer Hebrides. Proc. Roy. Soc. Edinb. 77B pp 495-503.

101. Boehme, L., Thompson, D., Fedak, M., Bowen, D., Hammill, M. O., Stenson, G. B. (2012). How many seals were there? The global shelf loss during the last glacial maximum and its effect on the size and distribution of Grey Seal populations. PLoS ONE 7 (12) pp 1-10. https://doi.org/10.1371/journal.pone.0053000

102. Boyd, J. M. & Boyd, I. L. The Hebrides. London: Collins New Naturalist Series. 1990, ISBN 0-00-219885-1.

103. McConnell, B. J., Chambers, C., Nicholas, K. S., and Fedak, M. A. (1992). Satellite tracking of Gray Seals Halichoerus grypus. J. Zoology 226 (2) pp 271-282.

104. Hammond, P. S., Hall, A. J., and Prime, J. H. (1994). The diet of grey seals in the

Inner and Outer Hebrides. J. of Applied Ecology 31, pp 737-746.

105. Hewer, H.R. (1974). British Seals. Collins New Naturalist Series (No. 57) London: Collins. ISBN 0-00-213032-7.

106. Darling, F. F. (1939). A naturalist on Rona: Essays of a biologist in isolation. Oxford: Clarendon Press.

107. MacAulay, J. M. (1998). Seal-folk and ocean paddlers: Sliochd nan Ròn. Cambridge: White Horse Press. ISBN 1-874267-39-1.

108. Caldwell, D.H., Hall, M.A., and Wilkinson, C.M. (2010). The Lewis Chessmen Unmasked. Edinburgh: National Museums of Scotland. ISBN 978-1-905267-46-0.

On land and sea - the Otters

109. Bonesi, L., Chanin, P., and MacDonald, D. W. (2004). Competition between Eurasian otter Lutra lutra and American Mink Mustela vison probed by niche shift. Oikos 106 pp 19-26. https://doi.org/10.1111/j.0030-1299.2004.12763.x

110. Clode, D. and MacDonald, D. W. (2002). Invasive predators and the conservation of island birds: the case of American Mink Mustela vison and terns Sterna spp. in the Western Isles, Scotland. Bird Study 49 (2) pp 118-123. https://doi.org/10.1080/00063650209461255

111. McDonald, R. A., O'Hara, K., and Morrish, D. J. (2007). Decline of invasive alien mink (Mustela vison) is concurrent with the recovery of native otters (Lutra lutra). Diversity and Distributions 13 pp 92-98. https://doi.org/10.1111/j.1366-9516.2006.00303.x

112. Bonesi, L. and MacDonald, D. W. (2004). Impact of released Eurasian otters on a population of American mink: a test using an experimental approach. Oikos 106 pp 9-18. https://doi.org/10.1111/j.0030-1299.2004.13138.x

113. Kruuk, H. (2006). Otters: Ecology, behaviour and conservation. Oxford: Oxford University Press. ISBN 0-198-565-879.

The island as a refuge

114. Leopold, A. (1949). A Sand County Almanac and sketches here and there. London: Oxford University Press. ISBN 978-0-19-500777-0.

115. Marten, G. G. (2003). Human Ecology: basic concepts for sustainable development. London: Earthscan. ISBN 1-85383-714-8. Also available online at http://gerrymarten.com/human-ecology/tableofcontents.html

116. Lauer, M. (2017). Changing understandings of local knowledge in island environments. Environmental Conservation 44 (4) pp 336-347. https://doi.org/10.1017/S0376892917000303

117. Smout, T. C. (2011). The Highlands and the Roots of Green Consciousness, 1750-1990. Chapter 2 in Exploring Environmental History: Selected Essays. Edinburgh: Edinburgh University Press. ISBN 978-0-7486-4561-9.

118. Rennie, F. (1986). The role of Conservation in Highland Land-use. Paper in Land: Ownership and use. Fletcher Paper, (Ed. John Hulbert). pp 20-8. Pub. by the Andrew Fletcher Society. ISBN 0-9511509-0-1.

119. Boyd, J. M. (1986). Fraser Darling's Islands. Edinburgh: Edinburgh University Press. ISBN 0-85224-514-9.

5.Ice Age to Iron Age

Muddling through the Mesolithic

120. Ralph, R. (Ed.) (2017). William MacGillivray: A Hebridean Naturalist's Journal 1817-1818. Stornoway: Acair. ISBN 978-0-86152-441-9.

121. Gordon, J. E. (1980). North-west coast of Lewis, in Ellis, N. V. (Ed.) Bowen, D. Q., Campbell, S., Knill, J. L., McKirdy, A. P., Prosser, C. D., Vincent, M. A., and Wilson, R. C. L. Geological Conservation Review. www.jncc.defra.gov.uk/pdf/gcrdb/gcrsiteaccount1450.pdf

122. Love, J.A. (2001). Rum: A landscape without figures. Edinburgh: Birlinn. ISBN 1-84158-224-7.

123. Wickham-Jones, C. R. (1994). Scotland's first settlers. London: Batsford. ISBN 0-7134-7371-1.

124. Burgess, C., Knott, C. and MacLeod, M. (2008). Ancient Lewis and Harris: Exploring the archaeology of the Outer Hebrides. Stornoway: Comhairle nan Eilean Siar. ISBN 978-0- 9519490-2-3.

Narrating the Neolithic

125. Barrowman, C. S. (2015). The Archaeology of Ness. Stornoway: Acair. ISBN 978-0-86152-534-8.

126. Anderson, J. (1892). Notice of a bronze sword, with handle-plates of horn, found at Aird, in the Island of Lewis. Proc. Soc. Antiq. Scotland 27 pp 38-49.

127. Anderson, J. (1911). Notice of a hoard of bronze instruments recently found in Lewis. Proc. Soc. Antiq. Scotland 45 pp 27-46.

128. Armit, I. (1996). The archaeology of Skye and the Western Isles. Edinburgh: Edinburgh University Press. ISBN 0-7486-0640-8.

The enigmatic dùns

129. Sharples, N. and Pearson, M.P. (1997). Why were brochs built? Recent studies in the Iron Age of Atlantic Scotland. pp 254-265 in Reconstructing Iron Age Societies: New Approaches to the British Iron Age, Gwilt, A. and Haselgrove, C. (Eds.) Oxford: Oxbow Books.

130. Thomas, F.W.L. (1890). On the Duns of the Outer Hebrides. Archaeologia Scotica, 5 (3) pp 365-415.

131. Royal Commission on Ancient and Historical Monuments and Constructions of Scotland, (1928). Ninth Report, with inventory of monuments and Constructions in the Outer Hebrides, Skye and the Small Isles. Edinburgh: HMSO.

132. Pearson, M.P., Sharples, N., and Mulville, J. (1996). Brochs and Iron Age society: a reappraisal. Antiquity 70 pp 57-67.

133. Robson, M. (2004). Forts and fallen walls: The duns of northern Lewis. Callicvol, Lewis: Michael Robson. ISBN 0-9534015-3-7.

134. Martin, M. (1981). A description of the Western Isles of Scotland. Edinburgh: James Thin.

135. Armit, I. And Fojut, N. (1998). Dùn Chàrlabhaigh and the Hebridean Iron Age. Stornoway: Urras nan Tursachan: . ISBN 0-9532906-0-3.

136. Armit, A. (1992). The Later Prehistory of the Western Isles of Scotland. BAR British Series 221. British Archaeological Reports. Oxford: Archaeological and Historical

Associates Ltd. ISBN 0-86054-731-0.

137. Pearson, M.P., Sharples, N., and Mulville, J. (1996). Brochs and Iron Age society: a reappraisal. Antiquity 70 pp 57-67.

Living in the land

138. MacGregor, A. A. (1967). The Enchanted Isles: Hebridean portraits and memories. London: Michael Joseph.

139. Edwards, A. J. H. (1924). Report on the excavation of an earth-house at Galson, Borve, Lewis. Proc. Soc. Antiq. Scot. 58, 1923-4, pp 185-203.

140. Wainwright, F. T. (1953). Souterrains in Scotland. Antiquity 27 (Issue 108) pp 219-232.

141. Baden-Powell, D. and Elton, C. (1936-37). On the relation between a raised beach and an Iron Age midden on the island of Lewis, Outer Hebrides. Proc. Soc. Antiq. Scot. 71 pp 347-365.

142. Stevenson, R. B. K. (1952). Long cist burials, particularly those at Galson (Lewis) and Gairloch (Wester Ross), with a symbol stone at Gairloch. Proc. Soc. Antiq. Scot. 1952, pp 106-15.

143. Hill, W. C. O. (1952). Human skeletal remains from a kitchen midden at Galson, Lewis. Proc. Roy. Phys. Soc. Edinburgh 23, pp 165-82.

144. Wells, L. H. (1952). A note on the human remains from the Gairloch and Galson cist burials. Proc. Soc. Antiq. Scot. 86 (1951-2) pp 112-115.

145. Ponting, M. R. & Bruce, M. (1990).Two Iron-age cists from Galson, Isle of Lewis. Proc. Soc. Antiq. Scot. 119, 1989-90, pp 91-100.

146. Neighbour, T., Knott, C., Bruce, F. M., & Kerr, N. W. (2000). Excavation of two burials at Galson, Isle of Lewis, 1993 and 1996. Proc. Soc. Antiq. Scot. 130 pp 559-584.

147. Armit, I. (2006). Anatomy of an Iron Age Roundhouse: The Cnip Wheelhouse excavations, Lewis. Edinburgh: Society of Antiquaries of Scotland. ISBN 0-903903-32-6.

148. Hothersall, S. and Tye, R. (2000). The lost wheelhouses of Uist. Isle of South Uist: Robert Tye. ISBN 0-9524144-1-4.

149. Campbell, E. (1991). Excavations of a wheelhouse and other Iron Age structures at Sollas, North Uist, by R. J. C. Atkinson in 1957. Proc. Soc. Antiq. Scot. 121 pp 117-173.

Here and Far Away

150. MacLeod, F. (Ed.) (1989). Togail Tir: Marking Time: The map of the Western Isles. Stornoway: Acair and An Lanntair. ISBN 0-86152-842-5.

151. McDonald, R. A. (2011). The kingdom of the isles: Scotland's western seaboard c. 110-1336. Edinburgh: Birlinn. ISBN 978-1-904607-79-3.

152. Hennig, B. (2014). Visualising wilderness, on the website "Views of the World" at www.viewsoftheworld.net/?p=4319

6.From the Settlers to the Clearances

The servants of St Brigid

153. MacDonald, I. (Ed.) (1992). Saint Bride. Edinburgh: Floris Books. ISBN 0-86315-142-6.

154. MacLeod, F. (2018). The Chapels and Healing Wells of the Western Isles. Stornoway: Acair. ISBN 978-1-78907-001-9.

155. McIntosh, A. (2018). Poacher's Pilgrimage: An island journey. Edinburgh: Birlinn. ISBN 978-1-78027-468-3.

156. Marsden, J. (1995). Sea-road of the saints: Celtic holy men in the Hebrides. Edinburgh: Floris Books. ISBN 0-86315-210-4.

Healing wells and hermits

157. Severin, T. (1978). The Brendan Voyage. London: Hutchinson. ISBN 0-09-133100-5.

158. Daniell, W. (2006). Daniell's Scotland : a voyage round the coast of Scotland and the adjacent isles, 1815-1822 : a series of views, illustrative of the character and prominent features of the coast by William Daniell, (2 vols). Edinburgh: Birlinn in association with the National Library of Scotland, 2006. ISBN 1-84158-317-0 (vol. 1); 1-84158-318-9 (vol. 2).

159. Robson, M. (1997). A Desert Place in the sea: The early churches of Northern Lewis. Habost, Lewis: Comunn Eachdraidh Nis. ISBN 0-953137406.

160. Moorhouse, G. (1983). Calcutta: The city revealed. London: Penguin. ISBN 0-14-009557-8.

Gabhsann becomes a named place

161. Oftedal, M. (2009). The village names of Lewis. Kershader, Lewis: The Islands Book Trust. ISBN 978-0-9560764-7-2.

162. MacIver, D. (1934). Place-names of Lewis and Harris. Printed by the Stornoway Gazette.

163. Carmichael, A. (1992). Carmina Gadelica: Hymns and incantations. (Single-volume edition reprint). Edinburgh: Floris Books. ISBN 978-086-3155-208.

164. Robson, M. (1989). The living voice. Essay, pp 97-104 in Macleod, F. (Ed.) (1989). Togail Tir: Marking Time: The map of the Western Isles. Stornoway: Acair and An Lanntair. ISBN 0-86152-842-5.

165. Fraser, I. (1974). The place names of Lewis - Norse evidence. Northern Studies 4 pp 11-21.

166. Webster, D. C. F. (1989) A cartographic controversy: In defence of Murdoch MacKenzie. In MacLeod, F. (Ed.) . Togail Tir: Marking Time: The map of the Western Isles. Stornoway: Acair and An Lanntair. ISBN 0-86152-842-5.

167. Fleet, C., Wilkes, M. and Withers, W. J. (2016). Scotland: Mapping the Islands. Edinburgh: Birlinn. ISBN 978-1-78027-351-8.

Fashion-conscious Vikings

168. Graham-Campbell, J. (1986). A late Celtic enamelled mount from Galson, Isle of Lewis. Proc. Soc. Antiq. Scot. 116, pp 281-284.

The Norse village

169. Nicolaisen, W. F. H. (1969). Norse Settlement in the Northern and Western Isles: Some Place-name evidence. The Scottish Historical Review 48 (No. 145, Part 1: Scotland and Scandinavia: Studies Commemorative of the Union of Orkney and Shetland with Scotland. Pp 6-17. https://www.jstor.org/stable/25528785

170. Thomas, F. W. L. (1861). "Notes on the Lews". Society of Antiquaries of Scotland Manuscript Collection (MS 28). 1861 (based on notes from papers by Rev. Gunn, minister of Uig.)

171. Williams, R. (1997). The Lords of the Isles: The Clan Donald and the early Kingdom of the Scots. Argyll: House of Lochar. ISBN 1-899863-17-6.

172. Schorn, B. and Quinn, J. (Eds.) (2014). The Vikings in Lewis. Languages, Myths and Finds Vol. 2. Nottingham: Centre for the Study of the Viking Age, University of Nottingham. ISBN 9780853582991. https://www.nottingham.ac.uk/research/groups/csva/documents/lmfpublications/lmf2-isleoflewis,thevikingsinlewis.pdf

173. Þórarinsson, G. G. (2014). The Lewis chessmen: the Icelandic theory. Chapter 2.7 pp 201-218 in The Lewis Chessmen: New perspectives. Caldwell, D. H. and Hall, M. A. (Eds.) Edinburgh: National Museums of Scotland. ISBN 978-1-905267-85-9.

174. Pringle, D. (Ed.) (1994). The ancient monuments of the Western Isles: a visitors' guide to the principal historic sites and monuments. Edinburgh: HMSO. ISBN 0-11-495201-9.

175. Barrowman, R. C. (2015). Dùn Èistean, Ness. Stornoway: Acair. ISBN 978-0-86152-539-3.

176. Stiùbhart, D. U., (2015). Local traditions concerning the late medieval history and topography of Sgìre Nis. in Barrowman, R. C. (2015). Dùn Èistean, Ness. Stornoway: Acair. ISBN 978-0-86152-539-3.

177. MacKenzie, W. C. (1974). The History of the Outer Hebrides. Edinburgh: The Mercat Press.

178. Neighbour, T. and Church, M. J. (2001). The eroding settlement and Iron Age cemetery at Galson, Isle of Lewis: Recording of the Erosion Face and Geophysical Survey. Report No. 635, Centre for Field Archaeology, Edinburgh (Unpubl.)

179. Sharples, N. and Pearson, M. P. (1999). Norse Settlement in the Outer Hebrides. Norwegian Archaeological Review 32 (1) pp41-62.

180. Etheridge, D., Hart, M., Heans-Glogowska, E. and Kupiec, P. (2014). Life at the coast. Chapter 2, pp 13-17 in Schorn, B. and Quinn, J. (Eds.) (2014). The Vikings in Lewis. Languages, Myths and Finds Vol. 2. Nottingham: Centre for the Study of the Viking Age, University of Nottingham. ISBN 9780853582991. https://www.nottingham.ac.uk/research/groups/csva/documents/lmfpublications/lmf2-isleoflewis,thevikingsinlewis.pdf

Of Pots and Bowls

181. Simpson, D. D. A., Murphy, E. M., and Gregory, R. A. (2016). Excavations at Northton, Isle of Harris. British Archaeological Reports, Series 208. Oxford: BAR Publishing. ISBN 978-1-8417-1936-8.

182. Lane, A. (2007). Ceramic and cultural change in the Hebrides AD 500-1300. Cardiff Studies in Archaeology, Special Report No. 29. Cardiff: Cardiff School of History and Archaeology. ISBN 0-9537793-9-4. https://core.ac.uk/download/pdf/42525207.pdf

183. Campbell, E. (2002). The Western Isles pottery sequence. Chapter 11, pp 139-144 in Ballin Smith, B. and Banks, I. (Eds.) (2002). In the shadow of the brochs: The Iron Age in Scotland. Stroud: Tempus. ISBN 0-7524-2517-X.

184. Barrowman, R. C. (2015). Dùn Èistean, Ness. Stornoway: Acair. ISBN 978-0-86152-539-3.

185. MacSween, A. (2002). Dun Beag and the role of pottery in interpretations of the Hebridean Iron Age. Chapter 12, pp 145-152 in Ballin Smith, B. and Banks, I. (Eds.) (2002). In the shadow of the brochs: The Iron Age in Scotland. Stroud: Tempus. ISBN 0-7524-2517-X.

186. Cheape, H. (1992). Crogans and Barvas Ware: Handmade pottery in the Hebrides. Scottish Studies, 31 pp 109-128.

Part of history's backdrop

187. MacDonald, D. (1978). Lewis: A history of the island. Edinburgh: Gordon Wright Publishing. ISBN 903065-23-1.

188. MacKenzie, A.M. (1958). The passing of the Stewarts. Edinburgh: Oliver & Boyd.

189. Barrowman, R. C. (2015). A local response to a wider situation: the archaeology of the clan stronghold of Dùn Èistean, Isle of Lewis. Post-Medieval Archaeology 49/1 pp 37-56. doi:10.1179/0079423615Z.00000000070)

190. Lawson, B. (2007). Croft History: Isle of Lewis, Volume 13. Northton, Isle of Harris: Bill Lawson Publications. ISBN 1-872598-51-X.

7. Two hundred years of standoff

The Farm

191. Richards, E. (2016). The Highland Estate Factor in the age of the Clearances. Laxay, Isle of Lewis: Islands Book Trust. ISBN 978-1-907443-70-1.

192. Hunter, J. (2015). Set adrift upon the world: The Sutherland Clearances. Edinburgh: Birlinn. ISBN 978-1-78027-268-9.

193. MacLean, M. and Carrell, C. (1986). As an fhearann: From the land. Clearance, Conflict and Crofting: A century of images of the Scottish Highlands. Edinburgh: Mainstream. ISBN 1-85158-036-0.

194. Devine, T. M. (1995). The Great Highland Famine: Hunger, Emigration and the Scottish Highlands in the Nineteenth Century. Edinburgh: Birlinn. ISBN 1-904607-42-X.

195. Prebble, J. (1969). The Highland Clearances. London: Penguin.

196. Grigor, I. F. (1979). Mightier than a lord. Stornoway: Acair. ISBN 0-86152-030-0.

197. MacPhail, I. M. M. (1989). The Crofters' War. Stornoway: Acair. ISBN 0-86152-860-3.

198. Richards, E. and Tindley, A. (2012). After the Clearances: Evander McIver and the 'Highland Question', 1835-73. Rural History 23, pp 41-57. https://doi.org/10.1017/S0956793311000148

199. Grimble, I. (1993). The trial of Patrick Sellar. Edinburgh: The Saltire Society. ISBN 0-85411-053-4.

200. MacKenzie, J. M. (1994). Diary 1851: John Munro MacKenzie, Chamberlain of Lewis. Stornoway: Acair. ISBN 0-86152--908-1.

201. Grant, J. S. (1992). A shilling for your scowl: The history of a Scottish legal mafia. Stornoway: Acair. ISBN 0-86152-898-0.

202. Lawson, B. (2008). Lewis, the West Coast: in history and legend. Edinburgh: Birlinn. ISBN 978-1-84158-386-6.

A Harvest of grain

203. Fenton, A. (1999). Scottish Country Life. East Linton: Tuckwell Press. ISBN 1-86232-066-7.

204. MacLeod, F. (2009). The Norse mills of Lewis. Stornoway: Acair. ISBN 978-0-86152-362-7.

The Final Clearance

205. MacLeod, J. (2010). None dare oppose: The Laird, the Beast and the people of Lewis. Edinburgh: Birlinn. ISBN 978-1-84158-909-1.

206. Paterson, N. (1963). 100 Years ago this month: Galson clearance recalled. Stornoway Gazette and West Coast Advertiser, Friday May 10 1963 p 7.

207. Inverness Courier, 16 July 1863, p 5.

208. Collier, A. (1953). The Crofting problem. Cambridge: Cambridge University Press.

209. Love, J. A. (2011). The island lighthouses of Scotland. Stornoway: The Islands Book Trust. ISBN 978-1-907443-26-8.

The Turning Point

210. Cameron, A.D. (1986). Go listen to the crofters: The Napier Commission and Crofting a century ago. Stornoway: Acair. ISBN 0-86152-063-7.

211. Napier Commission, (1969). Evidence (Volume 2) taken by the Royal Commission of Inquiry on the conditions of Crofters and Cottars in the Highlands of Scotland 1884. Irish University Press Series of British Parliamentary Papers (facsimile edition) Shannon, Ireland, 1969, Vol. 23, p 1012 Agriculture, SBN 7165-0856-7.

212. Hunter, J. (1976). The making of the crofting community. Edinburgh: John Donald. ISBN 0-85976-014-6.

8.Re-settlement to the present

Direct Action

213. Cameron, E. A. (1996). Land for the people? The British Government and the Scottish Highlands, c 1880-1925. Edinburgh: Tuckwell Press. ISBN 1-898410-291.

214. Buchanan, J. 1996). The Lewis Land Struggle: Na Gaisgich. Stornoway: Acair. ISBN 0-86152-166-8.

215. MacKinlay, D. (1878). The Island of Lews, and its fishermen-crofters. In a letter to Hugh M. Matheson, Esq. the Commissioner for Sir James Matheson, Bart., of Lews. London. Barrett and Co.: Seething Lane.

216. Glasgow Herald, (1888). The situation in Lewis. Visit to the Galson Farm. Saturday January 14, p7.

217. The Scotsman, (1888). January 17, The military and the police forces at Stornoway are idle.

218. The Scotsman, (1888). January 18, Another outbreak in Lewis and a conflict with the police, who were put to flight.

219. Aberdeen Press and Journal, (1888). The agitation in Lewis. Serious moonlight outrage. Conflict with the police. Wednesday 18 January p 5.

220. The Scotsman, (1888). January 19, Yesterday the police, supported by a strong military body, proceeded to Borve, and arrested five men...

221. The Scotsman, (1888). January 21, There is comparative quiet in Lewis.

222. The Scotsman 21 February 1888

223. Glasgow Herald, (1888). The rioting at Galson Farm. Trial of the crofters in Edinburgh. Verdict of not guilty. Tuesday 6 March, p 4.

224. The Scotsman, (1888). Trial of the Galson Crofters. Tuesday 6 March, p 3.

225. Grant, J. S. (1988). The battle of Galston Farm (In search of Lewis No. 387) Stornoway Gazette and West Coast Advertiser, week ending September 10, 1988, p 6.

226. Grant, J. S. (1988). A dawn swoop on Borve (In search of Lewis No. 388). Stornoway Gazette and West Coast Advertiser, week ending September 17, 1988, p 6.

227. Ross-shire Journal, A striking story. 26 October 1888, p3.

Will you give us the land?

228. McKichan, F. (2007). Lord Seaforth and Highland estate management in the First Phase of Clearance (1783-1815). Scottish Historical Review, 86 No. 221, part 1 pp 50-68. https://www.jstor.org/stable/25529952.

229. McKichan, F. (2018). Lord Seaforth: Highland Landowner, Caribbean Governor. Edinburgh: Edinburgh University Press. ISBN 978-1-4744-3848-3.

230. MacKenzie, F. H. of Seaforth, (1793). Letter to Lord Adam Gordon 27 April 1793, RH2/4/207

231. Logue, K. J. (1979). Popular disturbances in Scotland 1780-1815. Edinburgh: John Donald. ISBN 085976-037-5.

232. McKichan, F. (2011). Lord Seaforth: Highland proprietor, Caribbean Governor and slave owner. Scottish Historical Review, 90, No. 230, Part 2 pp 204-235. https://www.jstor.org/stable/23073285

233. Bunting, M. (2016). Love of Country: A Hebridean Journey. London: Granta. ISBN 978-1-84708-517-7.

234. Moireasdan, D. A. (Ed.) (2014). The going down of the sun: The Great War and a rural Lewis community. Stornoway: Acair. ISBN 978-0-86152-543-0.

235. Macdonald, M. and MacLeod, D. J. (2018). The darkest dawn: The story of the Iolaire Tragedy. Stornoway: Acair. ISBN 978-78907-024-8.

236. Nicolson, N. (1960). Lord of the Isles. Stornoway: Acair. ISBN 0-86152-215-X.

237. Leneman, L. (1989). Fit for Heroes? : Land settlement in Scotland after World War 1. Aberdeen: Aberdeen University Press. ISBN 0-08-037720-3.

238. Hutchinson, R. (2003). The Soap Man: Lewis, Harris and Lord Leverhulme. Edinburgh: Birlinn. ISBN 1-84158-184-4.

239. MacDonald, C. (1943). Highland Journey or Sùil air ais. Edinburgh: The Moray Press.

240. Stornoway Gazette, (1919). Land seizure (Borve and Mid-Borve News). 2 May 1919. p3

241. Highland News, (1919). Another farm seized. Saturday, 3 May 1919. p5.

242. Hunter, J. (2019). Repeopling emptied places: Centenary reflections on the significance and the enduring legacy of the Land Settlement (Scotland) Act 1919. Edinburgh: Scottish Land Commission.

The Auction

243. Knight, Frank, and Rutley, (1924). Catalogue for the sale of "the greater portion of the Island of Lewis in the county of Ross and Cromarty". London.

244. The Scotsman, (1924). March 5 p 8. Island of Lewis. Auction of Leverhulme Estates. Land at 2 1/2D an acre.

245. Jones, D.S.D. (2015). Galson: The story of a forgotten Lewis sporting estate. Back in the Day. (Historical newsheet). September 2015 pp 10-11.

The Map

246. Robinson, T. (1990). Stones of Aran: Pilgrimage. London: Penguin. ISBN 0-14-011565-X

Coming home

247. Stornoway Gazette, (1923). 5 April, p 4. Proposed Land Settlement at Galson.

248. Stornoway Gazette, (1923). 22 November p 5. Galson Farm to be Broken Up.

249. Stornoway Gazette, (1924). 28 August, p 5. Galson Crofting Settlement: The New Tenants.

250. Rennie, F. W. (1998). Land, Culture, and the Future of Rural Communities. The 1998 Rural Lecture. 15pp Pub. Lews Castle College. 1998 ISBN 0-9533808-0-7. Available on-line at http://www.lews.uhi.ac.uk/about/research/lecture1998.htm

251. Dodgshon, R. A. (1993). West Highland and Hebridean settlement prior to crofting and the Clearances: a study in stability or change? Proc. Soc. Antiq. Scot. 123, pp 419-38.

252. Dodgshon, R. A. (1998). From Chiefs to Landlords: Social and economic change in the Western Highlands, c. 1493-1820. Edinburgh: Edinburgh University Press. ISBN 0-7486-1034-0.

253. Campbell, S. D. (2009). Post-medieval settlement in the Isle of Lewis: a study in adaptability or change? Proc. Soc. Antiq. Scot. 139 pp 315-332.

254. Bignal, E. M. and McCracken, D. I. (1996). Low-intensity Farming Systems in the conservation of the countryside. J. of Applied Ecology, 33 pp 413-24. https://www.jstor.org/stable/pdf/2404973.pdf

255. Caird, J. B. (1990). Personal communication to the author.

256. Chalmers, A. H. C. (1988). Influence on land use in a crofting township: Galson, Barvas Parish, Isle of Lewis. MSc. dissertation (Unpubl.) University of Edinburgh.

257. Flynn, D. and Graham, K. H. R. (1994). The Crofters (Sotland) Act 1993. (Greens Annotated Acts). Edinburgh: Green/Sweet and Maxwell.

258. MacCaig, N. (1990). "A man in Assynt", in Collected Poems, pp 224-231. London: Chatto & Windus. ISBN 0-7011-3713-4. Also available at: http://www.scottishpoetrylibrary.org.uk/poetry/poems/man-assynt-extract

259. Rennie, F. (2000). Why bother about rural areas? Inaugural professorial lecture, 19 February, 2008. University of the Highlands and Islands https://www.lews.uhi.ac.uk/t4-media/one-web/lews/research/contact/prof-frank-rennie/professor-frank-rennie/WhyBother.pdf

260. Handley, S. (2013). Community consultation survey: Summary Report 2013. Urras Oighreachd Ghabhsainn (Galson Trust Estate).

261. Wemyss, R. D. (2011). A major wind farm development in a valued natural environment: A thematic discourse analysis of public responses to a proposed wind farm on the Isle of Lewis, Scotland. PhD dissertation (unpublished): The Open University and the University of the Highlands and Islands.

262. UoG (Urras Oighreachd Ghabhsainn) (Galson Estate Trust) (2017). Strategic Plan 2017-2037. www.galsontrust.com

263. Bryden, J. and Hart, K. (2000). Land reform, planning and people: an issue of stewardship? Paper presented at the RSE/SNH Millennium Conference, 'The future for the environment in Scotland: Resetting the Agenda?' Edinburgh. http://www.caledonia.org.uk

264. Hunter, J. (2012). From the low tide of the sea to the highest mountain tops: Community ownership of land in the Highlands and Islands of Scotland. Ravenspoint: The Islands Book Trust. ISBN 978-1-907443-28-2.

9. Human ecology in a crofting township

Perspectives

265. Gunn, N. M. (1978). The Drinking Well. Souvenir Press: London. ISBN 0-285-62330-3.

266. Tilley, C. (1994). A phenomenology of landscape: Places, Paths and Monuments. Oxford: Berg Publishers. ISBN 1-85973-076-0.

267. Stegner, W. (1993). Where the Bluebird sings to the lemonade springs: Living and writing in the west. London: Penguin Books. ISBN 0-14-017402-8.

On the landscape

268. Ritchie, E. (2017). Wild Land: alternative insights into Scotland's unpeopled places. https://www.communitylandscotland.org.uk/wp-content/uploads/2017/06/Wild-Land-alternative-insights-into-Scotlands-unpeopled-places-final.pdf

269. Smout, T. C. (2000). Nature Contested: Environmental history in Scotland and northern England since 1600. Edinburgh: Edinburgh University Press. ISBN 0-7486-1411-7.

270. Vitek, W. and Jackson, W. (Eds.) (1996). Rooted in the land: Essays on community and place. New Haven: Yale University Press. ISBN 0-300-06961-8.

271. Tait, J., Lane, A., and Carr, S. (1988). Practical conservation: Site assessment and management planning. London: The Open University in association with the Nature Conservancy Council. ISBN 0-340-49003-9.

272. Dwelly, E. (1973). The illustrated Gaelic to English dictionary. 8th Edition. Glasgow: Gairm

273. Brody, H. (1975). The People's Land: Eskimos and Whites in the Eastern Arctic. London: Penguin. ISBN 0-14-02-1813-0.

From the landscape

274. Milliken, W. and Bridgewater, S. (2013). Flora Celtica: Plants and People in Scotland. Edinburgh: Birlinn and the Royal Botanic Garden Edinburgh. ISBN 978-1-78027-169-9.

275. Beith, N. (1995). Healing threads: Traditional medicines of the Highlands and Islands. Edinburgh: Polygon.

276. Brody, H. (2002). Maps and Dreams. London: Faber and Faber. ISBN 0-571-20967-X.

277. Brody, H. (1989). Maps and Journeys; chapter (p133-136 in MacLeod, F. (Ed.) (1989). Togail Tir: Marking Time: The map of the Western Isles. Stornoway: Acair and An Lanntair. ISBN 0-86152-842-5.

278. Rennie, F. (2008). Human ecology and concepts of sustainable development in a crofting township. Folk Life(Journal of Ethnological Studies) 46 pp 39-57 https://www.lews.uhi.ac.uk/t4-media/one-web/lews/research/contact/prof-frank-rennie/prof-frank-rennie-publications/Galson_Paper.pdf

279. Best, J. and Mulville, J. (2014). A bird in the hand: Data collation and novel analysis of avian remains from South Uist, Outer Hebrides. International Journal of Osteoarchaeology 24 pp 384-396. https://doi.org/10.1002/oa.2381

280. Serjeantson, D. (1988). Archaeological and ethnographic evidence for seabird exploitation in Scotland. Archaeozoologia 2, pp 209-224.

281. Morrison, D. A. (Ed.) (2005). Traditions of sea-bird fowling in the North Atlantic region. Port of Ness: The Islands Book Trust.

282. Beatty, J. (1992). Sula: The seabird-hunters of Lewis. London: Michael Joseph. ISBN 0-7181-3634-9.

283. Best, J. and Mulville, J. (2016). Birds from the water: Reconstructing avian resource use and contribution to diet in prehistoric Scottish island environments. J. of Archaeological Science: Reports 6, p 654-664. http://dx.doi.org/10.1016/j.jasrep.2015.11.024

284. Campbell, A. (2013). Rathad an Isein/The Bird's Road: A Lewis moorland glossary. Glasgow: FARAM. ISBN 978-0-9571530-1-1.

In the landscape

285. Zenner, G. (2007). Indicators for sustainable development at the level of a rural community. Case studies: Galson township and South Dell, Isle of Lewis, Scotland. Unpublished Diploma thesis, Carl Von Ossietzky University, Oldenburg.

286. Barrowman, R. (Ed.) (2020). PLACE NAMES OF NESS AND THE WEST SIDE. Stornoway: Acair.

287. Lopez, B. (2019). Horizon. London: The Bodley Head. ISBN 978-1-847-92577-0.

288. Darling, F. F. (1948). Island years. London: Bell & Sons.

289. Smith, J. (ed.) (2019). Donald Smith: The Paintings of an Islander: Dealbhan le Eileanach. Stornoway: Acair. ISBN 978-1-78907-043-9.

290. Lawson, I. (2015) From the land comes the cloth. Ian Lawson Books. (3rd Edn.) ISBN 978-0-956872401.

291. Macdonald, A. and Macdonald, P. (2010). The Hebrides: An aerial view of a cultural landscape. Edinburgh: Birlinn. ISBN 978-1-84158-315-0.

292. Berry, W. (1990). What are people for? Essays by Wendell Berry. New York: North Point Press. ISBN 0-865-47437-0.

10. The distant shore

What next?

293. Heat-Moon, W. L. (1991). PrairyErth. Boston: Houghton Mifflin. ISBN 0-395-48602-5.

294. Scotese, C. R. (2004). The Palaeomap Project. https://www.youtube.com/watch?v=uLahVJNnoZ4

295. Merritt, J. W., Hall, A. M., Gordon, J. E., and Connell, E. R. (2018). Late Pleistocene sediments, landforms and events in Scotland: a review of the terrestrial stratigraphic record. Earth and Environmental Science Transactions of the Royal Society of Edinburgh, 53 pp 1-53. https://doi.org/10.1017/S1755691018000890

296. Sutherland, D. G. and Walker, M. J. C. (1984). A late Devensian ice-free area and possible interglacial site on the Isle of Lewis, Scotland. Nature, 309 pp 701-703.

297. Peacock, J. D. (1984). Quaternary geology of the Outer Hebrides. Report of the British Geological Survey16 (2), pp 1-26. Edinburgh: British Geological Survey.

298. Steers, J.A. (1973). The coastline of Scotland. Cambridge: Cambridge University Press. ISBN 0-521-08696-5.

299. USGCRP (2017). Climate Science Special Report. Chapter 12: Sea Level Rise. https://science2017.globalchange.gov

300. WCRP Global Sea Level Budget Group (2018). Global sea-level budget 1993-Present. Earth System Science Data 10 (3) pp 1551-1590. https://doi.org/10.5194/essd-10-1551-2018

301. Day, J. C., Heron, S. F., Markham, A., Downes, J., Gibson, J., Hyslop, E., Jones, R. H., and Yall, A. (2019). Climate risk assessment for Heart of Heart of Neolithic Orkney World Heritage property: An application of the Climate Vulnerability Index. Edinburgh: Historic Environment Scotland. https://www.historicenvironment.scot/archives-and-research/publications/publication/?publicationId=c6f3e971-bd95-457c-a91d-aa77009aec69

302. Falcone, E. A., Schorr, G. S., Watwood, S. L., DeRuiter, S. L., Zerbini, A. N., Andrews, R. D., Morrissey, D. J. (2017). Diving behaviour of Cuvier's beaked whales exposed to two types of military sonar. Roy. Soc. Open Sci. 54: 170629 https://dx.doi.org/10.1098/rsos.170629

303. Met Office (2019) UK Climate Projections (UKCP).https://www.metoffice.gov.uk/research/approach/collaboration/ukcp/index

304. Bennett, K.D., Bunting, M.J. and Fossitt, J.A. (1997). Long-term vegetation change in the Western and Northern Isles, Scotland. Botanical J. of Scotland, 49 (2) pp 127-140. doi: https://doi.org/10.1080/03746609708684861

305. Crawford, R. M. M. (2001). Plant community responses to Scotland's changing environment. Botanical J. of Scotland 53 (2) pp 77-105. doi: https://doi.org/10.1080/03746600108685016

306. Devine, T. M. (2018). The Scottish Clearances: A history of the dispossessed. London: Allen Lane. ISBN 978-0-241-30410-5.

307. MacKinnon, I. (2017). Colonialism and the Highland Clearances. Northern Scotland, 8 pp 22-48. https://www.euppublishing.com/doi/full/10.3366/nor.2017.0125

308. Masterson, V. A., Enqvist, J. P., Stedman, R. C. and Tengo, M. (2019). Sense of place in social-ecological systems: from theory to empirics. Sustainability Science 14 pp 555-564. https://doi.org/10.1007/s11625-019-00695-8

309. Adger, W. N. (2000). Social and ecological resilience: are they related? Progress in Human Geography, 24 (3) pp 347-364. https://pdfs.semanticscholar.org/6eb9/1fb61d5f29aee85ed1e62adcd80943c6bb85.pdf

310. Edwards, K. J., Whittington, G. and Ritchie, W. (2005). The possible role of humans in the early stages of machair evolution: palaeoenvironmental investigations in the Outer Hebrides, Scotland. Journal of Archaeological Science 32 pp 435-449. https://doi.org/10.1016/j.jas.2004.09.011

311. Lewis, S. L. and Maslin, M. A. (2015). Defining the Anthropocene. Nature 519 pp 171-180. https://doi.org/10.1038/nature14258

312. Delgado, J. D., Riera, R., Rodríguez, R. A. González-Moreno, P., and Fernández-Palacios, J. M. (2017). A reappraisal of the role of humans in the biotic disturbance of islands. Environmental Conservation 44 (4) pp 371380. https://doi.org/10.1017/S0376892917000236

313. Editor's Introduction, (2016). Fighting for Rural America: Overcoming the Contempt for Small Places. American Journal of Economics and Sociology 75 (3) pp 569-588. https://doi.org/10.1111/ajes.12148

314. Sutton, R. D. (2019). Discovering our Natural Heritage - Biological Recording in 2018. Outer Hebrides Biological Recording Pub.

315. Grant, J. S. (1984). The part-time holding - an island experience. The Arkleton Lecture 1983. Enstone: The Arkleton Trust. https://arkletontrust.co.uk/wp-content/uploads/2017/12/Arkleton-Lecture-1983.pdf

316. Marrs, S. J., Foster, S., Hendrie, C., Mackey, E. C. and Thompson, D. B. A. (Eds.) (2011). The Changing Nature of Scotland. Edinburgh: TSO Scotland. ISBN 978-0-11-497359-9.

317. Mullally, S. L. and Maguire, E. A. (2014). Memory, Imagination, and Predicting the Future: A Common Brain Mechanism? The Neuroscientist, 20 (3) pp 220-234. https://doi.org/10.1177/1073858413495091

318. Gunn, N. M. (1977). Butcher's Broom. London: Souvenir Press. ISBN 0-285-62288-9.

319. Thomson, D. S. (2004). Màiri nighean Alasdair Ruaidh [Mary MacLeod]. Entry in the Dictionary of National Biography. https://doi.org/10.1093/ref:odnb/17675

320. Newton, M. (Ed.) (2015). Seanchaidh na Coille: The Memory-Keeper of the Forest. Anthology of Scottish-Gaelic Literature of Canada. Sydney, Nova Scotia: Cape Breton University Press. ISBN 978-1-77206-016-4.

Appendix 1

The names of this place
(Places in the Gabhsann area or mentioned in the text)

A

A' Chlach Ghorm	NB 436 594
A' Ghràiseach	NB 429 591
A' Phàirc Ghainmhich	NB 437 594
A' Phàirc Churs	NB 421 584
A' Staile	NB 439 592
A' Ghil	NB 497 553
A' Mhaoim	NB 501 537
Abhainn Gabhsann bho Dheas .... South Galson River	NB 439 586
Abhainn Gabhsann bho Thuath .... North Galson River	NB 46 58
Aiginis	NB 48 32
Àird Dhail	NB 477 617
Àirigh a' Gheàrraidh Bhochd	NB 444 583
Àirigh Bhotair	NB 451 559
Àirigh Bhruthach	NB 477 563
Àirigh nan Uan	NB 445 573
Àirigh MhicLeòid	NB 453 592
Àirigh Nioscalaid	NB 453 592
Àirighean Bhìogaidean	NB 450 566
Àirighean Cearsabhat	NB 457 555
Allt an Mill	NB 465 584
Allt Grunndal	NB 424 571
Allt Meagro	NB 422 576
Allt Stiuacleit	NB 432 550
An Àird Garbh	NB 426 586
An Àth	NB 432 583
An Cnoc Aird	NB 535 644
An Druim bho Thuath	NB 45 59
An Gioban	NB 420 585
An t-Srùp	NB 438 593
An t-Slag Mhòr	NB 475 538
An Gleann bho Dheas	NB 478 571
An Taigh Mòr	NB 437 591
An Taigh-sgoile	NB 432 579
An Tobha Ghabhsainn	NB 452 603
An Tobha Mòr	NB 452 603
An Taobh Thuath	NF 98 90
An Tòl	NB 439 594
Ascalin	NB 475 574
Àsmaigearraidh	NB 464 604
Àth Bheag	NB 438 595
Àth Cheapach	NB 430 587
Àtharaig	NB436 595

B

C

D

Druim na h-Eige .... NB 425 573
Druim Thurstail .... NB 489 534
Dùn Bharabhat .... NB 462 597
Dùn Bhuirgh .... NB 419 580
Dùn Èistean .... NB 536 651
Dùn Sabhuill .... NB 443 595
Dùn Shiabhat .... NB 476 593

E

Eighe Sgeir .... NB 446 598
Eire .... NB 407 571
Eitacleit .... NB 464 585
Eòropaidh .... NB 515 650

F

Feadan Atagro .... NB 433 563
Feadan Bhotagro .... NB 448 570
Feadan Bhotargile .... NB 478 558
Feadan Dhruidnaspotair .... NB 461 575
Feadan 'Illechroisda Dhubh .... NB 469 536
Feadan Hiadagro .... NB 479 565
Feadan Loch a'Cheisteir .... NB 462 563
Feadan Loch Ruiglabhat .... NB 474 562
Feadan Loch Striamabhat .... NB 442 557
Feadan nan Cnàmh .... NB 501 536
Feadan nan Uan .... NB 502 536
Feadan Thurstail .... NB 487 537

G

Gabhsann bho Dheas .... South Galson................. NB 43 58
Gabhsann bho Thuath .... North Galson .... NB 44 59
Gàradh Dubh .... NB 479 569
Gèarraidh Amadal .... NB 463 579
Geàrraidh Eoruilltean .... NB 473 579
Gèarraidh Mòr Ghabhsann .... NB 426 585
Gèarraidh Mòr Mhealabost .... NB 417 582
Gearraidh na Sige .... NB 472 567
Gèarraidh Rathaclaid .... NB 445 579
Gèarraidh Roscalaid .... NB 446 581
Geodh a' Gharaidh .... NB 455 604
Geodh a' Phìobaire .... NB 459 606
Geodh an Tairbh .... NB 452 602
Geodh an Toabh .... NB 451 603
Geodha Gorm .... NB 412 582
Geodha na Faing .... NB 411 580
Geodha Ruadh .... NB 451 602
Gleann Ghabhsainn .... NB 482 572
Gleann na Sige .... NB 465 562

Gob an Eich .... NB 464 580
Gob an Eòin .... NB 432 592
Griais .... NB 50 42

H

Hèisgeir .... NB 435 577
Hiadagro .... NB 481 565

L

Leac a' Mhiosachain .... NB 427 590
Leacainn Eoruilltean .... NB 472 579
Lèana Bhàin .... NB 493 560
Lèana nan Caorann Fiadhag .... NB 474 590
Loch a' Cheisteir .... NB 463 559
Loch an Ime .... NB 427 582
Loch Beag Sanndabhat .... NB 499 530
Loch Bharabhat .... NB 462 596
Loch Carsabhat .... NB 457 551
Loch Ghearasaidh .... NB 467 582
Loch Leiseabhat .... NB 436 572
Loch Ruigleabhat .... NB 467 557
Loch Ruiseabhat .... NB 482 569
Loch Rumsagro .... NB 463 559
Loch Shiabhat .... NB 476 593
Loch Stiapabhat .... NB 528 643
Loch Striamabhat .... NB 447 554
Lochan Grasabhat .... NB 485 581
Loidse Ghabhsainn .... NB 455 591

M

Malagro .... NB 466 563
Meagro .... NB 428 582
Mealabost .... NB 41 57
Miosgalin .... NB 471 573
Mol Thòrsuig .... NB 441 597
Mol Thòrsaig Bheag .... NB 447 598
Mol Thòrsaig Mhòr .... NB 448 600
Mullach nan Slag .... NB 458 591

N

Niuclan .... NB 494 556

P

Pairc a' Ghlinne .... NB 438 590
Peiceir .... NB 444 575

R

S

T

Tobair Mhurchaidh 'An Bhàin .... NB 432 588
Tobair na Traith Bhàn .... NB 416 576
Tobair na Sùist .... NB 438 587
Tobair Reicean .... NB 447 592
Tobair Sgodaidh .... NB 436 591
Tobair Thormoid Sona .... NB 440 592
Tobair Thormoid 'an Ruairidh.. NB 439 586
Tobair Thuataidh .... NB 443 590
Tobair (unnamed) .... NB 443 594
Tobha Ghabhsainn .... NB 452 603
Tol .... NB 439 595
Tolastadh Chaolais .... NB 195 380
Tom a' Bhiudhair .... NB 457 563
Tom a' Mhile .... NB 439 574
Tom a' Mhonaidh .... NB 438 580
Tom an ime .... NB 428 583
Tom Atagro .... NB 430 560
Tom Grasabhat .... NB 481 579
Tom Leiseabhat .... NB 434 573
Tom Lomaidean .... NB 455 597
Tom na Bà .... NB 434 576
Tom Shiabhat .... NB 478 595
Tom Tip Tap .... NB 425 565
Tòrsuigabac .... NB 427 589
Tùlaigean .... NB 444 596

Appendix 2

Ways to describe a place in Gaelic

Gaelic is the language of this land. Through Gaelic, the many gradations of landforms and landscapes are described as well as named, and there are some fascinating observations on how these distinctions subtly alter, as well as, perhaps surprisingly, some terms which are differentiated in English but which are lumped together in Gaelic. This is a functional vocabulary, chronicling what the people dwelling on that land found useful - where to walk, where to avoid, where to find berries or good arable land. Although this is not an exhaustive list, there are 765 individual terms below by which we might describe a certain place - the nature or appearance of that piece of land. This does not even include the many terms for the flowers, plants, conditions of crops, or the working nomenclature of agriculture, peat harvesting, and hunting, nor the tools for working the land. Many of the words below are now used in common conversation only rarely, if at all, (and come from several different dialects of Gaelic) but devotees of topographical nomenclature are recommended to read Campbell (2013) or simply browse the comprehensive Gaelic-English dictionary by Dwelly.

A

Abar – a confluence of two streams
Abarachd – marshiness, bogginess
Àbhadh – a fold, hollow
Abhainn – a river
Abhainneach – fluvial, abounding in rivers
Abhnag – a little river
Abhsan – a hollow or furrow
Abile – a wooded hill
Achadh – a field, plain, meadow
Aibhneach – fluvial, full of rivers
Aigeann – an abyss, a deep pool
Aigheannach – a place where thistles grow
Ailbhinn – a flinty stone or projection
Àilean – a green, plain, meadow
Aileas – pleasant country
Aill – rugged, steep river bank
Àill-bhruachach – having steep or rocky banks
Aillte – a high, precipitous rock
Ailmh – a boundary stone
Aimhreidh – defiles, passes, straits
Àiridh – a summer residence for herders and cattle
Àirneagach – full of sloes
Aisgeir – a ridge of high mountains
Aisir – a defile
Aitheornach – land ploughed for a second crop
Aitionnach – a place where Juniper grows
Allt – a mountain stream
Alltan – a streamlet

An-fhosgladh – a chasm
Annamh – a wilderness
Ansgairt – a thicket of brambles
Aoineadh – a steep promontory
Aonach – a hill, a steep height
Aonachail – mountainous
Apainn – Abbey lands
Arbharach – abounding in corn
Àrdan – a height, eminence, hillock
Àros – a place of habitation
Àr-samhraidh – fallow ground
Artach – stony ground, a quarry
Àruinn – a deer forest
Asrus – a footpath
Àthan – a little ford or shallow part of a river reaching from bank to bank
Athar-dha – one's native country
Athar-thir – one's native country
Ath-thodhar – land remaining two years untilled

B

Bacan – a knoll
Bac-moine – a peat bank
Badanach – abounding in groves or thickets
Bailc – a strip of corn-land left fallow
Baile – a hamlet or farm
Baile-geamhraidh – infields, the low grounds of a Highland farm
Bairighean – flat ground
Ball-òtraiche – a miry place
Bàn – the left-hand side of a furrow in ploughing
Bàn-achadh – a waste field
Banbh – land unploughed for a year
Bàn-talamh – Lea ground
Beacanach – abounding in mushrooms
Bealach – a defile, passage, pass, or mountain gorge
Beanntach – hilly, mountainous, rocky
Beinn – a mountain or hill
Beinneach – full or mountains or hills
Beis – marshy ground
Beitheach – belonging to birch trees
Beò-ghaineamh – quicksand
Beul-shruth – a roaring stream, a cataract
Beul-àtha – a ford, a shallow part of a river
Beum-sleibhe – a mountain torrent
Beur – a pinnacle
Binnein – a pinnacle, the apex of a hill, a high conical hill
Bioda – a pointed top
Biorrag – a soft, marshy field or plain
Bior-shruth – the old bed of a river
Blar – a plain, a field, a level flat spot

Blianach – exhausted land or land covered in drift-sand
Blianag – a green level spot of land
Bòchar – ground turned to soft mud by the feet of cattle
Bog – marsh, swampy ground
Boglach – quagmire
Boigreanach – abounding in bulrushes
Boirb – the brow of a hill
Boiriche – rising ground, a bank
Boiteach – swampy ground
Bonnchart – land between two ridges
Bòrlum – a strip of arable land
Bothag – a reedy marsh, quagmire
Bòthar – soft mud
Bràigh – upland country
Bran – a mountain stream
Branar – fallow ground
Brannrach – borderland
Breòilleanach – abounding in darnel or rye-grass
Brioghach – hilly, mountainous
Broghag – a little ditch
Brucaich – to turn up the ground imperfectly
Bruthach – a steep hillside, brae, precipice
Buaile – a circular fold for sheep or cattle
Bugha – a green spot by (the windings of) a stream
Buidhinneach – a quarry for stones
Buigileag – a soft place, a bog
Buinn-shruth – a precipitous stream
Bunan – stubble
Bun-dubh – the underground root of bracken used as thatch for houses or corn-stacks
Bùnnsach – a place where willows grow

C

Cabhan – a field or plain
Cadha – a narrow pass/ravine at the side of a mountain
Caigeann – a rough mountain pass
Cailleach-baic – the outside peat in a peat bank
Caisleach – a footpath, a smooth place
Caitcheann – land common to all the crofters in a township
Camachag – a small bay
Cambar – a place of burial
Camhar – a little cave or cove
Camus – bay, creek, harbour
Caoinleach – corn stubble
Caoir-dhis – a thicket of thorns or brambles
Caoireag – a small dry peat
Caol – a narrow strait, sound, firth
Caol-abhainn – a narrow river
Caol-fairge – a strait, a narrow part of the sea
Caomh-shrath – a pleasant valley

Caoran – third or bottom row of peat cut from a bank with a tairsgear
Càrn/Cairn – a pile of stones loosely thrown together
Càrnach – rocky, stony
Càrr – a bog, fen, moss
Carraig – rock, cliff
Casach – the outlet of a loch
Cas-cheum – a footpath, a steep or difficult way
Cas-chreag – steep rock
Càthar – mossy, soft ground, the dry part of a peat bog
Ceannamhag – the part at the end of a field where the horses turn in ploughing
Ceannamhagan – scraps of grass adjacent to growing corn
Ceann-mhàg – the head ridge in a ploughed field
Ceann-tire – a headland, promontory, peninsula
Ceap – the top of a hill
Ceap-cinn – a peat cut with a spade
Ciobach – abounding in Deer's Hare Grass
Clach – a stone
Clachach – stony, rocky, pebbly
Clach-ghrain - granite
Clach-ghuail - shale
Clach-shloc – a stone quarry
Cladach – shore, beach, coast
Cladh – a burying place, trench
Cladhan – a channel, a very narrow stream
Cladh-shruth – a canal
Claigionn – the best field of arable land on a fram
Claiseach – furrowed, trenched, full of ditches or hollows
Claoin-leathad – a sloping hill
Cleiteadh – a ridge of rocks in the sea
Cle tig – a measure of croftland containing ½ pennyland [rent], one cow's grass
Cliata – a meadow
Cliatan – a level plain of ground
Cloichreach – stony place
Cluain – pasture, green field, meadow
Cluaineag – a retired field
Cluaranach – abounding in thistles
Cnap – a little hill
Cneas-mara – firth, a strait of the sea
Cnoc – a knoll or hillock
Cobhan – a hollow, small creek
Coig-crich – strange country
Coille – wood, forest, grove
Coillearnach – woody place, shrubbery
Coille-challtuin – a Hazel wood [and many similar terms for other species of trees]
Coille-dharaich – an Oak wood
Coille-dhearcag – a wood where brambles grow
Coille-ghiuthais – a Pine wood
Coille-shlat – a wood where wattles may be cut
Coinneachail – mossy

Coirceach – abounding in oats
Coire – a circular hollow surrounded by hills [such as carved by a glacier]
Coirean – a little circular hollow/dell
Coitcheann – Common Grazing
Comh-dhùthchas – the circumstances of belonging to or having a connection with
        the same country
Còmhnard – level ground or a field
Comh-shreabh – the confluence of streams
Comh-shrutha – the confluence of streams
Conasgach – abounding in Gorse
Connalach – stubble
Corpachaich – ground under which there is decayed wood
Corrach – steep, precipitous
Còrr-bheann – a steep hill
Corr-fhàd – the first or outermost peat cut from a peat bank
Corr-fhòd – the concluding or outermost furrow of a ridge or field
Còrsa – coast, shore
Còs – a cavern, cave, hole
Cosan – a footpath
Còs-shruth – a stream running partly underground or forming hollows in its course
Crà – a fish trap in a river for catching salmon
Cracan – a hillside
Crag/Creag – a cliff, rocky, a precipice
Craobharnach – shrubbery
Creachann – the summit of a rock
Creagach – craggy, rocky
Creatrach – wilderness
Crioch – a boundary land mark
Cro-sheilg - a hiding place for hunters
Crothaid – gravel
Cruach – a rounded hill standing apart
Cruaidh-rathad – a causeway
Cruailinn – mountainous rocky ground, hard ground
Crùlaist – a rocky hill
Cuairt-char - a meander
Cuanna – a hill
Cuinge – a narrow strait or passage
Cuithe – a trench, pit, or cattle enclosure
Cùlagach – abounding in turf
Cùl-cinn – outrun, common grazing
Cunglach – a cleft, a narrow defile
Curagh- a burial place
Currach – a bog where shrubs grow

D

Dabhach – a portion of land or farm to carry 60 cows or head of cattle
Daibhir – the common or worst pasture of a farm
Dail – field, dales, meadow
Dail-bhuntàta – a potato field

Dairbh – a nursery or grove of Oaks
Dàirteach – a field of clods
Damaisear – mud, mire
Damh-imir – a 20-acre field
Deanntagach – a place where nettles grow
Dearc – a cave, grotto, hole, grave
Dearcach – abounding in berries
Deisear – a place having a southern exposure
Diamhladh – a place of retreat or refuge
Dian-shruth – a rapid stream or torrent
Dìg – a ditch or drain
Dìleagach – abounding in flowers
Dilleanan – the depth(s) of the earth
Dìon-aite – a place of refuge or sanctuary, shelter
Diong – hillock
Dionnan – a little hill
Disd – a layer of stacked peats or turfs
Dìthreabh – the higher and less cultivated parts of a district
Dlùth-phreasach – full of thickets or thick bushes
Dob – a river or stream
Dobhair – the border of a country
Doch – one's native country
Doir-choille – a grove
Doirling – an isthmus, peninsula
Dornaidh – a narrow channel of the sea where it flows and ebbs and where at full tide
        a vessel can be towed to either side of the harbour
Dosach – bushy, full of thickets
Dris-choill – a thicket of briars of brambles
Drisearnach - a thicket of briars of brambles
Droighnean – a thicket of Blackthorns
Dromanach – ridged or furrowed land
Dronnag – the highest point of a ridge
Dronnan – the ridge of a hill
Druibheal – a dark place
Druim – the ridge of a hill
Dubhagan – the deepest part of a stream or pool
Dubh-fhàd – the second (level) or lowest peat
Dubh-ghlac – a dark valley
Dubh-ghleann – a dark valley
Dubhras – a gloomy wood
Dùcan – a little heap or little hillock
Dùcan-faimh – a mole-hill
Duibheagan – an abyss
Duibheid – a divot, a flat turf used for covering a cottage roof
Dùn – a heap, hillock, mound
Dunnsag – a large stone or boulder
Duslachail – earthy, dusty
Dùthaich – country, native-land
Dùthchas – the place of one's birth, one's hereditary right

E

Eabarach – muddy, miry
Eachrann – a place where brambles grow
Each-shlighe – a horse road
Eagmin – a meander (of a river)
Earghalt – arable land
Earrlait – rich soil, ground manured one year and productive the next
Eas – a waterfall
Easach – a dark, deep, rocky stream
Easaraiche – the boiling of a pool where a cascade falls
Easard – a cataract
Eascaich – a quagmire or fen
Easg – a ditch formed by nature
Easloch – a pool
Eibhir – granite
Eilean – an island
Eilgheadh – the first ploughing of land that requires a second ploughing for seed
Eilidh – fallow ground
Eisgir – a ridge of mountains
Eiteag – white quartz
Eithreach – wilderness
Eitre – a trench or furrow
Eòrnach – Barley-land
Eug-lios – a burying ground

F

Fàdach – abounding in peats
Fadhail – a hollow in the sand, formed by and retaining water after the egress of the tide
Fadhban – a molehill
Fadhlach – havig an extensive beach
Fadhlainn – an exposed place beside the shore covered with small white stones
Fad-seilbh – the handful of earth given by the seller to the buyer of land; possession
Faiche – field, meadow
Faileag – hillock, little meadow
Fàir – skyline, height, ridge, hill
Fairc – land sometimes covered by the sea, links
Fàire-druim – a saddle-back
Fairthir – the shelving slope between an old raised beach or other plateau and the
          present beach
Falach-fuinn – land-hiding; taking advantage of every natural feature in the landscape
          to hide
Fàladh – enclosing or covering with turf
Falaisg – moor-burning
Falc – sterile, barren ground, ground parched by heat
Famh-thòrr – a molehill
Faobhar – a ridge of a hill, edge of a precipice
Faoch – a field
Faoi – a noisy stream
Faoin-bheanntan – a sloping hill

Faontraigh – an exposed place, the open shore
Farbhalla – a buttress
Far-bheann – a cliffy mountain, pinnacle
Fàsach – a desert, wilderness
Fasan – homestead and cultivated ground around it
Fàs-choille – a young grove of trees in its first few years of growth
Fàsmhor – a desolate, lonely place
Fàth – a long narrow glen
Feadan – a small watercourse
Feannad – the surface peat (whiter)
Feanntach – the turf taken off a peat bog before commencing to cut peats
Fearann – land, earth, estate
Fear-breige – a heap of stones used as a landmark
Fearsach – full of little ridges in the sand
Fearsda – a pool, standing water
Featha – moorland
Feirsde – pits of water in the sand at low tide
Feith(ean) – rents in the moor or bog-land made by water, bog-channel(s)
Feodhail – a shallow estuary
Feòran – a mountain valley
Feurach – abounding in grass, a grassy place
Feuth – a peat hag
Fiadhach – abounding in deer
Fiadhair – lea land, green sward
Fiadh-àite – a wild desert place
Fiadh-ghleann – a wild glen where deer herd together
Fiadh-lann – a deer park
Fianach – moor-grass
Fidean – a green islet or spot uncovered at high tide
Fighdeach – links, land sometimes covered by the sea
Fineach – rank moor grass
Fineagach – full of crowberries
Fineamhnach – a place where vines grow
Fiodhach – a shrubbery
Fiodhagach – abounding in bird-cherries
Fionn-choille – a flourishing wood
Fionn-chòinneach – white moss
Fior-thobrach – abounding in perennial springs or wells
Fior-uachdar – a summit
Foid – clod, turf, sod
Foighe – a green or lawn
Foinnsidh – springs, wells, fountains
Foirb – land
Fòir-bhruach – pinnacle or precipice
Foirichean – boundaries, borders
Fòirinn – borderland, debatable land
Foithre – woods
Forrach – a perch (a measure of land equal to 5.5 yards)
Fothach – a lochan, marsh, pond
Fothargadh – a well of purification

Fraochach – heath-covered
Fraon – a place of shelter in the mountains
Freumhach – full of roots
Frìth – a deer forest
Frith-cheum – a by-road
Frith-choille – underwood, brushwood
Frith-eilean – a small island
Fuachasach – full of caves
Fuar-achadh – untilled land
Fuaran – a well or a spring

G

Gabhaltas – land rented from a landlord, land in tack, division of land among the clan
Gabhrach – abounding in goats
Gail-bheinn – a great or rocky hill
Gaineamh – sand, gravel
Gairbheal – coarse sand, gravel
Gamhann – a ditch
Gaotha – streams left at low water
Gàradh – the second row of peats taken from a bank
Gàradh-arbhair – a corn-yard, stackyard
Gàradh-an-arbh – a dyke surrounding arable land
Gàradh-baic – peats laid out on the edge of the bank, one over the other, to dry rapidly
Gàradh-cinn – the dyke separating arable land from the moor or common pasture
Gàradh-crìche – the boundary dyke between two properties
Gàradh-droma – a turf dyke
Gàradh-fàil – a turf dyke
Gàradh-gleidht – a defending wall
Garan – a grove, forest, thicket
Garbhachd – a rocky place
Garbhalach – stony or rocky ground
Garbh-allt – an impetuous torrent
Garbh-chrìoch – rugged country
Garbh-eas – a cascade, rough torrent
Garbh-ghaineamh – coarse gravel
Garbh-ghrinneal – gravel
Garbhlach – the more rugged part of a country, stony or rocky river bed
Garbh-leac – the rugged part of a country
Garbh-shlios – the rough side of a hill
Gàrd – a fenced place
Garran – a thicket, grove, underwood
Gart – a field of standing corn
Gart-ghlainte – an area cleared of weeds
Gead – a small spot of arable land
Geadach – abounding in little fields
Gead – an iron rod about 2m in length with the end bent into an oval to serve as a
        handle, used for determining the presence of tree remains in a peat-moss
Geadhail – a ploughed field or park
Geamhrach – a winter park or feeding area

Gearradh-aidhean – a summer grazing place for cattle

Gearraidh – a point of land, the land between the machair and the moor, enclosed grazing between arable land and the open moor

Geil -a fountain, well, spring

Geòdh – a creek or cove formed by surrounding rocks

Geòtan – a spot of arable land

Gil – a watercourse on a mountainside

Gilmean – a small green knoll

Giolaid – an inlet, little creek

Giùirne – a rocky knoll on the side of a mountain

Giuthasach – abounding in Scots Pine

Glac – a narrow valley

Glaibeach – boggy

Glaisbheann – a grey hill

Glas-choirean – a little green valley

Glas-ghort – a piece of lea ground

Glas-mhagh – a green field or plain

Glasrach – uncultivated land

Glasradh – pasture land

Gleann – a valley, dale, glen

Glomhas – a rock cleft

Gluis-gheugach – full of green boughs

Glumaid – a deep pool in a river

Gluta – a deep round pool

Gnàithseach – arable land under crops

Gobhlan - a river or burn where the stream divides

Gobhlannaidh – a hollow between two hills

Goibheinn – a little hill

Goirteanach – abounding in little fields, crofts, or patches of arable land

Gorm – a grassy or green plain

Gormanach – Full of green fields

Gorm-shleibhteach – green hilled

Gort – standing corn

Greallaich – clay, mud, dirt, mire

Grianan – a sunny spot

Grioth – a gravel-pit

Gròilleach – muddy

Gròiseideach – abounding in gooseberries

Grothal – sand or gravel

Gruaim-bheinn – a dark hill or gloomy mountain

Grunnan – a little heap or hillock

Guganach – abounding in buds, flowers, or daisies

I

I – an island

Iarspealadh – a second crop of grass

Igh – a small stream with green banks

Ilbhinn – a craggy mountain

Ingealtas – pasture ground, ground fit for feeding cattle

Inuilt – pasture
Innean – a rock or a hill
Innis – a sheltered valley protected by a wood
Innis-mhuir – an archipelago
Innseach – abounding in islands
Innseag – a little island, a detached field or pasture, a little patch of arable ground in
                hilly, wooded country
Ìochdaranta – a tributary
Ìoc-lusach – abounding in healing herbs
Iodhan – a small strip of land under corn
Iolar – the bottom of a loch or the foot of a hill
Iolla – a fishing rock, generally covered at high tide
Iollairce – a hiding hillock in deer hunting
Iomaireach – abounding in ridges of land
Ionailt – feed, grazing
Ion-àitichte – arable fit for cultivation
Ionaltradh – pasture
Ionbhar – the confluence of waters
Ironn – a field
Ithir – a cornfield, arable land
It-ros – a headland or promontory
Iubharach – abounding in Yew trees
Iùilean – a landmark at sea
Iumaidh – level ground, open country

L

Labach – swampy or boggy
Làimhrig – a natural landing place on the shore
Làirig – a pass between two mountains, a sloping hill
Lamhgair – a sunken ledge of rock covered with slippery seaweed
Làmh-ròd – a footpath or by-road
Lànaig – a narrow path for cattle through crofts in a township
Lann-gleidhte – an enclosure
Lanntair – landscape, a beautiful side of a country, full of woods and arable land,
     facing the sea
Laomach – a piece of land where corn falls flat from exuberant growth
Làpach – marsh, swamp, bog
Làr – the ground, earth
Làrach – the site of a building or ruin
Làthaich – moor, peat-moss
Leac – flat slab, a ledge of rock jutting out from a cliff
Leacann – the broad side of a hill, a broad slope
Lèana – a meadow or swampy plain, a field of luxuriant grass
Lèanach – swampy, marshy
Lèanag – a small meadow or lawn
Lèantach – a country of plains
Lear-dhromain – the ridge of a hill
Leargan – the sloping green side of a hill, steep pasture ground
Leig – a marshy or miry pool

Leig-chritheach – quagmire
Leitir – the slope of a hill or shore
Leth-rathad – a by-road
Linne – a pool, pond, or cataract
Lob – a puddle
Loch – a loch (lake)
Lochanach – abounding in little lochs
Loch-monaidh – a mountain tarn
Loch-uisge – a freshwater loch
Lochan-tàimh – a loch having no outflow
Lodach – abounding in pools or puddles
Lòin – a little stream or rivulet
Lòineanach – abounding in little meadows
Loireachan – a boggy or wet place
Lom – a bare surface or plain
Lon – a puddle, a meadow or small brook with marshy banks
Lonaig – a lane for cattle
Lorganach-shneachda – sufficient snow covering the land to show a track
Luachrach – full of rushes
Lùb-shruth – a winding or meandering stream
Lùib – an angular turning or bend of a stream
Lùibeach – full of little glens or creeks
Luim-dheirg – an abyss or deep channel of a river
Luimean – a barren hillock
Luisreadh – a plain abounding in herbs or plants
Lunndan – a meadow, marshy ground
Lusairneach – a place where weeds grow
Lusrach – a place well supplied with herbs

M

Machair – flat and sandy coastal grassland
Màg – a field that can be ploughed, a very broad ridge of arable land
Magh-aoraidh – a field of worship
Magh-uisge – a winter loch
Mainnir – a fold on the hillside for livestock
Maol – the brow of a rock, cape, or promontory
Maol-aodainn – a bleak hillside
Maor – a field
Marbh-shruth – a still stream
Màrr – a thicket in which to catch cattle
Meacanach – abounding in roots
Mealbhan – a stretch of sand dunes with sea-bent growing on them
Meall – a great shapeless hill
Meanntach – abounding in Mint
Meas-ghort – a fruit garden or orchard
Meiltreach – a smooth, level plain
Meuragach – abounding in small pebbles
Miadan – a grassy plain

Mianach – abounding in ore
Mi-chorrach – not steep, easy of ascent and descent
Min – a plain field
Mìn-fheurach – abounding in soft grass
Mion-chlach – gravel
Mion-chorrach – very steep ground
Mionnan – a small mound
Mire-shruth – a rapid stream
Mòine – a mossy place, peat
Mòinteach – moorland, a peat-moss
Mòirneas – a great cascade or waterfall
Moluach – marsh
Monachan – hills, mountains
Monadh – any hill pasture as distinguished from meadow and arable land
Morbhach – land liable to flooding by the sea
Morghan – gravel or shingle
Muc-ghaineamh – a sandbank, quicksand
Muileagach – abounding in Cranberries
Muinchinn – a headland
Muir-ghobhal – an arm of the sea
Mulagach – hilly or knolly
Mullach – a summit
Mùrach – a sandhill on the seashore

N

Near-àite – A place frequented by wild boars
Neas – a fortified hill; an isthmus, promontory, or headland
Neòineanach – abounding in daisies
Nios – a top or summit
Nochd-larach – a place that is laid waste

O

Òb – a bay, creek, or harbour
Ochdamh – four pennylands, an eighth of a davoch – a measure of land
Oil – a stone or a rock
Oirthir – the coast, shore, beach
Oitir – a bank or ridge in the sea
Òrd – a steep mountain with a round form
Os – a river mouth or outlet
Oth – a large body of water
Othainn – a large river

P

Pabach – full of refuse of flax
Pabadh – a luxuriance of grass
Pail-chlachan – a causeway
Pàirc – an enclosed field
Peighinn – one twelfth of a Scots penny; a measure of land (for rent)
Pìbhinneach - abounding in Lapwings

Pliad – a plot of ground
Plocach – abounding in pieces of earth, turf, or clods
Plòitean – downy peat
Plumag – a little, deep pool
Poll – a pole of land (301/4 square yards)
Poll – a hole, pit, pool with deep, stagnant water
Polldach – marshy ground
Poll-mòna – a peat hag
Pota – a hole from which peats have been cut
Preach – a bog, marsh, morass
Preas – a shrub or thicket
Preasarlach – coppice
Preasarnach – shrubbery
Priomh-abhainn – a large river
Pruchlais - a den or cave
Pulagach – abounding in round stones
Punnd – an enclosure to contain livestock that trespass
Pùtach – abounding in young Grouse

R

Raghar – arable land not in tillage; sometimes grazing ground enclosed between the arable land and the open moor
Raineachail – abounding in ferns
Ranach – a cave that gives an echo
Rang – the bank of a river
Rann – a promontory
Raointeach – meadowy, full of plains
Raon – a mossy field or plain
Raonadh – a way or road
Rasachd – shrubbery
Rastach – country
Rathad – a road, path, track
Reidh – a plain, meadow, level ground
Riasg – a moor or marsh
Riasglach – land that cannot be cultivated
Righe – a field, the bottom of a valley
Rinneach – abounding in promontories or headlands
Riomba – a semi-circular bay or beach
Rion – a way, road, track
Ritheadh – a grove
Ro-choille – a thick wood
Ro-chrannach – abounding in stately or lofty trees
Ròig – a den or a cave
Roilbheach – hilly
Roileag – a burial ground
Roimh – earth, soil
Roinn-ruithe – run-rig, a form of common division of the land for cultivation
Ruadh-bhuinne – a mountain torrent
Ruaimle – muddy standing water

Rucanach – abounding in stacks of corn
Ruadha – a point of land, a promontory
Ruimneach – a marsh
Rumach – a marsh
Rustan – a hillock

S

Sàileagach – abounding in creeks, bays, or inlets of the sea
Sàilean – a little inlet or arm of the sea
Sàilear – a cavern or grotto
Samhnach – a deer park or winter park
Saothair – a low promontory covered at high tide
Seann-talamh – fallow land, or land long unploughed
Seasgan – moor-like ground
Seidean – quicksand
Seileachean - a place where willows grow
Seilisdeireach – abounding in Yellow Iris
Seisgeach – abounding in bog reeds
Seisgeann – boggy country
Seisreinn – as much land as can be ploughed with one plough in a year
Seolas – a passage for boats cleaned of stones
Sgàil-ionad – a bower
Sgailp – a den or a cave
Sgair – any place where a thing is laid to dry
Sgairg – a gravelly bottom
Sgàirneach – scree; a continuous heap of stones covering a mountainside
Sgaoilteich – ground on which to spread anything to dry
Sgàrdan – scree
Sgarta – a cleft, cave, or recess in rock in which to hide
Sgeachrach – full of bushes, thorns, or briars
Sgeilp – a shelf or a cliff of rock
Sgein – a hiding place
Sgeir – a rock in the sea
Sgirbh – a rocky ford; a stony bottom
Sglèatach – a slate quarry
Sgoirm – the brow of a hill
Sgòr – a sharp, steep hill; a precipitous height on another hill or mountain
Sgoraban – a little pointed rock
Sgòr-bheannach – rocky, hilly
Sgòr-bheinn – a mountain cliff
Sgòr-eild – a hill frequented by Roe Deer
Sgòr-shruth – a rocky stream
Sgoth – an abrupt hill
Sgreagach – parched, rocky soil
Sgreagan – hard, rocky ground
Sgribhinn – the rugged side of a hill
Sgriodadh – shingle
Sgriodan – a stony ravine on a mountainside
Sgriogalach – bare mountain top beyond the line of vegetation

Sgrioth – gravel
Sguit – a piece of land cut off from another
Sgùrr – a high, sharp-pointed hill
Siaban – drifted sand
Sionn – here
Sith – a hill-mount
Sithean – a little hill or knoll
Siuchag – a small patch of smooth green sward amid rough heathery ground
Slàib – mire by the side of a stream
Sleibhteach – mountainous, hilly
Sliabh – an area of dry moorland on a mountain
Sligearnach – a place abounding in shells
Sloc – a hollow or hole
Slodanach – full of little pools or puddles
Slorag – a dell
Slugaite – quicksand
Smalanach – full of hillocks
Soilleagach – abounding in willows
Sonann – fertile land
Sorchan – a little hillock
Sòrnach – a great heap of boulders at the foot of a precipice
Spad-thalamh – unproductive or fallow ground
Spàrdan – a level shelf on a hillside where one would naturally rest
Spitheagach – full of pebbles or small stones
Srath – a valley through which a river runs; low-lying country along a river
Srathanach – abounding in little valleys
Sròn – a promontory or headland (like a nose) running from a mountain ridge
Sruamach – the meeting of streams
Sruthan – a stream or rivulet
Stac – a precipice or high, projecting rock
Staing – a ditch or trench
Stair – stepping stones in a river
Stalla – an overhanging rock; a ledge on the face of a cliff
Stang – a pool of standing water
Starran – a place for crossing a river
Steall – a cataract or mountain torrent
Steud-shruth – a rapid stream
Stobanach – abounding in small stumps
Stòr – a steep, high cliff
Stuadh – the summit of a mountain
Stuaic – a small rounded promontory
Stùc – a little hill jutting out which is steep on one side and rounded on the other
Stùc-bheinn – a rocky mountain
Stuirichd – a pinnacle
Stùrr – the rugged point of a hill
Sùil-chritheach – deep bog, quagmire
Sùthanach – quicksand

T

Tàirbhealach – a defile, pass, or narrow mountain valley
Talamh-toll – the opening over a burn running underground
Tanalach – shallow water
Tathag – a small in-bye field
Teil – fertile ground
Tiadhanach – abounding in little hills or mounds
Tiobairteach – abounding in springs
Tir – the land
Tobhtag – a small yard containing a stack or two of corn
Tochar – a causeway
Tochlad – a quarry or mine
Tom – a round hillock or knoll
Tòrr – a hill of abrupt or conical form
Tràigh-cheum – a path along the shore of the sea or a loch
Treabhachas – an arable farm
Troimchill – sanctuary
Trusganach – abounding in Lady's Mantle
Tuathair – countryside with a northern exposure
Tuilmean – a little knoll
Tuineadh – a dwelling place
Tulach – a hillock or a knoll
Tum-àite – a bathing place
Tum-ionad – a bathing place
Tung – an enclosed family burial ground
Turloch – ground covered with water in the winter and dry in summer

U

Uachdar – summit or upper part
Uaghaidh – a cave, cavern, or den
Uaigh – a grave or tomb
Uar – a waterfall
Uchdach – a brae, a steep ascent
Uchdan – a hillock, a raised bank or terrace
Ùdrathad – free access to the common land
Ughtraid – a side road or byway
Ùidh – a ford; the part of a stream which leaves a loch before breaking into a current;
          slow-running water between two lochs
Uig – a solitary hollow or nook
Uirigh-creige – a shelf of rock
Ùirlios – a walled garden
Urard – a high place, high ground
Urlar – a low place in the landscape

Appendix 3

Species mentioned in this book (or noted in Gabhsann)

English	Scientific	Gaelic
Mammals		
Arctic Fox	*Vulpes lagopus*	Sionnach an t-Sneachda
Arctic Lemming	*Dicrostonyx torquatus*	Lemming an t-Sneachda
Badger	*Meles meles*	Broc
Brown Bear	*Ursus arctos arctos*	Math-gamhainn
Common Hedgehog	*Erinaceus europaeus*	Gràineag
Common Porpoise	*Phocoena phocoena*	Pèileag
Common Seal	*Phoca vitulina*	Ròn
Ferret	*Mustela furo*	Fearaid
Field Vole	*Microtus agrestis exsul*	Feurlagan
Fin Whale	*Balaenoptera physalus*	Muc-an-sgadain
Grey Seal	*Halichoerus grypus*	Ròn Mòr
Humpback Whale	*Megaptera novaeangliae*	Muc-mhara chrotach
Long-tailed Field Mouse	*Apodemus hebridensis*	Luch-fheòir
Lynx	*Lynx lynx*	Lincs
Mink	*Mustela vison*	Mionc
Minke Whale	*Balaenoptera acutorostrata*	Muc-mhionc
Mountain Hare	*Lepus timidus*	Geàrr a mhonaidh
Orca (Killer whale)	*Orcinus orca*	Madadh-cuain
Otter	*Lutra lutra*	Dòbhran
Pine Marten	*Mustela martes*	Taghan
Polecat	*Mustela putorius*	Feòcallan
Pygmy Shrew	*Sorex minutus*	Fionnag-feòir
Rabbit	*Oryctolagus cuniculus*	Coineanach
Red Deer	*Cervus elaphus*	Fèidh
Red Deer	*Cervus elaphus*	Damh (Stag)
Risso's Dolphin	*Grampus griseus*	Leumadair Risso
Roe Deer	*Capreolus capreolus*	Earbh (Male)
Roe Deer	*Capreolus capreolus*	Eilid Female)
Reindeer	*Rangifer tarandus*	Rèin-fhèidh
Sperm Whale	*Physeter macrocephalus*	Muc-mhara spùtach
Walrus	*Odobenus rosmarus*	Each-mara
White-beaked Dolphin	*Lagenorhynchus albirostris*	Leumadair geal-ghobach
White-sided Dolphin	*Lagenorhynchus acutus*	Leumadair cliathaich-bhàin
Wild Boar	*Sus scrofa*	Torc fiadhaich
Wildcat	*Felis silvestris*	Cat-fiadhaich
Birds		
Arctic Redpoll	*Acanthis hornemanni*	Deargan-seilich an t-sneachda
Arctic Skua	*Stercorarius parasiticus*	Fàsgadair
Arctic Tern	*Sterna paradisea*	Steàrnal
Barnacle Goose	*Branta leucopsis*	Cathan

Black-headed Gul	*Larus ridibundus*	Faoileag a' chinn duibh
Blackbird	*Turdus merula*	Druid
Bonxie	*Stercorarius skua*	Fàsgadair mòr
Buzzard	*Buteo buteo*	Clamhan
Chough	*Pyrrhocorax pyrrhocorax*	Cathag dhearg-chasach
Corncrake	*Crex crex*	Traon
Canada Goose	*Branta canadensis*	Gèadh Canadach
Carrion Crow	*Corvus corone corone*	Feannag-dhubh
Common Gull	*Larus canus*	Faoileag-bheag-an-sgadain
Common Sandpiper	*Actitis hypoleucos*	Fìdhleir
Common Snipe	*Gallinago gallinago*	Naosg
Common Tern	*Sterna hirundo*	Steàrnag
Coot	*Fulica atra*	Lach-bhlàir
Cormorant	*Phalacrocorax carbo*	Sgarbh
Corncrake	*Crex crex*	Traon
Cuckoo	*Cuculus canorus*	Cuthag
Curlew	*Numenius arquata*	Guilbneach
Dotterel	*Eudromias morinellus*	Amadan mòintich
Dunlin	*Calidris alpina*	Gràillig or Gille-feadaig
Fulmar	*Fulmarus glacialis*	Eun crom
Gannet	*Morus bassana*	Sùlair
Glaucous Gull	*Larus hyperboreus*	Muir-mhaighstir
Glossy Ibis	*Plegadis falcinellus*	Ìbis-lìomharra
Golden Eagle	*Aquila chrysaetos*	Iolair
Golden Plover	*Pluvialis apricaria*	Feadag
Great Black-backed Gull	*Larus marinus*	Farspag
Great Northern Diver	*Gavia immer*	Muir-bhuachaill
Great Skua	*Stercorarius skua*	Fàsgadair mòr
Greenshank	*Tringa nebularia*	Deoch bhiugh
Grey Heron	*Ardea cinerea*	Corra-ghritheach
Greylag Goose	*Anser anser*	Gèadh-glas
Guillemot	*Uria aalge*	Eun-dubh-an-sgadain
Hen Harrier	*Circus cyaneus*	Clamhan nan Cearc
Herring Gull	*Larus argentatus*	Faoileag an sgadain
Hooded Crow	*Corvus corone cornix*	Feannag
Iceland Gull	*Larus glaucoides*	Faoileag-liath
Jackdaw	*Corvus monedula*	Cathag
Kestrel	*Falco tinnunculus*	Clamhan ruadh
Lapland Bunting	*Calcarius lapponicus*	Gealag Lappaich
Lapwing	*Vanellus vanellus*	Curracag
Laughing Gull	*Leucophaeus atricilla*	Faoileag Ameireaganach
Lesser Black-backed Gull	*Larus fuscus*	Faoileag bheag
Magpie	*Pica pica*	Pioghaid
Mallard	*Anas platyrhynchos*	Lach riabhach
Marsh Harrier	*Circus aeruginosus*	Clamhan-lòin
Meadow Pipit	*Anthus pratensis*	Snàthag
Merlin	*Falco columbarius*	Mèirneal
Oystercatcher	*Haematopus ostralegus*	Gille brìghde

Peregrine Falcon	*Falco peregrinus*	Seabhag
Puffin	*Fratercula arctica*	Buthaid
Raven	*orvus corax*	Fitheach
Red Grouse	*Lagopus lagopus*	Coileach fraoich
Red-necked Phalarope	*Phalaropus lobatus*	Deargan-allt
Red-throated Diver	*Gavia stellata*	Learga dhearg
Redshank	*Tringa totanus*	Cam-ghlas
Redwing	*Turdus iliacus*	Sgiath-dheargan
Ringed Plover	*Charadrius hiaticula*	Trìlleachan-tràghad
Rock Dove	*Columba livia*	Calman creige
Rock Pipit	*Anthus spinoletta*	Gabhagan
Rook	*Corvus frugilegus*	Ròcais
Shag	*Phalacrocorax aristotelis*	Sgarbh an sgumain
Skylark	*Alauda arvensis*	Uiseag
Snowy Owl	*Nyctea scandiaca*	Comhachag bhàn
Starling	*Sturnus vulgaris*	Druid
Stonechat	*Saxicola torquata*	Clacharan
Swallow	*Hirundo rustica*	Gobhlan-gaoithe
Wheatear	*Oenanthe oenanthe*	Brù-gheal
White-tailed Sea Eagle	*Haliaeetus albicilla*	Iolair-mhara
Wren (Hebridean)	*Troglodytes t. hebridensis*	Dreathan-donn

Fish

Basking Shark	*Cetorhinus maximus*	Cearban
Cod	*Gadus morhua*	Trosg
Herring	*Clupea harengus*	Sgadan
Horse Mackerel	*Trachurus trachurus*	Cnàimh-rionnach
Ling	*Molva molva*	Langa
Lythe	*Pollachius pollachius*	Liùbh
Mackerel	*Scomber scombrus*	Rionnach
Megrim	*Lepidorhombus whiffiagonis*	Leabag-cheàrr
Saithe	*Pollachius virens*	Saoidhean
Sandeel	*Ammodytidae*	Siolag
Whiting	*Merlangius merlangus*	Cuiteag
Witch	*Glyptocephalus cynoglossus*	Leabag-uisge

Plants

Alder	*Alnus glutinosa*	Feàrna
Bell Heather	*Erica cinerea*	Fraoch a' Bhadain
Bog Asphodel	*Narthecium ossifragum*	Bliochan
Bog Pondweed	*Potamogeton polygonifolius*	Lìobhag Bogaich
Bog Sedge	*Carex limosa*	Seisg na Mòna
Bogbean	*Menyanthes trifoliata*	Trì-bhileach
Carnation Sedge	*Carex panicea*	Seisg a' Chruithneachd
Carrageen	*Chondrus cripsus*	Cairgean
Common Butterwort	*Pinguicula vulgaris*	Mòthan
Common Cottongrass	*Eriophorum angustifolium*	Canach
Cross-leaved Heath	*Erica tetralix*	Fraoch Frangach
Crowberry	*Empetrum nigrum*	Lus na Feannaig
Dark-leaved Willow	*Salix nigricans*	Seileach na Duilleige

Duirche	Deergrass	*Trichophorum cespitosum*
Cìob		
Dioecious Sedge	*Carex dioica*	Seisg Aon-cheannach
Downy Birch	*Betula pubescens*	Beith Charraigeach
Dulse	*Palmaria palmata*	Duileasg
Dwarf Willow	*Salix herbacea*	Seileach Ailpeach
Eared Willow	*Salix aurita*	Seileach Cluasach
Early Marsh-orchid	*Dactylorhiza incarnata*	Mogairlean Lèana
Feathery Bog-moss	*Sphagnum cuspidatum*	Còinneach-bhoglaich chleiteach
Few-flowered Sedge	*Carex pauciflora*	Seisg nan Lusan Gann
Frog Orchid	*Coeloglossum viride*	Mogairlean Losgainn
Goat Willow	*Salix caprea*	Geal-sheileach
Great Sundew	*Drosera anglica*	Lus a' Ghadmainn
Grey Willow	*Salix cinerea*	Dubh-sheileach
Hare's-tail Cottongrass	*Eriophorum vaginatum*	Sìoda Mhonaidh
Hawthorn	*Crataegus monogyna*	Sgitheach
Hazel	*Corylus avellana*	Calltainn
Heath Spotted-orchid	*Dactylorhiza maculata*	Mogairlean Mòintich
Heather	*Calluna vulgaris*	Fraoch
Hebridean Spotted-orchid	*Dactylorhiza fuchsii*	Urach-bhallach
Lustrous Bog-moss	*Sphagnum subnitens*	Còinneach-bhoglaich lìomharra
Magellanic Bog-moss	*Sphagnum magellanicum*	Còinneach-bhoglaich Magellan
Many-stalked Spike-rush	*Eleocharis multicaulis*	Bioran Badanach
Marsh Marigold	*Caltha palustris*	Lus buidhe bealltain
Northern Deer Grass	*Trichophorum cespitosum*	Cìob
Northern Marsh-orchid	*Dactylorhiza purpurella*	Mogairlean Purpaidh
Oblong-leaved Sundew	*Drosera intermedia*	Dealt ruaidhe
Pale Butterwort	*Pinguicula lusitanica*	Mòthan beag bàn
Papillose Bog-moss	*Sphagnum papillosum*	Còinneach-bhoglaich Papillose
Purple Moor-grass	*Molinia caerulea*	Fianach
Red Bog-moss	*Sphagnum rubellum*	Còinneach ruadh
Round-leaved Sundew	*Drosera rotundifolia*	Lus na feàrnaich
Rowan	*Sorbus aucuparia*	Caorann
Scots Pine	*Pinus sylvestris*	Giuthas
Sheep Sorrel	*Rumex acetosella*	Sealbhag nan Caorach
Silver Birch	*Betula pendula*	Beith Dhubhach
Slender Cow-horn Bog-moss	*Sphagnum subsecundum*	Còinneach
Slender Sedge	*Carex lasiocarpa*	Seisg Choilleanta
Soft Bog-moss	*Sphagnum tenellum*	Còinneach-bhoglaich tais
Soft Rush	*Juncus effusus*	Luachair Bhog
Spearmint	*Mentha spicata*	Meannt gàrraidh
Tea-leaved Willow	*Salix phylicifolia*	Seileach-tuathach
Tormentil	*Potentilla erecta*	Cairt làir
Thyme	*Thymus praecox*	Luibh-na-macraidh
White Beak-sedge	*Rhynchospora alba*	Gob-sheisg
White Water-lily	*Nymphaea alba*	Duilleag-bhàite Bhàn
Woolly Fringe-moss	*Racomitrium lanuginosum*	Còinneach-ghruaige ola
Yellow Iris	*Iris pseudacorus*	Seileastair

Invertebrates

Azure Damselfly	*Coenagrion puella*	Cruinneag liath
Cryptic Bumblebee	*Bombus cryptarum*	Seillean-dìomhair
Dragonfly	*Cordulegaster boltonii*	Tarbh-nathrach òrfhàinneach
Garden Tiger Moth	*Arctia caja*	Leòmann-tìgeir mòr
Great Yellow Bumblebee	*Bombus distinguendus*	Seillean-mòr buidhe
Heath Bumblebee	*Bombus jonellus*	Seillean-mòr a' bhlàir-fhraoich
Large Red Damselfly	*Pyrrhosoma nymphula*	Cruinneag dhearg
Limpet	*Patella sp*	Bàirneach
Midge	*Culicoides impunctatus*	Meanbh-chuileag
Moss Carder Bumblebee	*Bombus muscorum*	Seillean càrdair na còinnich
Mussel	*Mytilus sp*	Feusgan
Northern Colletes	*Colletes floralis*	Seillean-talmhainn
Northern White-tailed Bumblebee	*Bombus magnus*	Seillean-mòr earball-bàn a' chinn a tuath
Red Admiral	*Vanessa atalanta*	Àrd-sheòladair dearg
Scallop	*Aequipecten opercularis*	Creachan
White-tailed Bumblebee	*Bombus lucorum*	Seillean-mòr an earbaill bhàin
Winkle	*Littorina sp*	Faochag

Appendix 4 <small>206 & 320</small>

There are eight surviving verses, but no title.

B'e siud bliadhna na h-éiginn:
Shil na speuran na frasan,
Bha an crodh air na stéillean
Ri dol eug leis an acras;
Cha robh connadh ri fhaotainn
Air gach taobh do'n bhaile,
Is chaidh gach bruthach agus garradh
Chur gu làr air son teine.

That was the year of extreme difficulty:
Rain showered down from the skies,
Cattle were carried on biers,
Dying from hunger.
No fuel [peats] could be found
Anywhere around the village,
And so every hillside and dyke
Was razed down to feed the fires.

Dhùilt an siameurlan sìol dhuinn
Air son biadh na sìol-cura;
Is rinn na ceannaichean cumhnant
Gun làn a dùirn 'thoirt do dhuine;
Mura pàigheadh sinn sìos e
Leis an iasg bho'n an dubhan,
No le crùna na Rìoghachd,
Cha deidheadh sgrìobag air duinte.

The Factor refused to give us seed
In order to sow food crops
And the merchants entered an agreement
Not to give a fistful of it to anyone;
If we could not pay for it
With the fish from the fishing-hook,
Or with British crown coins,
No one would have as much as a scratch.

'S ann bho Loch an Dùnain a sheòl sinn
Air ar fògradh á Alba;
Is iomadh neach a bha tùirseach
Nuair a chaill sinn Mùirneag 's an an-moch;
Am bàta-iarainn gu sunndach
Null leinn gu fairge
Dh'ionnsaigh Baile Doire an Éirinn
Far an d'fhuair sin té'ile gu falbh leinn.

It was from Loch an Dùnain that we sailed
Expelled out of Scotland;
Many a person was mournful
When we lost sight of Mùirneag in the
    twilight;
The iron boat cheerily going over with us
    to sea
Towards Derry in Ireland
Where we got another boat to take us away

Ealasaid bhòidheach
Is i an òrdugh gu guanach,
Le cuid chroinn agus ròpan
Dol a sheòladh a' chuain leinn;
Dh'ionnsaigh fearann Cholumbuis
Air an turas bu luaithe dhi,
Far na sgap sinn uile
Mar bhucas chuileag 'déidh 'fhuasgladh.

Lovely Elizabeth, giddily made ready
With her masts and ropes,
Going to sail the ocean with us
Toward the land of Columbus
Making the trip as quickly as she could,
Where we all parted ways like a box of flies
after it is opened.

Bliadhna trì fichead sa trì -
Gur tric a bhios 'nam chuimhne -
Nuair fhuair Tòmas an t-earraid,
An cabhaig, an lùb sinn;
Ach leamsa gum bu shòlasach
A bhith seòladh gu Quebec
Ann am bàta gun cheanna-bheairt
Làn de gharbh-chlachan muille.

I often recall the year of 1863
When Thomas got the sheriff's order
That hurriedly overpowered us;
But I thought it gladdening
To be sailing to Quebec
In a boat without sailing gear
Full of rough-hewn stones.

Tha dà cheannaiche làmh ruim
Anns a' cheàrnaidh seo do'n talamh:
Fear ann an Lingwick tàmh dhiubh
Is fear a' fàs ann an Winslow;
Is cuimhnich ma thig thu
Bidh thu aca 'nan ìnean
Mar gun spìonadh tu 'chearc '
Is gun leigeadh tu i 's an Fhaoilleach;
Chan eil rian agad dhol ás bhuapa
Gun 'a bhith air t'fhad anns an Legion.

There are two merchants next to me
in this region of country:
One man lives in Lingwick and the other
flourishes in Winslow;
And remember if you come they
will have you in their grip
Just as you would pluck the chicken
and let it go in January;
There is no way for you to escape from them
Without being fully involved in the Legion.

Ma chluinneas tu mo dhàn-sa,
An àite tàimh anns am bheil thu,
Thoir am muir agus an tràigh ort
Mus tig thu dh'àiteach 'na coille;
Chan eil saidhbhreas ri fhaotainn
Air an taobh seo de'n Atlàntic
Ach coille mhór do'n speur
Fad 's as léir dhomh ri 'fhaicinn.

If you hear my song
in your current dwelling place,
Go to the sea and the shore [of Scotland]
before you come to farm the forest [in Canada]
There are no riches to be had
On this side of the Atlantic
Only an enormous forest reaching the sky as
far as I am able to see.

'S e Eilean Leódhuis an t-eilean
Anns a bheil gach goireas tha feumail;
Pailteas airgid an tasgadh
Am banca Ghlaschu is Dhùn Éideann,
Is trì bancannan eile
Chùl air an sin ag éirigh:
Stìmearan snasail,
Tarraing bho fhéilleirean.

Lewis is the island in which every
advantageous resource can be found;
There is plenty of money stored up in the
banks of Glasgow and Edinburgh,
And three other banks besides
Are being developed there:
Stylish steamers
Are hauling loads from merchants.

Iain Greumach mac Mhicheil Thormoid   John Graham (son of Michael Norman)

251